Kristine
I treasure our
Frienship!
Love
John

THE
Forgiving
DREAM

JOHN HARRISON TAYLOR

BALBOA.
PRESS

A DIVISION OF HAY HOUSE

Author photograph by Karen Taylor

Balboa Press books may be ordered through booksellers or by contacting:

Balboa Press
A Division of Hay House
1663 Liberty Drive
Bloomington, IN 47403
www.balboapress.com
1 (877) 407-4847

Print information available on the last page.

ISBN: 978-1-5043-4463-0 (sc)
ISBN: 978-1-5043-4464-7 (e)

Balboa Press rev. date: 12/14/2015

Special thanks to Brigitte Weeks. whose editorial expertise, gentle guidance—and especially her friendship—were blessings as I wrote.

"Love one another."—Yeshua (John 13:34)

PART ONE

Chapter 1

"Dear God! What's wrong with it!"

Eleanor held the slippery infant upside down by ankles smaller in her experienced hands than any other she had held in her forty years of midwiving Randall's Bow's newborns. A little too boney perhaps, but well shaped. Yet...something was missing. Something that should be there, wasn't. She felt the hairs stand up on the arm that held the babe and a heaviness, a kind of dread, settled in the pit of her stomach. Eleanor slapped the tiny bottom and waited for the quick, life-giving intake of breath followed by a cry that would tell her his little lungs were working fine in the new surroundings that were too cold, too noisy, and too bright after the warm, quiet darkness of his mother's womb.

The infant hung limply in her hand.

Eleanor slapped his bottom again, this time a little harder, and waited.

"What's wrong with you? Why won't you cry?"

She slapped him a third time and lifted him higher, his face close to hers, and looked at his eyes, shut tightly against the world. He was beginning to breathe now in little sucking gasps, but still there was no cry.

Something was missing. Something was terribly wrong.

Eleanor looked at the young woman on the cot against the wall, crudely constructed from fallen branches and tied together with rawhide thongs.

She was not much more than a child herself, tangled in the coarse, blood-soaked linen sheets and so near death that she wasn't really alive any more, alone in that place between heaven and earth where she belonged to neither. It would be no sacrifice for her to leave the barren coldness of the small cabin, no more than a shelter, really, made of logs with nothing between the spaces to keep out the wind and rain beating against it. And even under the best of circumstances, it was hard, if possible at all, for a woman without a husband, and with a child to care for, to be strong enough to withstand the silent condemnation of the people of Randall's Bow and make a home here.

Lightning forked down into the forest nearby. Thunder shook the cabin and the wind howled like a hungry beast, tearing a branch from the loosely constructed roof. Rain sprayed down through the hole in the roof onto the bed, turning the bloody sheets into a pale, almost pretty pink, a delicate, pastel bier for the dying young mother.

Eleanor bent over the infant to protect him from the rain. He stirred slightly, taking in air with shallow little gasps, but still he made no sound. She turned him upright and looked at his pale, wrinkled face. His eyelids flickered as if he was having a bad dream, his hands balled into two little white fists tucked tightly against his boney chest. Better he was born dead. Then at least his mother would have someone waiting for her on the other side—heaven or hell, who was she to say? But he was alive. Not much more than his mother, but alive still.

She looked toward the door of the shed just off the bedroom where her daughter stood at the rough stone fireplace, stoking a fire under a kettle of water, coaxing it to a boil.

"Leyla! Bring me a blanket!"

Leyla stepped back from the fire and looked in the direction of her mother's voice. She had heard no cry, so the baby hadn't been born yet... what could Eleanor want? Perhaps the child had become twisted somehow inside its mother. Leyla was no stranger to difficult births. Though scarcely fourteen, she had been helping her mother deliver the babies of Randall's Bow since she could walk, standing obediently at the bedside while Eleanor impatiently snatched hot, wet cloths from her little outstretched hands. And before that, Eleanor would take Leyla with her, sit her on the floor next to the bed and describe what was happening and what she was doing as she worked. By the time Leyla was eight, she could midwife an uncomplicated birth by herself, and often did, with Eleanor at her side in the event something should go wrong.

By the time she was twelve, Leyla could handle any emergency by herself and her mother no longer felt it necessary to be present at every birth. No one seemed to mind. Some even requested Leyla to be with them when their time came, risking whatever Eleanor might think about that, which was usually relief, if the truth be known. Forty years of midwiving under every conceivable circumstance left her nothing to prove, to herself or anyone else.

It was obvious to all who saw her, even from the time she was still in the cradle, that Leyla was a special child. She smiled and cooed for those who stopped by the cottage for one of Eleanor's remedies from the forest for whatever ailed them. She began to walk before she was a year old, and from her very first steps she moved with an uncommon grace and sureness far beyond her age.

Unlike her mother, a woman of average height and sturdy build, with thick, chestnut-colored hair and deep brown eyes that spoke of gentleness and welcomed you into her life, Leyla was tall for her age and slender of figure. Her black eyes flashed and danced and covered you with silent laughter. Unless she was angry. Then the laughter left her eyes. Fire would take its place and her words would sear you with their fury.

Then, suddenly, her anger would disappear and her laughter would return, the point of it all forgotten. But the ones who felt her wrath would remember and be more wary with their words the next time. Once was enough to be the target of Leyla's angry tongue.

"Leyla!"

There was an unfamiliar urgency in Eleanor's voice as Leyla hurried into the bedroom and handed her mother a small, dirty blanket. "This is all I could find. Give him to me and I'll bathe him before we show him to his mother."

"No." Eleanor's voice was strangely flat. She took the blanket and quickly wrapped the infant, covering his head and face with one of the coarse, filthy folds. Then she pushed the bundle into Leyla's arms.

"Get rid of him. Take him into the forest and leave him." Eleanor's voice shook as she spoke, and she avoided Leyla's eyes.

"Leave him! What are you saying? What's wrong?"

"Get it out of here!" Eleanor pushed Leyla out of the bedroom to the door of the cabin.

"Mother! No! We can't just leave him. What's wrong? The child…"

"Child? Devil child!"

5

Eleanor shoved the door open and pushed Leyla out into the night. Rain slashed across her face and the wind tore another branch from the roof and sent it flying across the small clearing.

"Go!" Eleanor's voice was a whisper now, a prayer, pleading with her daughter to ask no questions and do as she was told. "Into the forest. Quickly!" Eleanor stepped back into the cabin and slammed the door shut. Leyla heard the plank slide into place, barring the door from the inside, and she knew she had no choice but to do as her mother said.

She reached into the rain barrel under the eaves, full to overflowing now from the storm, and dipped her fingers into the cold water. Raindrops hit its surface like little stones, splashing the blanket that covered the infant. Dark splotches appeared where the water was already beginning to soak through the porous fabric unto the unprotected little body within its folds. Leyla pulled the blanket back and looked at his face, his eyes shut tight as if he was trying with all his little might to block out what was happening. It was as if he knew that his life was almost at an end and that his time in this wet, unpleasant place into which he had been abruptly squeezed and pulled against his will, only to be unwanted and discarded in the cruelest of ways when he finally arrived, would be short.

Leyla wet her fingers in the rain barrel again and drew a small, damp cross on the infant's forehead. The wrinkled skin felt brittle to her touch. She pulled her hand back quickly and looked at his face more closely. Perhaps her mother was right. This one was different from all the others.

"I'm sorry," she whispered. "God bless you, whatever you are."

His eyelids fluttered briefly, and it seemed to Leyla that he had looked at her for just an instant before he quickly shut his eyes tight again, but she couldn't be sure. She pulled the blanket back over the now wet, wrinkled little face and ran into the forest.

* * * *

Lightning streaked across the sky and for an instant the forest was light as day. The path that would lead Leyla away from the berrying places where the people of Randall's Bow gathered in the season of harvest lay before her. She looked forward to those times, when differences and old resentments were laid aside for the several days ahead and sometimes even for good. The only things that mattered were the juicy, ripe raspberries, blackberries, and blueberries that were to be picked for cooking and canning, to bring a little of summer's flavor to the repetitious winter fare of boiled game and potatoes.

But tonight was not a night for picking berries. Tonight belonged to death, and Leyla had a part to play. She wanted this terrible thing she was about to do behind her and done with. She had no choice—she wanted to believe that—and she would, no matter how much her breaking heart cried out against it.

She had no choice. That was true, wasn't it? Her mother had told her to leave the infant in the forest to die, hadn't she? Her mother was the one. And Eleanor knew all about these things, so she had to be right, didn't she?

Leyla felt the infant move as she held the bundle tightly against her chest. Oh, she wanted to be rid of this thing she held in her arms! She had heard no sound through the tightly wrapped blanket, but she felt a slight rhythmic movement beneath the pressure of her arms as tiny breaths were taken in and then exhaled.

But this was not murder; this was not a human child that she held like a mother, tightly but gently cradled in her arms. This wasn't even a baby at all. It was a devil child. Eleanor had called it that. And only her mother and she would ever know about this night, and they would never speak of it. Never. And soon they would forget and it would be as if it had never happened. This thing she was doing had to be done. In the name of mercy, it had to be done!

God himself would say so.

Lightning flashed and grotesque shadows jumped out from behind the trees and surrounded her. She ran faster, deeper into the forest. Her lungs burned from the cold, wet night air until she thought she couldn't take even one more breath.

But still she ran.

Suddenly a branch with sharp thorns lashed out at her, waving back and forth in front of her like an arm with hundreds of tiny swords instead of hair covering its skin. She put her hand up to protect her face and felt the sharp point of one of the thorns rake across her palm

"Oh!"

Lightning flashed again and she saw a thin red line of blood oozing across the width of her hand.

This was the end of it. She would end it now. Leyla ran into a large clearing and stopped on the soft, wet grass. Lightning forked down and a tree crashed to the ground at the far end of the clearing. Smoke curled from the shattered stump, flames licking hungrily at the wet wood. She ran to the fallen tree, knelt and laid the bundle beneath one of the branches.

"Help him. Please help him," she whispered, bending close to the infant to tuck a loose fold of the blanket back in place. A tiny, pale white, perfectly shaped hand reached out from beneath the blanket and grabbed the gold locket dangling from a chain around her neck.

"No!"

Leyla pried at the tiny white fingers, but their grip would not loosen. They held the locket tightly, as if they were a part of it. She let go of the hand and tried to back away but the chain pulled taut, holding her to the spot. What was she to do? Eleanor would be furious if she lost the locket, especially like this. The rain came down harder now in blinding, ice-cold sheets, and lightening struck again, lighting up the clearing clear as day. She saw the infant's hand protruding from the blanket and nausea gripped her stomach. She had to leave this place now, no matter what the cost.

Leyla bent her head and slipped the locket's chain from around her neck. The hand disappeared back into the folds of the blanket, taking the locket with it. She touched the blanket where the hand had been as lightning flashed again. Thunder filled her head as if it was a physical thing, and she covered her ears with her hands. It was beyond anything she could stand, and she knew the locket was lost to her forever. It was his now, whoever or whatever he was.

She ran to the edge of the clearing, then turned back to look one last time at the bundle. It was still. Perhaps he was dead already, the strength of his grip a last desperate attempt to hold on to a life so short that it could not be said to really exist at all.

Then, in an instant, the storm ended. The slashing rain became a light sprinkle, hardly more than a mist. Leyla felt a gentle breeze move over her as the clouds that covered the moon drifted away into the night sky. She looked up at its shining fullness, lighting up the clearing as bright as the mid-day sun. She felt a tingling in her hand and looked down at the gash the thorn had torn across her palm and watched in disbelief as it slowly disappeared until there was no trace of it at all.

A low, snarling sound came from the direction of the bundle, and, as the last of the bloody stripe faded from her palm, she looked at the place where she had left the infant. A wolf looked out at her from the edge of the clearing just behind the fallen tree, ears flattened back against its large gray head, its fur matted from the rain. Teeth bared, the wolf raised his snout and sniffed the moist night air, then slowly moved, slightly sideways, around the still-burning stump and stepped into the clearing. He looked at Leyla, then at the bundle, then back at Leyla

For a moment, neither of them moved. The wolf's yellow, unblinking eyes burned with an eerie light as he considered the silent challenge of Leyla's frightened stare, locked with his. He snarled again, lower now than the first time, and less threatening. He took a step toward Leyla then stopped, his paw held suspended in mid-air as if pondering his next move.

Leyla took a step backward, and then another. Then another. The wolf lowered his paw to the ground, but held his place. With one last look at the bundle and then the wolf, Leyla turned and ran out of the clearing, back towards Randall's Bow and the safety of the manor. Surely Eleanor would know the meaning of this night and what had happened here.

But as she ran, Leyla knew she would not tell her mother everything.

Chapter 2

Old Man stood silent and unmoving at the edge of the clearing and watched the girl disappear down the moonlit, overgrown path toward Randall's Bow. When she was out of sight, he walked toward the fallen tree where he had seen her place a bundle among its branches. He focused his attention on the spot where the bundle lay, scarcely acknowledging the wolf's whimperings and wet licks on his hand. This was not to be an ordinary night, he knew. He felt a surge of energy of the kind he thought was long lost, rush through his body as a small cry, barely audible but clear nonetheless, came from the bundle. He walked quickly toward the cry, his breathing quiet and steady, mind and heart focused on his target.

He pulled the branches away from the tiny bundle and smiled. He knew what he would find within its folds. What he did not know was the nature of the child he would find. And in the years to come, he would often remember this moment and ponder the events that came after. He would wonder, had he been given the gift of knowing the future, whether he would still have taken the child to raise and nurture as his own, as he did on that night of shining moon and stars, there on the forest floor beneath the heavens.

* * * *

Old Man hurried toward his cave on Panther Mountain, the bundle cradled gently in his arms. The wolf took the lead.

"That's right, my friend. You lead and I'll follow. Your eyes are mine tonight." Old Man knew the forest as well as the wolf, but the moonlight sometimes played tricks on him and he wanted to reach the cave quickly and without incident.

Many years before—he had chosen to forget the number—he had become sick at heart and soul and had followed the insistence of the words that often called to him from a sacred text, *"See that you make all things according to the pattern shown you on the mountain."* He had lost his faith—no great tragedy had beset his life, but unanswered prayers and unrepentant sinners were all he saw as he stood in the rough-hewn pulpit in the tiny, sparsely attended church Sunday after Sunday and preached what to him had become an empty dream—the inherent goodness that was in the core of each of us. He had fled from Randall's Bow to seek the silence and solitude of the forest to find whatever pattern would be revealed to him on Panther Mountain, if anything at all.

He had found his answer. In an instant. Rather, it had been revealed to him by some power far beyond his comprehension. He had been transformed in a moment of grace, however defined, for he now knew grace to be real. The sun had just set when he had fallen to his knees, defeated and without hope, his guts convulsing with whatever little was there, spewing green and bitter bile on the ground in front of him. His chest ached as he sobbed the words to whomever or whatever might be there to hear him. "Help me." Over and over, for how long he had no idea, he had said just those two words. And then there came a silence and he sensed a presence standing over him. Within him. Outside of him. He didn't know. Tall and gowned in hooded reddish-brown, with sword in hand, the point touching the back of his neck. And then the words. Steady. Unrelenting. No more choice left. "Alright. It's over. Get up and let's go." And that was all. He had gone to the back of the cave and washed his face in the clean, cold water of the spring, laid down on the pallet of pine boughs and furs, and slept until well past sunrise the next morning, when the wolf's rough tongue licked across his face. From that moment, ten years past now, he was a changed man. He had received the help he had begged for—what it was or where it came from he didn't know. But it was, and is, real. As real this moment as that night so long ago.

Old Man opened the blanket to allow the infant room to breathe more freely. He bent close and felt little warm puffs of breath coming from the slightly parted lips. But why hadn't it cried again? Its breath was coming in a strong and steady rhythm, but it had made no sound at all, other than the single small cry in the clearing. And although its cheek was strangely dry to his touch, almost like parchment it seemed, it had the warmth of life. He was curious about the tiny face, but the darkness of the forest prevented him from seeing all but a vague outline in the moonlight.

He felt the flat terrain begin to steepen and he was climbing, the forest thickening the higher he went. The sweet smell of the pines, soaked through by the storm, filled his nostrils. He would be into the spruce soon, the hardier ones who could survive on the rocky surface of Panther Mountain, and the soft, often slippery, cushion of pine needles on the ground would disappear. It wouldn't be long now before he reached the sanctuary of the cave. "We're almost home, my friend," he called to the wolf. And then he whispered softly to the infant in his arms, almost to himself, "And you, too, my little friend. You're almost home, too." When the trunks of the trees became so close together that he had to turn sideways to get between them, he knew the clearing in front of the cave was only several yards away. It was just behind the gentle rise ahead that concealed the entrance to a cavern that was more than twice the size of most of the log cabins in Randall's Bow, several miles to the south on the banks of Cold River.

Old Man skirted a thick outgrowth of brush heavy with thorns and paused at the edge of a small clearing. He watched as the wolf paused in the middle of the clearing, raised his snout and sniffed the wind, his head moving up and down in a quick little rhythm to mark each breath. He turned to look at Old Man for a moment, then trotted to the entrance of the cave and went in.

Old Man followed behind the wolf and entered the cave, stopping to light a series of large tallow candles as he made his way to the back and the small pool of water that was fed by a spring beneath the cavern floor. The origin of Cold River, it overflowed its stone basin through a natural trough worn over hundreds, perhaps thousands, of years and formed a stream that flowed out of the back of the cave and made it's way in an ever-widening, ever faster rushing river down the mountain.

He gently laid the infant on a pallet of pine boughs covered by a variety of soft furs, than gathered twigs from a pile of tinder nearby and began to build a small fire. As the tinder and twigs caught the sparks of his flint, he added wood cut to lengths and sat next to his tiny charge and watched the flames grow. "Well, my little one, let's see what you look like." He gently pulled the folds of the blanket back until a boney little chest was revealed. "We'll have to put some meat on you, that's plain to see." Old Man opened the blanket further, freeing the infant's arms and legs. "What's this? Ah! You'll grow to be a man, I see."

The infant began to move his stick-like limbs. Clenched in one of his tiny fists was a gold locket on a chain, glistening in the firelight. Old Man gently pried the delicate little fingers open, took the locket and held it near the flames. Engraved on one side was an ornate *R* and on the other side, a *J*. Two small hinges indicated that there was a compartment inside, Old Man pried the locket open and read the words engraved within: *To my Judith. My heart is yours. Randall.*

"Well. What am I to make of this? You've come to my mountain with a little wealth, at least. Perhaps one day we'll know the meaning of it. But for now, I'll put it away for safe keeping. I suspect that you have little to say on the subject at the moment." In truth, he knew those names in another time. Yes. Another time.

Old Man went to the wall of the cave behind the spring and placed the locket on a small, natural stone shelf, then returned to the pallet. Afterbirth had dried into a thin crust on the infant's fragile little body, and the soft glow of the fire gave his skin a translucent sheath of varying hues of reds and grays. He noted that the mucous had been removed from the infant's eyes, ears and nostrils, so the basics of survival, however temporary, had been attended to. He filled a kettle with water from the spring and hung it from an iron rod suspended over the fire, than turned back to his charge. He was beginning to stir now, in short, jerky movements. But still, he uttered no sound.

"Are you hungry? I'd be surprised if you're not. You've had quite an adventure, and a not so pleasant one, I'd venture to guess. Well, we'll see what we can do."

Old Man walked to the entrance of the cave and went outside. He whistled sharply and waited, looking at the trees at the far end of the clearing. After a few moments, he heard a bleating sound and a white nanny goat emerged from the forest, paused at the edge of the clearing, then crossed the clearing and stopped in front of Old Man.

He picked up a small wooden bucket near the entrance of the cave. "I know it's not time, but we have a guest and he's very hungry," he said softly, kneeling and pulling at her with firm yet gentle strokes, coaxing the sweet, warm milk from her udder into the bucket.

"Give generously, now. I know this is a highly unusual time for us to be doing this, but we have a little guest. The only thing I can tell you about him is that he is newborn and was left in our forest to die. And there is a strangeness about him—a lack, somehow—that I can't name, and which I think is the cause of his abrupt exit from Randall's Bow. Not unlike ourselves, you say? Perhaps. I had thought of that, too. But this is a forest of life, not death, and your sweet, warm milk will make it so for him."

Old Man stood up and looked at the contents of the bucket. "Thank you. You are a good goat. You can come with me, if you like, and watch while I feed him. I'm sure you'll be pleased." He returned to the cave and placed the milk near the fire to keep it warm until he was ready to feed the infant, who, by this time, was complaining loudly. "Well. You have a voice, after all. Cold and hungry, are you? Welcome to the human race." Old Man lifted the kettle from over the fire, dipped a cloth into it and began to gently bathe the shell of afterbirth away.

"There now," he declared, as he worked the last vestiges of the infant's mother from his body. "I'm giving you your freedom, and it's going to be a little uncomfortable at first. But that's only because it's new and unfamiliar. You'll get used to it and you'll even begin to like it very soon. But I talk too much, I know. To Goat. To the trees. The birds. And when they've had their fill of my ramblings, even to myself. And our friend, the wolf, wherever he is. See? You've chased him away with that strong voice of yours. But he'll be back. Now let's get you something to eat."

Old Man loosely tied off one end of a small deerskin pouch and punctured the nipple-like protrusion with a piece of sharpened bone to make four tiny holes. He filled the pouch with milk, placed a few drops on the infant's dry lips with his finger then gently pushed the soft leather nipple into the already eagerly sucking mouth.

* * * *

14

"He was alive, mother! He grabbed the locket and he wouldn't let go! Please! Why won't you believe me?" Leyla pleaded through her tears. Why couldn't her mother understand what had happened? Why couldn't she understand the terror of it—that she couldn't stay there for even one more instant?

"Shhhh, child. Someone might hear." Eleanor stepped closer to her daughter and put her hand on Leyla's arm. It was late and the manor was probably empty, but she didn't want to take the chance that one of the servants might be eavesdropping. Randall was off somewhere to the south with his small army of men, answering the call of a caretaker of his land under siege by another who was eager to enlarge his fiefdom. Randall was, in truth, a man of noble causes. In truth, also, he was a mercenary, though he would reject that role as an accusation, for he would see is as such. Rashan, her husband, was with him, so she didn't need to be concerned about them. But the servants—she could never tell. They loved to get something on a person, especially her, and then run to Randall with their gossip, hoping to gain favor in his eyes. Would they never understand that Randall detested gossip, and that the bearer of it lost whatever favor they had with him? And, without fail, the time would come when Randall would gently ask them to seek employment elsewhere.

"Judith's locket—where is it now?" Eleanor's voice was calm, though her heart was pounding. That locket was precious to Randall, and if he noticed it was missing, and he would, she or Leyla would have to tell him the truth. Randall was not a man you could lie to without him knowing. He could always tell.

Randall had given the small gold heart to his beloved Judith only a few days before she died giving birth to Merrill, their son and only child. He had given it to her as a sign of his love before he rode off to defend another's land. For a price, of course, although he had no idea at the time that whatever he was paid in gold would pale beside the personal price he would pay for being absent at his son's birth. He had promised Judith that his victory would be swift and that he would return to the manor in time. But Judith had died shortly after Randall returned, and the locket was the most precious thing he had to remember her by. She had cradled it gently in her hand as she breathed her last.

Randall had given the locket to Leyla on her twelfth birthday. The gift was as much to honor Eleanor who, at Randall's request, had taken over the duties of mistress of the manor and Merrill's surrogate mother, as it was to honor Leyla's entrance into womanhood.

"He wouldn't let go of it!

"And you left it there?"

Leyla was almost hysterical now. Why couldn't her mother understand what she was trying to tell her?

"If someone finds it, Leyla. If Randall finds out what we've done...."

"There was a wolf. He saw me. He saw the baby...."

"That's enough! He's dead, then, like his mother. They're both better off for it. Now, we've got to go back and get the locket before Randall returns."

"No!"

"Yes, Leyla." Eleanor's voice was unforgiving and Leyla knew they would go to that place. And they would go tonight.

*   *   *   *

Leyla retraced her steps through the forest, Eleanor following closely behind. The air was thick with the smell of wet pine. Dawn was approaching and time was short. When they reached the clearing, Leyla stopped at its edge where she had stood only a few hours before and pointed to the fallen tree, still smoking in the early morning mist.

"There. I left him under that tree.." Her voice trembled, and she looked at the palm of her hand where the wound had been. Nothing was there.

"Show me," Eleanor said sternly, pushing Leyla ahead of her. "Let's find the locket and be gone from this place."

"But the wolf...."

"The wolf's long gone by this time, his belly full, God forbid. Or frightened off by what he found, which I suspect to be the case."

Despite her words, Eleanor quickly looked around the clearing and the edge of the forest that bordered it. She didn't like this. She didn't like this at all. But they had to retrieve the locket, and that was all there was to it. Soon they would be back at the manor enjoying the comfort of a mug of hot tea. But now....

"He's gone!"

"What?" Eleanor stepped around Leyla and looked under the branch, expecting to find a bloody blanket and whatever the wolf had left. Nothing was there.

"Are you sure this is the place? It was dark, and...."

"Yes, I'm sure," Leyla said through her tears. "Look. There's where I put him. And there are the wolf's tracks."

Eleanor bent down and laid the palm of her hand in the grass. Leyla was right. There was a small indentation in the shape of the bundle where the blades were bent down and dryer than the grass around it. And nearby, on a bare patch of wet dirt, were the fresh tracks of a large wolf.

Eleanor walked around the clearing, looking for the blanket, but found nothing. She returned to the fallen tree, bent down again and ran her fingers through the wet grass, hoping to find the locket, but found nothing. She looked at Leyla in silence. Confusion and fear were on her daughter's face, reflecting back her own, she was sure of that. What were they to do? What could they do?

Return to the manor before the rest of the servants came to her kitchen to be given their duties for the day. That was the first thing. Everything had to appear normal. Then she would have time to think. There was a reasonable explanation for this—there had to be—and she would find it.

From far off in the distance, somewhere near Panther Mountain, came the howl of a wolf. Low at first, so it could hardly be heard, then slowly rising in a long, soulful lament, then falling and fading until, like a song that had reached its end, there was silence. But strangely, it stayed with Eleanor and, stranger still, she was comforted by it. Then her stomach clenched like a fist, ready to defend itself. Something was happening in this forest, something that was out of her realm of experience. Something she couldn't control. She didn't like it, and it frightened her. And she knew somehow that her part in it was not yet done. Eleanor took Leyla's hand. "Come," she said. "Let's leave this place. Let's go home."

Chapter 3

Randall smiled as he surveyed his work, but he felt no joy in his heart. Soldiers who had fought bravely and long littered the battlefield before him—soldiers who had wives and children at home waiting for them. People who loved them and worried for their safety. Those few who were still alive and had the strength begged for a warrior's death, by arrow, ax, or sword. Death by the sword would be a great honor to them, Randall knew—especially his sword, for he was the greatest warrior who rode amongst them. The smell of death was all around him. The one who said that victory was sweet had never tasted victory on the battlefield. There was no sweetness here. A sudden wind blew dust into his face and he covered his eyes with his arm until it faded, then looked around once more. No. There was no sweetness here.

None got what they wanted. The wild people, as they were known, had come to steal his horses, his land, and what women they could find, if they could get away with it, and they knew well the price for that. They had come across the borders of his land, a small kingdom really, many times before and the result had always been the same. Death. No quarter given. And as long as he drew breath, that is the way it would be. And after him, Merrill, his son, would give them the same.

Randall felt the muscles of The Great Black War Horse stiffen beneath his thighs. The horse stopped without Randall's urging, raised his head and sniffed the wind. He whinnied softly, then bolted forward, almost throwing Randall from the saddle. Randall didn't see the arrow, but felt the sting of its feathers as it brushed the back of his neck. A horseman with an arrow protruding from his thigh came at full gallop off Randall's right shoulder, sword raised as he bore down on the young archer kneeling on one knee and struggling to fix another arrow onto his bow string.

"Rashan! No!" The horseman pulled his mount to a stop and looked at Randall then back at the archer, who had laid his bow on the ground in a gesture of surrender. Rashan lowered his sword but kept his eyes on the young man, ready to deliver the death blow should he so much as move toward the bow on the ground in front of him.

Randall was beside them now, and pulled The Great Black War Horse to a halt. He looked down at the fallen archer. "How old are you, son?"

"Twenty-four, sir. Randall."

"You know who I am, then."

"Yes, sir."

"Twenty-four? I have a son who's twenty-four. Would that he was about such things as you. A good soldier. You are that, I think." Randall and the young man looked at each other in silence. The archer lowered his eyes for a moment, then looked back up at Randall, his eyes full of defiance. "I'm ready to die, sir," he said, his voice strong and steady.

Rashan looked at Randall, then back at the archer. He raised his sword. "Sheath your blade, Rashan." Randall said. "This young man shall live."

"He wanted your life, Randall, and he would have had it if the horse hadn't….."

Randall raised his hand to silence Rashan, then looked down at the archer. "Get up," he said, and there was no kindness in his voice now. "Go back to your people and tell them that what they see before them is the last act of mercy they will ever get from me. If you cross my borders again, I will kill you all. All who come to fight here on my land, and when I have completed that, I will go to your land and kill all I find alive. Men, women, children, your animals. And I will torch your homes. Nothing will be spared.. Go to your people with what I say and know that I tell the truth. Rashan! Bring this boy, for that is what he is although he thinks differently, a horse. Now."

"But Randall…."

"Now!"

They watched the young man as he rode away. He paused once to look back at them, then kicked his mount into a gallop and disappeared into the forest. Randall surveyed the battlefield one last time. A fog was rolling in like smoke to give comfort and a bit of privacy to the dead. He turned to Rashan. "You and my men bury the dead from both sides. If any are still alive, kill them. If they belong to us, bring them back and we'll see what we can do."

Then, seemingly without urging from his rider, the Great Black War Horse wheeled and began a brisk trot in the direction of Randall's Manor, a day's journey if the weather held.

*   *   *   *

"Boot lickers!"

Merrill stood in the middle of the tavern and raised a tankard of frothy ale above his head. He was drunk, not unusual when Randall was off on one of his sorties against one vandal or another, usually gangs of wild people who coveted his precious horses and were foolish enough to try and steal some of them. Randall would catch up with them, kill the would-be thieves and return home with what meant most to him in all the world—his horses bred from The Great Black War Horse, the stallion he had brought with him from Ireland thirty years ago. Those who saw for the first time this one the stallion had sired, could only stand and observe the animal in a kind of reverential silence, his grandeur was so overpowering. And there was something else, something besides the physical beauty of the animal, that no one had been able to describe. The horse had never been named, and was known only as The Great Black War Horse, for there was not a name noble enough to cover him, He was the one Randall loved most, except for Judith. Even more than he loved Merrill, his only child.

Merrill crossed the now silent room and put his hand on the shoulder of a man at least twenty years his senior who was known to possess great physical strength and a will to win at sport that was unmatched. The man pulled back and smiled."When the ale wears off, my friend. Then it will be a fair fight. Or at least as fair a fight as it can be." Then he leaned close to Merrill's ear. "Back off, son," he whispered. "You're in no condition to take on anyone, least of all me."

Merrill tightened his grip on the man's shoulder and pushed him into a chair at a nearby table. He sat down across from him and put an elbow on the table, his arm perpendicular to its surface, palm open. "My father's slowest mount means more to him than you," he sneered, spitting as he spoke.

"You don't speak for Randall, Merrill.," the man whispered. He paused and looked at those crowding around them, then back at Merrill. "And you never will." He put his elbow on the table next to Merrill's and the two men locked hands. "Call it," the man said to no one in particular.

"Now!" someone shouted, and the man slammed Merrill's arm down on the table's surface.

Merrill slumped back in his chair. He rubbed his shoulder then emptied his tankard in one long swallow. Someone shoved another tankard toward him. He sipped from it slowly and looked at the other man still sitting across from him, a slight smile on his face. Merrill held his eyes for a moment, saying nothing. Silence filled the tavern.

"Bring me another tankard." Merrill's words were slurred, his eyes half closed now. A full tankard was placed next to him and he shoved it toward his conqueror. "Drink with me," he said softly. It was an order, yet, at the same time, a plea.

The man lifted the tankard and took a long drink, keeping his eyes on Merrill. When the tankard was empty, he spoke. "On a good night, you might be able to take me."

"It's true. I've had a little too much," Merrill laughed. "But we'll meet again, my friend, And then we'll see. We'll see." He shoved his chair back, almost falling, then stood up and staggered to the door. He turned and faced the silent crowd. "Randall uses you like oxen, and you don't even know it!" he shouted. "You are sheep!" Then he lurched out into the night and pulled himself up into the saddle of his waiting mount.

Merrill whipped the horse to a full gallop through the main thoroughfare of the settlement, a narrow dirt road lined with log cabins, their size determined by their function—business establishment or dwelling. When he reached the center of Randall's Bow, he pulled his horse to an abrupt stop next to the village green, a large, grassy circle surrounded by ancient trees and bordered on the far side by Cold River. He half slid, half fell to the ground and looked at the church that had been boarded up during a famine years ago when the people had despaired of any help from heaven. He crossed the road and pressed his hands against the roughly hewn doors, then turned and slowly made his way onto the village green and toward a grave at its center. He fell to his knees when he was several yards away, crawled to the gravestone and pressed his head against its cold, smooth surface. After a few moments, he pulled away and slowly read the words carved deep into its granite surface, his lips moving soundlessly.

Judith
Is buried here
And with her
The heart of Randall
Forever

Merrill put his arms around the gravestone, and began to weep. "Father," he whispered, and sank to the ground, falling into a restless, drunken sleep.

Chapter 4

"Take this in to Randall. He's in the Great Hall. Don't wake him if he's asleep, just set it next to him and leave." Eleanor handed Leyla a tray that contained a pot of strong tea, a bowl of hot corn meal smothered in butter and maple sugar, and a pitcher of fresh milk.

"What did he say?" Leyla asked.

"Say? About what?".

"About the baby and the locket. Mother...you told him, didn't you?"

"No."

"When will you?"

"When the time is right—if it ever is."

"What do you mean?"

Eleanor's voice was firm and unyielding now. Leyla had heard it like this many times before when her mother had made a decision and there would be no more discussion about it.

"I mean the time may never come. What good would it serve? If he asks about the locket, I'll tell him we put it away for safe keeping. And he doesn't need to know about the child, if that's what it was. Now take this in to Randall. He and your father arrived before dawn and he's very tired. He needs to get his strength back."

* * * *

The first rays of the morning sun fell on Randall as he sat in front of the fireplace in the Great Hall. He was tired. He raised his eyes, heavy from the hypnotizing power of the flames, to the life-sized portrait of a man and woman above the stone mantle. Standing half-a-hand taller than six feet, the man was elegantly dressed in a dark green velvet coat that narrowed at the waist, then slightly flared as it ended at mid-thigh, its brass buttons brought to a high polish. He was proud of his figure, and his form-fitting tan trousers tucked into brown boots that ended just below his knee, showed it off. His dark brown eyes looked into the distance, as if at a dream desired but not yet realized. Thick, reddish-brown hair streaked with gray brushed his shoulders. His hand rested on the silver handle of a sword protruding from beneath the coat.

A beautiful woman with long black hair cascading down the back of her crimson gown stood next to him. She was Randall's beloved Judith, dead these twenty-four years since Merrill's birth. It had been a terrible trade, her life for their son's. He loved her still, as deeply as ever, more perhaps, than he ever had. She looked down at him now with blue eyes approaching violet—directly at him no matter where he was in the Great Hall. He frequently came here to talk to her and it oftentimes seemed that she was actually there, listening to him and talking to him in her silence. Perhaps she was. He liked to think it was true.

It seemed, sometimes, that she was still alive when he would awaken at night from a fitful dream and sense her presence in their bed or hear her voice in one of the manor's distant rooms. He would hurry there, one of his hounds at his heels, knowing he would find nothing yet hoping that it was her death that was a dream and he would see her smiling face once again. So full of love for him. So knowing of his heart, so accepting of who he was. But of course, there would be nothing but an empty room.

"Randall..." Leyla's voice was soft behind him. He turned, hoping to see her beautiful smile and she didn't disappoint him. He loved Leyla as a daughter and sometimes wished that she was his child, and not Merrill.

Leyla placed the tray on the small table next to him. "Welcome home," she said. "You must be hungry."

"More tired than anything else." Leyla brought out the honesty in him. She always had, even when she was a small child. Her directness, like her mother's but softer, made him feel vulnerable somehow, and he was always truthful with her. He looked up at Judith in the painting, then back at Leyla. She was fast becoming a woman, and so much like Judith, it seemed. But no. He was exhausted and his foolish thoughts were born of that. No one was like his beloved Judith. No one would ever be like her.

"Is Merrill home yet?" He couldn't conceal the contempt in his voice, and he regretted at once that he had asked.

"No."

"Your father is in the stables, tending to the horses...and to himself. He saved my life. He took an arrow in his thigh that was meant for me."

"Is he alright? Does my mother...."

Randall cut her off. "It went deep, but it missed the bone. All the way through, so we pulled the arrow the rest of the way, cleaned the wound and bound it tight for the ride home. Your mother doesn't know. Rashan asked me not to tell her yet. Perhaps you might, so she can work her ways with his wound. He'll forgive you...he wouldn't forgive me."

Randall watched Leyla as she left the Great Hall, turning to her left toward the front door and the stables. Eleanor and her herbs could wait, apparently. Leyla would go to her father and see for herself how seriously he was wounded, then she would bring her assessment to Eleanor. With a remedy, more likely than not. It was her nature to heal and she had a great gift for it. Greater than her mother's. Even Eleanor would tell you that.

Randall turned to the breakfast Leyla had brought him. A hot cup of Eleanor's strong tea would feel good in his stomach, still tight and churning from the battlefield. These forays seemed to come more often now than in years past, and, truth be told, he was tired of it. And there was something else. Merrill. His gut tightened as he listened for the sound of hooves in the courtyard, a sound that would signal his son's return from a night of carousing, he was sure. He wished with all his heart now that it had been Merrill whom death had claimed, and not the only one on this earth that he had ever truly loved. God forgive him, but he would take his own son's life in an instant if it would bring his beloved Judith back.

"Randall! Mother!" Leyla's voice rang throughout the manor. Randall walked to the windows overlooking the courtyard and looked out. Where was she? He heard her call again, this time louder. Her voice seemed to come from the steps leading from the front door of the manor to the courtyard, but he couldn't see her.

Randall and Eleanor reached the front door together, Randall guiding Eleanor ahead of him out the door and into the early morning where Leyla stood on the steps. At her feet was a basket. And in the basket was a baby.

"This was with it." Leyla handed a scrap of paper to Randall. Her hand was shaking.

"Randall. This is your son's child," Randall read aloud. "By the time you find him, we will have taken his mother—our cherished daughter though Merrill thought of her only as a lowly barmaid—from this place. If we stay, the disgrace your son has brought upon us would be too much for us to bear. I pray that your son, and you, will pay as dear a price for this as we." There was no signature.

Randall bent over the basket and pulled the blanket back. There before him lay an infant. He looked healthy enough, his eyes closed in what seemed to be contented sleep, a growth of black hair on his little bare head. Like Judith. Randall was startled at the strangeness of the thought. And like Merrill, who, in appearance, was his mother's son. There was no doubt that Merrill was the father of this child.

"Only a day or two old, from the looks of him." Eleanor spoke from behind him. "Let's get him into my warm kitchen and take a closer look. He's beginning to wake up and he's probably a little wet." She bent and took the basket, then started toward the kitchen. Her eyes met Leyla's, but neither of them spoke.

"Go in and eat your breakfast," Eleanor said to Randall as she passed him on the steps. "Merrill will be home soon, and I suspect you'll need your strength." She turned to go, then hesitated and turned back to face Randall. "I saw Rashan. He came to the kitchen. A poultice and a tight bandage for a time and he'll be alright." Her voice was calm yet accusing.

"I didn't want to worry you..."

"You didn't want to face me, you mean. That's the truth of it. You were afraid I would blame you, and I do. That's the truth, too." She let a moment's silence stand between them, then stepped toward him and touched his arm, her eyes welling with tears. "I'm glad you're safe, Randall. Rashan will heal like new, so it's a small price to pay for what might have been. Now let's get this grandson of yours inside and see what needs to be done to make him welcome here at Randall's Manor."

*　*　*　*

Randall had no appetite for food. Now, he fed off the anger that seized his gut and sent its energy throughout his body. He crossed the courtyard to the stables and headed for the last stall in a long row of stalls that housed his beloved horses. The Great Black War Horse would be feasting on the grain he hadn't tasted in several days and Rashan would surely be nearby. He heard a soft whinny of greeting as he approached the stall. The Great Black War Horse's large head, ears thrust forward as he heard the familiar footsteps of the one he carried into battle so many times, looked out over the single rope barrier that hung loosely from each side of the open entrance of his stall. He whinnied again, this time louder, almost joyously it seemed, and pawed the straw in front of him.

"You're ready to go to war again, aren't you?" Randall whispered, rubbing the horse's soft muzzle that pressed against his chest. "That's what you're bred for. To go to war, large or small, and when you're not in the thick of the fight life gets boring. Well. Keep your ears sharp. I sense a battle. Not the kind you'd like, but a battle nonetheless. We have a newborn of the human variety at the manor, and when I confront the father I don't think he'll take the news any too cheerfully. I may need your help." Randall laughed softly through his anger, then turned toward the narrow cot at the rear of the stables, where a man rested, a makeshift bandage covering the wound on his right thigh.

"Eleanor and Leyla will be arriving soon, I'm sure." Randall told him. "They're probably arguing right now about whose poultice will have you on your feet faster right now."

Rashan pushed himself up on one elbow. "Best they leave me to my own device, if you ask me, " he said through clenched teeth. He slowly swung his legs over the edge of the cot until his feet rested on the floor. "I've had worse, and come through it better than ever tending to it myself." He hesitated, then continued. "One of the men told me he saddled a horse for Merrill last night." Randall looked around the stable to see which one of his horses was missing. "Did he say where he was going?"

"No. But he was in a hurry, like all young men."

"My horses can barely stand when he's finished with them."

"Sometimes he pushes them…."

Shouts and the sound of hoofbeats of a horse at full gallop clattered across the cobblestones of the courtyard. Randall strode to the door of the stables, Rashan limping behind him, just in time to see Merrill pull an exhausted buckskin stallion to a sliding stop. He wheeled the horse in small circles, reining hard and cracking his whip above his head, unaware that Randall was watching until he saw his father's hand on the bridle. Merrill dropped the reins and slid to the ground, greeting Randall with a low, mocking bow.

"Good morning, father," Merrill said, bowing once more, his words slurring from the night's ale. "Are you making sure the world is in order at this early hour—or at the very least, that it's to your liking? Long live King Randall!"

Merrill abruptly turned and started across the courtyard toward the manor. Randall put his hand on Merrill's shoulder and roughly turned his son around to face him. He pointed to the exhausted stallion, barely able to stand on his splayed, trembling legs. The animal was unable to lift his head and drink from the bucket of water Rashan had placed in front of him. His body was white from withers to hocks with foamy sweat and his breath came in heaving gasps, his painful grunts echoing across the cobblestones. The bloody whip marks on his flanks glistened in the early morning light. The horse was so broken that Randall feared he might have to put him down. One thing was sure—if he survived, he would never again allow a rider on his back.

"You've nearly killed another one of my horses." Randall's voice was dangerously low and without expression.

"Leave him alone, Rashan!" Merrill shouted. He stepped around Randall, pushing him out of the way, and cracked his whip, curling the long lash around the handle of the bucket in front of the stallion. He pulled on the lash and watched the water spill onto the cobblestones. He cracked the whip again, narrowly missing Rashan's face. "Shall we see a little blood?" he said laughingly. He brought the whip back for a second strike.

Randall came up behind Merrill and held his arm. "This is finished," he said quietly.

Merrill pulled away, threw the whip at Randall's feet and started toward the manor. Randall watched his son stagger across the courtyard. He knew in his heart that he was not without responsibility for what he had become. "Go into the kitchen, Merrill, and greet your son," he shouted after him.

*   *   *   *

Merrill pushed open the door to the kitchen and slowly walked toward the large wicker basket that rested on a table in the center of the room. This was Eleanor's domain and the aroma of a stew simmering in an iron pot on the stove mixed with the one next to it, filled with a special combination of herbs she was preparing for the poultice that would cover Rashan's wound. The basket moved slightly and Eleanor gently lifted a blanket-wrapped bundle from the makeshift crib and placed it in Merrill's arms. He didn't resist, but took the bundle without comment. She watched him with an amused smile on her lips. She had raised this troublesome son of Randall's since birth and she loved him. And Merrill loved her, she knew that beyond any doubt. And he, in turn, was well aware of Eleanor's love. That was one of the few things in this world of which he had no doubt.

Eleanor held Merrill's eyes with hers for a moment then lifted a corner of the soft blanket that covered the infant's face. "Isn't he beautiful?" She asked, almost singing the words.

Merrill looked closely at the small pink face that was lost in sleep, his eyes closed tightly against the early morning sun streaming into the kitchen through a open window nearby. "Yes," he said, returning Eleanor's smile. A tear slowly made its way down his cheek. "Yes. He's beautiful."

And in that instant, Merrill became father to his son. "I'll name him Jude," he whispered, gently kissing the baby's cheek. "I'll name him for my mother."

*   *   *   *

Jude grew to be a loving child. Merrill and his son rode the countryside together each morning, Jude cradled in his father's arms. And as Jude grew older, Merrill would put him in the saddle in front of him to give him the feel of the rhythm of his mount's body as he went from walk to trot to canter to full gallop, all the while in the safety of his father's arms around his little waist. He loved it, laughing and squealing with delight as the horse went from gait to gait, picking up speed.

Then came the day—Jude had yet to reach his fourth year—when he and his father went to the stable together to prepare for their morning ride, and there beside Merrill's mount stood a pony the color of the sky on a cloudy day, its rich, gray coat shining from Rashan's loving brush. Rashan lifted the toddler into the small saddle and, as father and son rode together out of the stable and into the courtyard in the morning mist, like two adventurers setting out to see what the world might hold for them, a grandfather stood in the shadows behind the stall of The Great Black War Horse, a smile upon his lips and a curious sadness that he could not name in his warrior's heart.

Merrill and Jude were a joy to all in Randall's Bow who saw them together and they felt the power of the love they felt for each other, although they could not name the thing that filled their hearts.

All but Randall felt this power. It was sadness that filled his heart, and he knew the reason why, after a time. To see between Merrill and Jude what he and Merrill never had pained him greatly. He knew that his grandson was but a reflection of what Merrill had become—one who could truly love and was truly loved in return. And Randall knew that he was not a part of that and never would be. It was too late.

Somehow, Merrill had been transformed in that moment when Eleanor had placed his infant son in his arms and he gave the child his mother's name. The mother he had never known. The wife Randall had loved, and still did, with all his heart—so much that there was no room to love anyone else, unless it was his horses. And in his deepest heart, Randall blamed Merrill for Judith's death, though it made no sense and he knew that. Yet, he couldn't erase the blame, the anger, and yes, the rage he held against his son—why not name it for what it was. And now, what was supposed to have been a travesty in Merrill's life had instead become a blessing and had changed him in ways that Randall had been unable to realize in his own life.

Merrill's joy greatly vexed Randall. There was laughter in the manor now, for the first time since Judith's death, and Randall was not a' part of it. He would not allow himself to be, no matter how the others tried to coax him into their circle of joy. And he couldn't understand why he refused. From time-to-time, Eleanor and Leyla invited him into one of their games, but he would have none of it. He felt only a vague sense of rejection of himself in their play, though what he felt made no apparent sense. After a while, Eleanor stopped trying, and he would walk away and brood in silence in the Great Hall, sitting beneath the portrait of himself when victory over any challenge was his daily fare.

* * * *

As Randall looked into the flames, he saw himself from long ago, dismounting from his horse to drink deeply from that place upon the river that was shaped like the warrior's bow slung across his back. While the horse drank, he had looked around him at the lush beauty of the forest. He was on an aimless journey now, and he was weary of the world and his place in it. A warrior by profession, he was without a battle to fight for the first time in a long time, and there was no king to whom he owed allegiance. He was free. But he was not a happy man.

He had knelt upon the river bank and drank his fill from the river's waters, clean and cold and good, then stood and looked around him once again, and he knew that his battlefield had changed. He would stay here and begin anew. No more would he spend his life in the service of others, fighting their battles, avenging or upholding or restoring their honor and their wealth. No more would he kill and maim and plunder for others. No more would he wonder where the next blood that he would cause to spill would come from or who would be the man whose gold would decide for him the banner he would carry.

Twenty-six years had passed since that day. He had looked at his reflection in the water, in a quiet place upon the river, and he had known that the life of war and killing were over for him, except to protect what was his own. He had stood and looked around him for the third time and breathed in the richness of the place with its tall, strong oaks, hickories, and sycamores. Some had surely stood for a hundred years or more. And then, untying the battle ax that was lashed behind his saddle, he had sunk its blade deep into the wood of an ancient oak that stood hardly an arm's length away, working through the day until it had fallen at last to the forest floor.

He had built a crude shelter for himself upon the riverbank, and soon he was joined by others who were looking for a place to begin a new life too. By the end of the first year, more than two hundred people had settled along the gently curving banks of the river that had come to be known as Randall's Bow.

Randall had gathered the people together as they were passing through. He spoke to them of the beauty of the place, the rich soil, the clear waters of the river. It was not so much what he said as who he was as a man, as someone they immediately trusted and accepted as their leader. Within five years after that first tree had fallen, more than two thousand people had settled there and Randall's Bow had become a place of plenty for all,

And Randall had found his Judith. She and her family had come to Randall's Bow during the second year, and had settled on some of the most fertile land along the river. Because of her father's vast knowledge of agriculture, he had soon become Randall's most important ally. Randall found himself spending as much time in the cabin of Judith's father as he did his own. And it wasn't solely for the purpose of obtaining advice on how to get the maximum yield of wheat, oats, barley, and potatoes from the land that brought him there nearly every day. Judith would serve Randall and her father hot tea and brandy with sweet cakes she had made, and, in truth, it had been the blush on her fair cheeks when he remarked on their sweetness that drew him there so often. And she knew, and Randall knew that she knew, that he wasn't only referring to the sweetness of the cakes. Within a year they were wed.

And within a year of their wedding, Judith was dead, bleeding to death after the birth of their son one day before her twentieth birthday.

Randall sat staring into the fire, a bitter man who had come to know that it was he who was his enemy now, and he felt powerless before it. He had failed as a father to his only child. He had failed as a father to the son his beloved Judith had left in his care.

Chapter 5

Old Man was not a stranger to newness, but his days were now new to him in ways he had never known before. He was aware of a difference—a strangeness—about the child that he could not quite locate or define. The infant was alert and none of his senses seemed to be impaired, as Old Man tested them with sounds and touches and sudden movements. His appetite was healthy to say the least, and he welcomed Goat's milk with contented sighs and little gurgles as he greedily sucked its warm sweetness into his little round stomach, made to appear even rounder somehow by a subtle lack of form or substance in his chest and limbs. Yes, something was lacking. Something that should have been present and apparent to the eye was missing.

Then suddenly, the cycle of seasons was completed and Joshua, as Old Man had named the child after that prophet of old who had taken up the staff of Moses to lead his people into the Promised Land, was a year old. Old Man felt a new power stirring within his heart during their first year together. It was like the newness he had experienced during his first year in the forest where, alone, he had faced himself and who he really was, for the first time. He had felt a power then, too, as he became more and more aware that his reality was strong and good, and the weakness and despair he had felt in Randall's Bow were but the burdens of a life that was contrary to this reality. And now, with Joshua, new levels of awareness— might he even call them revelations—were being reached and revealed as they moved across the forest floor and through the seasons together.

Old Man carried Joshua with him throughout the day, talking to him softly and describing the wonders of the forest as he went about the daily chores that assured their survival. He had constructed a sling of from a piece of strong yet supple deer hide that held Joshua securely. It was comfortable for both of them whether worn in front or on his back, depending on the task or inclination that occupied him at the moment. As Old Man walked through the forest, Joshua resting in the sling, he saw his environment with a new perception of the protection it would give them both. And he felt the beginning of a journey that would be new to him, the nature of which he sensed but could not even begin to imagine or speculate upon. He knew that this journey had been made possible because of the arrival of this little one who was now the center of his life.

From their first day together, Joshua became quiet and almost motionless whenever Old Man was near him. The infant would move his eyes toward the presence that he sensed, as if he understood what was being said, as Old Man spoke to him as a friend he wished to instruct in ways and customs that he loved. Joshua would gurgle baby sounds in response until he fell asleep. Then, with the talking done, Old Man would sit in the cave, enveloped in a silence that felt as if he was surrounded by a presence that was invisible yet physical. He would be filled with an exhilaration that lasted far into the night, its power making sleep impossible. It was during these times that he missed the books he had left behind in Randall's Bow. He had come into the forest without them because he had wanted nothing that would remind him of the life he had left behind. Even his clothes had been eventually discarded in favor of animal skins and furs. As dawn approached, peacefulness would come upon him. He would crawl between the furs that covered a bed of fragrant evergreen boughs and sleep late into the morning, awakened only by the pleading cries of Joshua and Goat, one to be fed and the other to be relieved of sweet milk that had become a burden in her swollen udder.

As the child grew, Old Man puzzled over the stirrings he felt within himself. It was the truth he was after—not some vague something that he wished for—but the truth. The truth about what? He didn't know. Whatever it was, it was all unknown to him, and it was unsettling because he had thought he had found all the answers he would need. And then this child had somehow led him onto a different path, a path that was strange to him because now he had to share his life, which he hadn't ever done before. The secrets that would lead him to whatever truths there were, Old

Man suspected, were not really secrets at all, but obvious to one of more pure perception into the nature of things than he.

Old Man looked at Joshua and Goat as they sat together on the soft green grass near the edge of the garden. Rays of early afternoon sunlight shone through the trees, bathing the two in its golden warmth. Joshua gently scratched his dozing companion behind one of her ears. We are indeed a curious combination, Old Man mused. An old hermit and a little boy who is beginning to look as ancient as his protector. It's as if nature has given him an excess of an element in the formula from which we humans are made.

There were times when Old Man seemed unaware of Joshua's presence because of his own longing for solitude on the ledge among the cliffs. In the past, when he descended to the forest floor once more, he would turn his attention to the child with new insights. Then, with a start, he would fix his gaze upon Joshua as if he was seeing him for the first time. He would feel a gnawing sickness in his belly as he realized that once again, in his absence, brief though it was, years, sometimes it seemed like decades, had entered the body of the little one he loved so much. He would stand rooted in the coldness of his dread, unable to move or speak as he realized that Joshua was becoming more and more like himself in appearance. As each cycle of the moon passed, Joshua came to increasingly resemble a little old man. His arms and legs were thin and stick-like, covered with wrinkled skin that felt like dried parchment. They looked as if they would snap in two like brittle twigs at the slightest pressure. And when he walked, he looked as if he carried the weight of a lifetime on his bent little back, a lifetime that had been long and hard and was coming to a merciful end.

And yet, all of this was scarcely noticed when Joshua spoke. His voice had a piping sound, almost like music from a flute. He seemed to speak in a kind of natural melody that swept away the appearance of his deformity. And when Old Man looked into Joshua's eyes, he saw not worry and concern, but love and trust and a wisdom that was budding and about to blossom in his youth, yet ancient in its depth and power. Only beauty was extended from this little one so loving. And so innocent.

Old Man spoke of the wonder of the forest to Joshua as the two of them explored it together. Joshua would look in the direction of Old Man's pointing finger—into the blue sky between the tree-tops—and watch as

35

a hawk swiftly imprisoned its small-bird prey in its talons. At the precise geometric bottom of its swooping downward arc, with not the slightest decrease in velocity, the instant of perfect capture would be completed. The hawk would then effortlessly glide back to its lair high in the rocky cliffs behind the cave and devour its newly captured meal. Old Man would then call Joshua's attention to a doe giving suck to her fawn, or a mother skunk leading her litter single file behind her to nearby bushes bent over with the plump, juice-filled berries of summer. And he and Joshua would look into each other's eyes, into the awareness of how the events that had just occurred before them were equal in their beauty and were the same, somehow.

As Joshua grew older and his powers of observation and intuition developed, their experiences in the forest bonded them in spirit and intellect. But they felt a lack, too. The energy between them seemed to have no direction or purpose except for its own sake, its own progression and growth. And its capacity seemed to be infinite, constricted only by their own abilities to comprehend and move within its limitless bounds.

The need to survive in an environment that was sometimes harsh, even cruel, to those unable to provide for their own food, shelter, and protection, proved to be a blessing that kept them in touch with the everyday realities of life. It gave them tasks of a definite nature to begin, to bring to fruition, and to partake of the benefits. It was a part of life that made their existence one of joyous fulfillment and accomplishment.

Their garden was a delight. It gave them food and a place to go each day and be a part of the miracle of life. They ate mostly vegetables, supplemented by fish from the river. Old Man would dip a net of tightly braided rawhide into the water and bring up a large and meaty fish that he had seen hovering lazily and unafraid near the river bank and close to the shallow bottom. He would clean and filet his catch, covering it with Goat's milk and flour made from wheat that grew in a small field at the far end of the clearing, and, finally a tasty seasoning made from a mixture of the many herbs that grew nearby. The fish would be cooked in a large, flat pan over the fire, filling the cave with a fragrant, smokey cloud that would last for hours. It was a special treat for both of them.

As Old Man and Joshua worked each day in the early morning, pulling weeds, loosening the rich, dark earth, and supplying water to the spots that were a little too dry, they talked of life and what might come after, and the truths they were searching for. Their work was like a prayer, and the new life they observed springing from the soil as they participated in the garden's growth were the answers.

Their love for each other was a sacred thing, a holy thing that made their work productive and their garden grow, transforming that piece of ground from just a garden to a paradise where sin was not yet known. The two of them were like man when first created, once again upon the earth when the sin that is now called original had not yet been committed, and all was peace and harmony in the forest.

Even the animals knew it. They knew no fear as they grazed or sunned themselves nearby, or played with their young as the two who walked upright worked and softly conversed throughout the mornings. As the sun reached its midpoint in the sky, Old Man and Joshua would straighten up from their work without speaking and return to the comfort of the cave where cool water from the river's source and food, followed by an hour's nap, awaited them before they would once again walk together across the clearing and into the forest.

Oftentimes, neither one of them would speak a word throughout the rest of the afternoon. Their minds and senses would feast upon the miracles before them, and silence was their cradle. In late afternoon, they would return and carry mugs of strong tea to a ledge upon the cliffs above the cave and watch the sun set on the perfection below, while in the distance, in a spot downriver, smoke from the cooking fires in Randall's Bow slowly rose into the darkening sky.

Chapter 6

"Grandfather!"

Randall reined The Great Black War Horse to a stop and watched Jude running toward him across the courtyard. He felt his impatience rising— he didn't like the routine of his daily rounds interrupted, and he was anxious to feel the power of the his mount beneath him as he urged him from walk to trot to canter to a charging gallop across the early morning meadows. As he watched Jude approach, he was surprised at how much the boy had grown. More than a decade had passed since that morning when he had arrived on the steps of the manor and, despite his impatience, Randall felt a pulling at his heart as Jude ran to his side and put his hand on his stirruped boot. Tall and strong for his age of nearly eleven years, he was as handsome as his father, and, like Merrill, he had the black hair and eyes of Judith. For the first time—he wondered how he had missed it—he saw how much the boy looked like her. The resemblance was so striking, how could he not have noticed it before? Their faces were identical. Randall's thoughts were interrupted by the insistent voice at his boot.

"Grandfather! I'm going with you!"

"What? What did you say, Jude?" Randall, lost in memories of long ago, brought his attention back to the eager young face looking up at him. He was startled that it was here before him now, and not another dream from which he would awaken, his body soaked with sweat and desire and a choking sob in his throat.

"This morning, I will ride with you, Grandfather. It's what I've decided. And every morning after this one, too." Jude looked at Randall high above him, and there was no question in his handsome face. It had been decided.

"So. You've decided this." Randall smiled down at his grandson. Amused. Not taking him seriously. "Tell me more." And as Randall spoke, his amusement disappeared before that young, unyielding determination, and it brought him back to his own youth so long ago. "Tell me why." His voice said that he accepted Jude's decision. Randall's daily rides about the countryside were sacred to him. That was known to all. To have that sanctity violated by someone saying they were going to accompany him was unthinkable. Until this moment, when Randall knew that Jude's presence would not be a violation. No. It would be a blessing. Randall sat astride The Great Black War Horse in an attitude of acceptance of Jude's decision and Jude knew that.

"Yes. I've decided to be like you, Grandfather."

Randall was really curious now. "Oh, really. And what is that? What am I?"

Randall felt a smile coming to his lips and struggled to hold it back, to maintain the seriousness of the situation.

"A great warrior and a great leader of men, Grandfather." Jude removed his hand from Randall's boot and stepped back, as if to get a better look at him.

"Oh? And who told you that?" Randall was smiling now, aware that this beautiful boy before him—his own grandson, his own blood—was perhaps seeing his grandfather smile for the first time in his life.

"My father, sir. My father told me. He said you are a great man. That you have a quality that brings out the very best in those who follow you. And if I want to be the best I can ever be, I would do well to follow you and learn your ways and listen to your words. He said that I should learn to be like you."

Randall was stunned at Jude's words. How could this be? Had Merrill really told him this? But the boy had no reason to lie to him. Randall looked toward the manor and saw Merrill standing in the window, looking at the two of them. His face was passive, without expression, as nearly as Randall could observe at that distance. But then, suddenly, the two of them were looking at each other, he was sure of that, and Randall knew. Merrill had indeed told Jude these things about him. And Merrill was telling him something through Jude. They looked at each other without moving for a moment, and Randall remembered that he was still smiling.

He kept it there as he and Merrill locked eyes. He remembered that time, years ago, when Eleanor had gently placed Jude in Merrill's arms for the first time. Randall was experiencing now what he had seen and envied then in Merrill. The thing he thought he would never know. He knew now that he had been wrong for all these years, and in that instant, Randall became father to his son.

Randall saw Merrill return his smile, then turn away and disappear from sight. And for the first time, he noticed another figure in the window who had been standing next to Merrill, watching too. He would not have seen Eleanor at all had it not been for the flash of white as she raised her handkerchief to wipe away her tears.

Randall looked down at Jude. "Go tell Rashan to put your saddle on the roan mare," he said. "If you would be a man like me, you must forsake your pony now, love him as you do."

As Jude ran off toward the stables calling for Rashan. Randall watched him go, and wondered at the joy that filled his heart so full that he thought that he would burst from the power of it.

Chapter 7

"Joshua!" Old Man called to the boy at the far end of the garden.

Joshua raised his head and smiled, revealing an incomplete set of teeth, crooked and crowded within the small mouth supported by a chin so small and receding as to be almost nonexistent. His large round eyes, dark brown and shining, focused on Old Man, the only other human being he had ever known.

Joshua loved Old Man with all the love his little heart could hold. And he knew that Old man felt the same toward him.

Old Man watched as Joshua hobbled toward him, his stride and posture resembling that of a man who had lived decades more than this dear little one whom he so greatly loved and feared for. Old Man, who was barely five feet tall, looked down at the shining face before him. The hairless, oversized head, its scalp covered with a network of prominent veins, barely reached the level of Old Man's chest. His thin arms and legs, tanned and leathery in texture, protruded awkwardly from his tunic of soft deerskin. Enlarged and stiffened joints gave him the look of one who had been put together by a poorly trained puppeteer whose object was to entertain by exaggeration. Joshua's thin chest labored under his tunic as he recovered from the short walk across the clearing from the garden.

What beauty there is in this little one, Old Man thought. There was laughter in Joshua's voice as he spoke to Old Man. "So tell me, my teacher, what is more important than the removal of the weeds that are at this very moment attempting to deprive us of the vegetables we've worked so hard to grow? If the weeds win, you know what will happen. No more soup. And if there's no more soup, you know what will happen. No more supper. And if there is no more supper, you know what will happen. No more pleasant evenings by the fire, filling our bellies and discussing what the day has given us. And if such evenings are to be no more, you know what will happen. Or do you? Perhaps I have overestimated your powers of perception and the ability to foresee the consequences of your actions. But I will withhold my judgment until you reveal to me whatever profound truth has caused you to pull me most unwillingly from the work so necessary for our survival. And which, I might add, you are most reluctant to do yourself."

The mock formality with which Joshua spoke, and the impish look in his eyes brought laughter from Old Man, despite his efforts to look stern, and he hugged the boy to him. He held him with a feeling of love and protection, and looked to the cloudless sky as a swooping hawk was taking yet another tiny victim to its lair. Old Man felt a chill run through him.

Joshua pulled away from Old Man and looked at him with concern. "Are you cold, Old Man? I felt you shiver as if you're cold."

"Cold? In a calculating way, do you mean?" Old Man joked, to keep the mood light between them despite a deep foreboding that had been triggered by the hawk and its helpless prey. "Cold? Yes, if that's the kind of cold you mean, the answer is a definite yes. I am in awe of the methodical brilliance with which you were wielding that hoe down at the other end of the garden. Not particularly effectively, mind you, but methodically, most certainly. Where, if my inquiry is not an intrusion upon your talent for creating illusion, did you learn to flail that agricultural artifact so artlessly? Surely, from one even more adept at such overt fakery than yourself?"

"I learned it from you!," Joshua laughed, and stepped away from Old Man. Of all the tasks required to keep their garden, hoeing weeds was the one both of them disliked the most. There seemed to be something wasteful—even judgmental—about it. They were convinced that even weeds could contribute to their lives if they were astute enough to discover how. In the meantime, they contented themselves with the exercise that the hoeing provided, and the monotony of the work allowed room for private thoughts and daydreams because it required no thought at all.

In truth, Old Man was using the weeding of the garden today as a diversion from a recent and persistent line of questioning from Joshua. More and more, the boy was asking about the world beyond the forest. His questions had begun a few years ago, whenever Old Man entertained

Joshua with stories about his own life in Randall's Bow. His questions then had been those of a curious child. The true nature of the place itself was of no interest. The truth about Randall's Bow, at least as Old Man experienced it, was not important to one so young.

But in time, the nature of his questions changed. Questions about where and when changed into how and why, until at last there was but one purpose to his interrogations.

"Why can't we go there, Old Man? I want to see Randall's Bow for myself."

"Please stop asking, Joshua. It's not a good place. People do harm to each other there."

"But how can I know the truth if I don't see for myself? What kind of harm?"

"You don't want to know, Joshua. You must believe me. You really don't want to know."

"But it's not right for you not to let me see for myself. How can I really know the value of what we have here if I don't know what that other life is like?"

"You know what it's like because I've told you."

"No, Old Man. You're the proof that I have to experience both places for myself. You wouldn't know how good this place is if you hadn't experienced the other place."

And for that, Old Man had no answer. He raised his hand, turned and walked away in silence, leaving Joshua staring after him with tears in his eyes. But they were not done with this. Old Man knew that.

Joshua was innocent. He had never been hurt by another human being. He had no idea that something was very wrong with him—that in the world beyond the forest he would be an abomination of nature, to put it in the cruelest terms, ridiculed, laughed at, even feared. To be laughed at was a concept as foreign to Joshua's experience as was a lie. The use of laughter in any way other than the sharing of a joke or a moment of happiness with Old Man was unknown to him. Old Man knew that Joshua's fate in Randall's Bow would be one of ridicule and rejection— perhaps even physical harm. That experience was no more real to Joshua now than the experience of surviving in a body like Joshua's was real to

43

Old man. Joshua had never had to learn to protect himself simply because he was different, and Old Man was determined to protect him from that.

The cliff above the cave would give him time to sit in solitude and listen for the guidance he craved from his inner guide—the voice that never failed him if he would sit in silence and truly listen...

"Joshua," he said, "I must go now."

*   *   *   *

Joshua looked up from his weeding in the garden at the speck on a ledge of rock in the cliffs high above the cave. The speck seemed not to have moved at all during the seven days and seven nights that had passed since Old Man had told him that he would climb to his solitude there. The announcement was not a new one. In the past, there had been periods of time when Old Man had become irritable and out of sorts and the days had become long and unpleasant for both of them. Old Man would scold him for little things that, at other times, would go unnoticed. Then suddenly the scolding would stop and Old Man would spend his days working silently in the garden, seemingly unaware that Joshua was there at all. It was if he didn't exist. Even Goat was ignored and was herself made irritable because the milking had to be done by Joshua, and she would have to endure the rough clumsiness of his hands. Several times during the day, Old Man would look up from his work as if distracted by a sudden noise. He would stand and stare into the distant sky as if looking for some far off place that existed just beyond the farthest point that he could see. Yet, so near, if only he could find a way to reach it. If only he could go there. If only he had wings to fly along the path that stretched invisibly before him. He knew it was out there somewhere beyond his sight, but not beyond knowing. It shouted its reality, more real even than the forest that enclosed and sheltered them both. Then he would remember that what he longed for was not beyond him, but within him. It was not a place to fly to, somewhere beyond the horizon. He had to search within himself and trust the inner voice he sometimes heard in quiet times upon the cliffs. His gaze would leave the sky and focus sharply on the child before him. His voice would tremble as he spoke. And the words were always the same.

"Stay close by the cave and you'll be safe. I'll be up there where you can see me. If you sense danger, fly the red cloak from the tree where Goat is grazing and then go quickly into the cave. Take Goat with you. I'll see the cloak and come down to be with you. I must go now."

And Old Man would go. Starting at the bottom of the cliffs next to the cave, he would slowly climb up the small, natural stone steps to a protruding shelf of rock high up on the face of the wall, where he would sit in silence looking out over the forest.

In previous times, Old Man had always descended from the cliffs after a day or two. The longest he had stayed on the shelf until now had been three days and two nights. Now seven days and nights had passed, with only rain water collected in the rock's crevices to sustain him, and Joshua was afraid. His fear would lessen sometimes, when he remembered the peaceful look in Old Man's eyes when he returned to the cave the times before. Surely, this longer stay could only mean Old Man was reaching new and deeper places of awareness. He would share it with Joshua, and the two of them would laugh about the fear that he was feeling now.

Joshua looked once more at the figure, barely discernable, perched high above him, and then he returned to his weeding. He wished that the pounding of his heart would soften, and that his breath would come easier, instead of in shallow gasps.

Chapter 8

Many were dying in Randall's Bow. There wasn't a family who hadn't lost at least one to the fever. It had come suddenly, announcing itself through the cries of a baby in the middle of the night. The child's mother had left her bed to attend to what she thought was nothing more than a bad dream. There had been a little difficulty in weaning the infant from her mother's milk to the milk of the cow that grazed quietly in the small clearing behind the cottage, but cries in the night had been unusual of late. This one was her fourth child, so she had experienced this before. The weaning would be done in a week or two, and she would be able to sleep through the night undisturbed.

She gently lifted the baby from its cradle and brought it close to her lips to kiss her forehead. "There now," she crooned softly. "It's alright. A little pat on the back and up it comes. You'll feel better then." She patted the small back and waited for the bubble of air that was causing the discomfort to escape in a not so subtle little burp. Putting her lips to the baby's forehead to gently kiss it, she quickly drew back. The child's skin was dry and hot. It was not what she had thought. This was not some routine colicky discomfort that needed only a little bit of a mother's patting to help relieve the pressure. Something was very wrong.

"What's wrong?" Her husband, awakened by the baby's crying, walked over to where she was standing and held a lighted candle close to her face. His wife looked at him, unable to speak. He saw the terror in her eyes as she looked helplessly from him to her crying child and then back at him, silently pleading with him to make what was happening go away. To make this terrible thing that was happening part of a bad dream from which they would awaken.

But it wasn't a dream, and she knew that. Her husband took the baby from her and pressed his cheek to her forehead. Then, holding her in front of him, he looked into her glazed, half-shut eyes, Her head rolled to one side then and her eyes closed. Her body went limp.

"She's gone." He brought the infant close to his chest and looked at his wife.

"What? What do you mean, she's gone?" Her voice was almost a scream.

"She's gone," he said again, his voice shaking. "She died. She just died. Here in my arms."

"Give her to me!" She pulled the limp little body from her husband's arms and brought her face close to the child's. "How can she be gone? She's burning up with fever!"

"She'll soon be cold." He left the room.

It had come quickly, the thing they called the fever. It had come without warning, precipitated by neither flood nor cold. Suddenly, it was in their midst. That was all. It was there, and it was killing them. The very young died quickly, usually within a day or two, their small bodies unable to withstand the all-consuming heat of the fever that drained them of their fluids. The older ones went more slowly. It required several days and much pain for them to die. Nothing could relieve their suffering. The best that could be done for them were cold compresses on their burning foreheads to give a little relief for a few minutes before the cloth, too, became warm from their body's heat. The comfort was more for the those who applied the compresses, to make them feel less helpless, and to provide the illusion that they were doing something more for their loved ones than simply standing by and watching as they suffered and died. But the dying were not comforted. They slowly burned away, their lips cracked and bleeding, unable to keep down even a drop of the water they craved so much.

Randall had to see for himself. Someone had summoned Eleanor that night because a child was sick with fever, and she had told him about it at breakfast. He sent Jude on his way alone, telling him it was time he tried the ride by himself, and he had ridden off in great excitement and importance through the manor gates. Randall left shortly afterward, riding slowly along the deserted road on The Great Black War Horse until he reached the cottage where the sick child and his family lived. As he dismounted, he saw a shutter open up a crack and then close quickly,

"Please open the door. You have nothing to fear." Randall spoke softly until the child's mother answered his knock and opened the door. Randall was no stranger to her. She had seen him ride by many times before. But seeing him now, standing at her door and asking her if he could come in was so unexpected that she didn't recognize him at first.

"What do you want? My child is ill, and I...."

Randall gently interrupted her. "That's why I've come. I'd like to see your child. Please. It's most important. Perhaps I can help, or find someone who can. You see, there may be danger...."

"No, there's no danger. What do you mean by danger? My child is ill, that's all. He'll be better in a day or two. Who are you? What do you want here? Why do you want to see my child?"

"I'm Randall. There's no need to be afraid. Please. Take me to your child."

"Randall." Her voice filled with relief as she said his name. "I'm so afraid. Something is happening to my baby, and I'm afraid he'll die. Come. In here.. Look at him and see. I don't know what's wrong with him. Please." She led Randall into a small, dark room at the back of the cabin. As he entered the room where the child lay, he smelled the stench that he remembered now, when his soldiers had fallen like rotted trees from the fire of the enemy he couldn't see. Or defeat. Before he even saw the child, that smell so wet and hot and heavy in the room told him that the sickness was the same as then. It had struck again, as quickly and without warning. Before he reached the child, he saw the father standing helplessly by the cradle and he knew he was too late, that the child had died. The father watched Randall with suspicion as he placed his palm on the forehead of the still little body. Even in death, its skin was hot.

"It's water that he wants," the mother whispered, "but he can't keep it down. He drinks so much that his stomach becomes swollen with it and he vomits it back up. And when I try to give him just a little bit instead, he cries until I can't stand it anymore, and then I give him more until he's sick from it again. Help him, Randall. Please, help him. We don't know what to do."

"Eleanor. You summoned her here last night. She told me this morning. Has anyone else been here since she left?"

"No. Just the ragman. The rags I bathed him in last night and put around him to cool him. I wanted them gone from here. Out of my sight. And when I heard the ragman's bell, I put them in a pile beside the road. He took them away." She looked at Randall with eyes that pleaded with him not to tell her that she had done something wrong. And she knew by his look that she had.

Randall looked at the father. He knew the child was dead and had been dead for a while now, he was sure. He held his tongue, but he knew, and he wanted Randall to know that he knew. He shook his head and Randall nodded.

So, it was done. There would be no stopping it now. To slow it down and try to contain it within a certain area until it disappeared again was their only hope, and now that hope was gone. The ragman, unbeknownst to him, was doing the fever's bidding. Death would be upon this place. There was no cure for what was before them now. They could only wait until the fever had run its course and disappeared. There was nothing else they could do.

Randall held The Great Black War Horse to a walk as he returned to the manor. He was in no hurry to confirm to Eleanor what she already knew. Is there really nothing to be done, he wondered? There had to be another way than bolting windows shut, hoping death would claim a neighbor and not tarry at their own door. There must be a way to fight this thing. In his heart, he swore to Judith that he would find it. And he asked for her help, if she heard, and if she could give it.

Chapter 9

The wind was strong in Old Man's face as he sat upon the ledge and looked out over the forest. His thoughts were on the child working in the garden far below him. Joshua was just a speck from where he sat, but, within his heart, there seemed to be room for nothing else. I love him so very much, he thought. His eyes followed a dark line though the treetops that marked the course of Cold River, coming to rest on a shadowed place that marked the settlement of Randall's Bow. He thought back to the night he had fled that place. He had almost let it destroy him with its hypocrisy. No. Rather, he had accepted its lessons until they became so much a part of him that he was the instrument of his own destruction. Oh, not his body. Not his physical self. He would still be alive if he had stayed there, and most probably prospering in their way. But he would have lost his soul—if he had one—in the bargain. He knew that. Trite as it may sound, were he to speak it, it was the truth. Half-truths and whole lies would have been his currency of exchange, and he would have been respected and feared because of the wealth and power his deceits would have brought him.

He knew he had that gift, if you could call it that. The gift of gold in return for the use of his intellect in pursuit of profit. But the pain had become too great. He had endured it until he could endure it no more. Abruptly and dramatically, he had changed the course of his life. He had abandoned everything he had and all he knew and entered the forest, taking only Goat, the clothes on his back, and a few cooking utensils with him.

He had settled on the word "grace" to explain it. Whenever he spoke the word aloud, he felt what he had experienced that night when, alone in his cabin as he always was because he had never married, he was suddenly and without warning overcome with the certain knowledge that this was wrong. His life was wrong. And that very night, without a moment to waste, was his last chance. That night was the only chance he would ever have to leave Randall's Bow. He was free to go tonight. Tomorrow, that freedom would be gone. He didn't know where he would go. It didn't seem important to know, because, on some level, that decision had already been made and would be revealed to him as soon as he made the final choice that was his alone to make. To leave. His chances to make that choice were gone—all but one. The one of now. To stay would be to commit his life to a living death. Not to the merciful silence of a lifeless corpse, but to a death that was wide awake and breathing, thriving on lies and corruption, with pride and the blindness that it breeds as its nourishment as it feeds upon itself.

And now he had another choice to make, and he would return to Randall's Bow. He would take Joshua to that place from which he had fled those many years ago. How many was it? Twenty-four. Yes. Twenty-four. He remembered the number now. A number that meant nothing anymore, if it ever did at all. They would go to Randall's Bow. It was inevitable. Joshua was too intelligent and inquisitive, too mentally and spiritually demanding for him to give in on this point. They had talked about Randall's Bow many times, and Joshua insisted that he see it for himself. He wanted to experience Randall's Bow. He wanted to see for himself the evil from which Old Man had fled to save his life. To save his soul. He wanted to walk its roads—he had never seen a road. Such innocence was almost inconceivable. How could it be possible to protect such innocence when they arrived? And Old Man was the only other human being Joshua had ever seen. What had he created in his isolation? But what else should he have done? Left the child to die, that night in the forest? No. He was sure of that. But what of his sickness, if that's what it was? What about this strange arrangement of nature's design that produced the appearance of a man even older than himself now, in a child of only eleven years? Did those years, the beauty and wonder of those eleven years, justify saving the life of this aberration of nature that he loved so much? There was nothing else to call him, love him even as he did. Left on his own, this one whom he had named Joshua would not have survived that first night in the forest. And even now, how much longer would Joshua live before some natural force decided to drop him to the ground like a wormy piece of fruit exorcised from the tree of life in order to protect the fit and the healthy?

These were harsh questions to ask about the living thing he held most dear in all the world. He had asked the questions and now he would listen for the answers.

Old Man sat wrapped in silence upon the ledge, the only sound coming from the wind as it gently caressed him in perhaps the deepest solitude he had ever known. And he heard. He heard the voice he was longing for—the guiding voice from deep within that never failed him if he would but still himself and listen—if he allowed the obstructions of fear and willfulness to be removed, his answer always came.

His mercy was justified. His life with this innocent one, this innocent of innocents, was blessed by the power that had put them both in the same place and time on that night so long ago.

He would stay upon this ledge among the cliffs a while longer. He would sit and listen, for there was more for him to learn. He would stay and surrender. And when he surrendered, the answers would be given to him.

*   *   *   *

Nothing. Darkness, yes. Blisters on his lips from the scorching sun, yes. And silence. That was all.

Old Man felt a dull ache behind his eyes and his belly cramped from lack of food. There was nothing except his body's pain to sustain him and to convince him that he was still alert enough to hear his inner voice when it spoke, as he knew it would. If only he knew its source, he could summon it and be done with this. But no—struggle was not the way. He knew that. He must surrender to something, but to what, he didn't know. He couldn't control this thing that was happening to him. He couldn't even name it. There was a will that was not his own and he must accept that mystery. He must trust it.

Silence and fasting were the only keys he knew to unlock the door that sometimes opened to let him hear the guiding voice that had never failed him in its wisdom. It had never shown him deceit or anger, or even impatience. Or lied to him. Never. It had shown him only truth, and gentleness, and hope. And love. Above all, love. His inner voice had brought only love into his life if he would but persevere.

Eight days had passed and Old Man was midway through the eighth night, with its quarter-moon beginning to fade and show signs that dawn was not far off. He was exhausted. Water from a source somewhere above him slowly dripped into a small earthen bowl he had brought with him the second time he had climbed to the ledge. Water was the only nourishment he had allowed himself, and it was not enough. The bowl had been filled just four times with the passing of each night and day, and it was not enough to sustain him without solid food for much longer. He would have to make the treacherous descent back down the cliffs when his quest had ended, and he couldn't wait much longer. Very soon, he would not have the strength to make it down without falling.

The ninth day came and went, and still there was only silence. The pain was becoming unbearable. Old Man had put his life in danger because of his physical weakness, and, in doing so, had also endangered the life of Joshua. The boy would not be able to survive in the forest without him. Physically, he was frail and misshapen, susceptible to sickness when the forest was cold and wet during the season of rains. Old Man carefully tended him during these times, keeping him within the cave most of the time and near the fire. Old Man would entertain him with stories of Randall's Bow, and they would drink tea and eat the thick, flavorful soup that was kept simmering over the fire. But always, Joshua's strength of spirit would dominate the sickness, and soon he would be well and at Old Man's side, walking with him through the forest once again.

But time was passing quickly, and he would not live forever. Another decade or so at the most, if he was fortunate enough to remain near the point of strength, spiritually and mentally, he had come to in these last few years. He was stronger now than he had ever been, and it was not only in his mind and spirit that his strength had manifested. His body, too, had found new life and vigor in the harmony of the forest and with the little one at the center of his life. But plans for the future welfare of Joshua must be made. Truth and wisdom and growth of spirit were not the only concerns here. Joshua's life, his very survival, was at stake. The future must be considered. Slowly at first, because it would be painful for both of them to think of one without the other. And confusing, too, because, in truth, Joshua might be the first to pass on. He knew he must discuss the possibility, the inevitability, of death with Joshua. Both their deaths. He didn't need guidance from his inner voice to know that.

Soon. It must be soon. So much pain was in him. He couldn't bear it much longer. He didn't have much time left until the pain would claim him as its own.

And still the silence thundered in his ears.

He remained awake throughout the ninth night, his eyes focused on a star high above the forest. As dawn broke, the aching in his joints eased a bit, and he felt his muscles relax amidst their throbbing until he slowly slipped to the hard rock floor of the ledge. He was on his back, legs straight and arms at his sides. He closed his eyes, his attention turned inward, and he saw himself as he was in spirit, without pain or discomfort any longer. His mind was alert and clear, at rest and knowing that the time had come. His breathing slowed so that his chest and stomach scarcely moved

And then he slept—and dreamed.

*   *   *   *

In the dream, Old Man walks with Joshua in the time and place toward which they are moving like arrows aimed at the heart of truth. The heart will burst and bleed when the arrows hit their mark, and its contents would spill out, to be revealed at last.

The streets of Randall's Bow are dark. No rain has fallen to cleanse the dirt from the houses and to nourish the flowers on the village green, where announcements are made each day of who has died and who has been taken to the infirmary.

Rain begins to fall, but this is not the soft, warm wet of springtime rain that soaks the streets of Randall's Bow. No. This is not only the wet of rain at all, beneath the feet of those who walk here. No. It is the stinking wet of mud and slime that is on these streets, and it sheaths Randall's Bow in all its days and nights now. Death is the crop it feeds, and the harvest is most bountiful. The stench of rotting flesh is in the air, and the only movement is that of wild dogs and rats as they feast on the yet unburied of death's harvest from the day before. There is no sun, but a kind of daylight comes as the eclipsed moon slips from behind the shadow of the earth and gives blank-faced witness to the atrocities on the earth below.

The once-green earth is black and wet now, soaked with vomit from the hearts and souls of the creatures that dwell here. They can no longer be recognized as men or women. Their gender cannot be distinguished, one from the other, their bodies and countenances reflecting only what is in their hearts, becoming more grotesque each day as their actions take direction from that beating horror within their breasts that pumps a blood boiling with the darkest of passions through their swollen veins. He cannot call those he greets human as he pauses to ask about their welfare each time he thinks he recognizes a feature or expression from the past.

And little Joshua. What lessons is he learning from the horror in these streets of Randall's Bow? His innocence is drained from him by the ridicule and vicious curses hurled at him as he passes by. The screeching laughter of the monsters peel from his face and very being the peace that Old Man and the forest has so lovingly nurtured with their teachings.

And the body of little Joshua is battered by the blows that fall upon him. That face of beauty, so deformed to the eye until one sees the love that's there. That little face, once so sweet, now bears the look of one betrayed to death. And still he looks upon Old Man with love.

I forgive you, the eyes of Joshua say. You would gladly die for me, my friend. I know that. But the time is mine, not yours, and you must have courage. You must not flee from this place again. The time for that is done, and there is no time nor reason for retreat or cowardliness. Yours is not that way, as it once was.

Your way is what you have taught me, the way of true sight. True voice. True action, the eyes of Joshua say. The place of solitude, our beloved cave, is no longer enough. The forest now is not enough. Now we must be here to do what we are led to do—yes, were born to do—and trust that all is what it is meant to be, though what we see would tell us differently.

There are things for us to do together before I go, the eyes of Joshua say. Yes. Before I go. And you must stay, my beloved friend and protector. I go before you, Old Man. We would not have guessed that truth, that sacred night you found me on the forest floor. The forest was too kind to tell us that, though if we looked closely enough we would have seen that those like me go passing quickly to the place beyond our knowing. But we were not ready, and so we could not *see. We could not know. Now we see because we must, because it's time, and we can bear the pain this knowledge brings, because we must.*

You do no wrong, old friend, the eyes of Joshua say. And you must be brave when the time has come for me to go and you to stay. Awaken now, and descend the cliffs. You have taught me well, and I have more to learn still, as you give me what is in your heart. Our guiding inner voices will keep us safe if we but listen, and we will know when the time has come for us to go to Randall's Bow.

*   *   *   *

Old Man is awakened by his screams. He does not know whether he has slept or whether extreme exhaustion has obliterated his resistance and let the voice pierce through his struggle when his surrender became total and absolute.

His body shakes and runs wet with sweat. His mouth is dry and parched and his head holds pain inside his skull like white-hot coals. He fears the pounding that he feels throughout his body will bring his death if it continues for much longer.

Sleep. Despite the pain, he knows that sleep will come quickly now. And when he awakes, the cliffs will be waiting for him. Old Man takes the half-filled bowl of water and drinks its contents. He looks eastward and sees the rising sun, its golden rim pushing above the horizon. It is the last thing he sees before he falls back upon his bed of stone and into a deep and dreamless sleep, not knowing that Joshua, too, has dreamed the dream

Chapter 10

Mid-afternoon. The handle of the hoe in Joshua's hand is dark and wet with sweat as he applies his efforts once again to the ever-present weeds. He's grateful for the work. It occupies his time and requires only mindless repetition. The monotony of the task allows his mind to wander in fantasy about what lay in store for him twelve miles to the south in Randall's Bow. He has a feeling that he can't explain—restlessness, anxiety, misgivings. Fear. Excited anticipation. The feelings have been with him since he awakened suddenly at dawn and knew that his life had changed, or was about to change somehow, although everything around him is the same.

But he is different. He knows Old Man will take him to Randall's Bow. That struggle is over, he is certain of that. And there is something he heard—a voice that spoke to him from within. His guiding inner voice had come to him in a way that was different from the way he heard the sounds of the forest. It had come from a place even deeper than his mind. Separated from it, somehow. His heart? No. It was from somewhere else even beyond that place. It was from a place in the middle of him, something like his heart, but not. He had walked in a dream with Old Man and it had told him that Randall's Bow was not so far away today. He would go there with Old Man and see the things he had only heard about.

He had much to give to the people of Randall's Bow.

His inner voice had told him so.

Joshua looked up at the cliffs, his eyes resting on the place where he had last seen Old Man. He wasn't there. For a moment, Joshua was frozen with the fear that Old Man had fallen from the ledge during the night. What could he do? He had purposely not looked up at the ledge this morning when he left the cave to milk Goat and collect the eggs still warm in the nest of the quails that lived nearby. And throughout the day, he had kept his eyes on the ground while he worked because it would only cause him pain to see Old Man so still and waiting. Today he had decided to spare himself the scene above, and try to ease the worry that the passing days had brought. How many? He had lost count. He hadn't searched the wall for the little speck that marked Old Man. Until now.

Then, to the left of the edge of the shelf and slightly below it, where the climbing places were that made the shelf accessible, something moved. So slowly moved. Old Man was coming down.

"His quest has ended," Joshua whispered, and then he heard his inner voice whisper back in answer, "No. His quest, and yours, have just begun."

And on the cliffs, Old Man heard these words, too.

*   *   *   *

The descent was hard. Nine days and nights with only water to sustain him, and the torturous experience of his dream, had left Old Man without much strength, mentally or physically. The sun was hot and burned through the skins that covered his back and shoulders. The heat felt good on his tired muscles, but the sweat caused his hands to slip from the rocks as he tried to steady himself. It was almost impossible. He must proceed slowly or he would surely fall.

Time wasn't important anymore. His perception of time had changed during his dream, and later that morning while he had slept. He felt less urgency about the fate of Joshua and what the boy would do without him. He didn't know why, but he knew it was connected somehow to his dream, despite the horrors that had been revealed to him. He was confused about it, and, strangely, he was grateful for that. The terror he had felt upon awakening this morning, and the pain that had gripped his body and his stomach convulsed with violent retching were still vivid in his mind. Much of the pain was still with him. Old Man breathed a silent prayer of thanks for the cloud that draped his memory, and proceeded with the only thing that mattered now—his safe descent to the ground and then rest within the safety of the cave.

As soon as he saw that Old Man had started his descent down the rocky wall, Joshua ran to the spot where he would first put his foot upon the forest floor. Because of the many protrusions of rock formations and shrubs that blocked his sight, he could barely see the small figure slowly coming towards him. Then, as if by magic made by some wizard of the forest, Old Man was standing there before him, his face gray and drained of strength.

Old Man felt a surge of energy and a clarity swept through him as he turned from the wall and looked at Joshua. The two of them rested as one, enfolded in the silent presence of their love for one another. They were destiny's children now, safe along its path no matter what the outcome, or how others would judge it if they knew it. They would continue their journey within the forest and speak its truths for a little while longer, until the time came for them to leave this place of peace for Randall's Bow.

The silence was broken by Goat's annoyed bleating, whose udder was swollen with the sweet results of the day's grazing. She had missed the soft voice and gentle hands of Old Man for much too long to suit her. Now that he had returned, she was impatient for his touch upon her once again. Joshua was not a patient receiver of her gifts, pulling and tugging to hurry a process that would not be hurried, no matter how hard he tried. It was slowed down, truth be told, by angry kicks when his pulling at her became too rough for her to endure.

Old Man smiled despite his weariness. He knew Goat's preference when it came to being milked, and he was sure that Joshua knew it too, but refused to change his ways. It was a battle of wills, and patience was a lesson that Joshua had yet to learn. He would come to know, in time, that nature's ways, and Goat's, cannot be changed by force of will, and that to try served only to delay life's perfect pace and process.

There were many other lessons to be learned, and Joshua would not be the only one to learn them. Something had changed between them. They were equals now, Old Man knew, and they must trust each other and learn together, each teaching the other with his special gifts that complemented what the other lacked and gave more power to who the other was. Old Man was able to sense a little of it now, but most of it was a mystery, and once again he felt gratitude for not knowing. To know more now would be to know more than he could bear. He felt again the terror and the pain he had felt upon the ledge when he awakened with this morning's dawn. He turned away from Joshua, to shield him from his fear.

But Joshua knew, and Old Man knew that. And suspected that perhaps the boy knew more than he.

Old Man walked slowly across the garden to where Goat was grazing. He knelt next to her and whispered into her ear, "Once more, my friend, and then I will be the one to come to you in gratitude for your sweet gift of milk. But not today. Today I have no strength for that. I spent my last upon that wall of rock you watched me crawl down like an ant upon a giant boulder. An ant in size only, I'm afraid. Agility is not my strength, the passing years have seen to that. I'm here and safe, and soon must sleep. But not until you have given Joshua your sweet milk so that I might sleep with a full, warm belly. And while I sleep, my strength will be restored from the nourishment you have given me. And when you awaken tomorrow, I will come to you, and again we'll talk and be together, and my hands will warm you in the morning's coolness. I go to rest now, and wait for Joshua to bring your milk to me."

Old Man stood and turned away from Goat. The entrance to the cave looked very far away.

"Come. I'll help you." Joshua put his arm around Old Man waist. "You're very weak and tired and only sleep will bring you back to me the way you were before. So full of wisdom and new things to teach me to fill my mind and heart. And laughter. Laughter, the best of all. And truths that sometimes make me happy and sometimes make me sad, too. But never make me sleep." Joshua's laugh was like music to Old Man, and he could feel the peace and quiet that he longed for begin to return as he leaned on Joshua and they started a slow walk toward the cave. The sound of his own laughter, too, was music to his ears.

Old Man entered the cave, leaving Goat's protesting bleats behind as Joshua knelt to milk her for the last time. She doesn't know, Old Man thought, how much Joshua loves her and that the hardness and clumsiness of his hands are caused by a cruelty not his own. And he knows so little himself. The dream has shown him that.

Old Man surveyed the warm interior of the cave. A fire burned brightly at its center, and there was a smaller fire burning near the two pallets of soft skins and furs where he and Joshua slept. He knelt by the small cooking fire and lifted the lid from a kettle resting nearby. As he had hoped, the kettle contained the herbal broth that eased them into sleep on nights when sleep was slow in coming. He sat down and stared at the dancing flames. His eyes grew heavy from the warmth and his mind receptive, almost without thought, non-resistant to the images that came before him. He saw again the fleshless face of Joshua, as he had in his visiondream. His body stiffened and he uttered a small cry as tears slowly crept down his cheeks and his heart began to race with the terror he had felt when he had awakened this morning. Was it only this morning? It seemed so long ago.

"Old Man!" The high-pitched music of Joshua's voice brought Old Man back to the present, and he slowly opened his eyes. Joshua was standing in front of him, a look of concern on his face. "Are you alright? Goat's milk is here, and sleep is close by, too. I've been calling you, but you didn't hear me. Do you feel sick? You need some milk and broth, and then sleep will come." Joshua's eyes became full of light and laughter as he anticipated their conversation. His smile revealed the amused, elf-like expression that he so often wore.

But fatigue had claimed Old Man and there was no room for the conversation Joshua so eagerly craved. Not even room for happiness with this one he loved so much. He had nothing to give and was too tired to receive.

"Not now, Joshua," Old Man whispered. "Just a few sips and then I must sleep. We'll talk later after I've rested. I have much to tell you. And much to ask, perhaps. There are things that are beyond my understanding."

Joshua watched as Old Man slowly took a few sips from each of the two earthen bowls of milk and broth and then lowered himself onto the soft furs and fell into a deep and instantaneous sleep.

Old Man did not hear the words that Joshua softly spoke to him from trembling, unsmiling lips. "And I, my friend, have much to tell you. It will take the two of us, and maybe others who now dwell downriver, to learn the meaning of this day."

Chapter 11

Joshua and Old Man are fast asleep by the fire. Old Man sleeps peacefully, but Joshua tosses and turns as he dreams of a meadow engulfed in a thick cloud of mist.

*   *   *   *

Joshua walks into the meadow and sees Old Man waving to him in the distance. The mist begins to clear and, as he walks towards Old Man, The Great Black War Horse suddenly appears, standing at Old Man's side. When Joshua reaches them, they stand unmoving together and watch as scenes unfold before them.

A horse-drawn wagon piled full of bodys moves slowly through Randall's Bow. People along the road draw back, weeping and wailing in their grief. The wagon stops. The driver and another man jump down from the wagon and pick up a body laying outside the door of a cabin, carry it to the wagon and throw it on top of the others.. The driver's helper returns to the cabin and draws a yellow X on the door. Rats scurry along the ground, clawing at the door, trying to get inside as the wagon continues down the road and disappears into the mist.

The scene abruptly shifts to Joshua standing in front of a man dressed in a long black cloak. A hood hides the man's face. He holds a whip in one hand and a sword in the other. The man swirls the whip's lash high above his head and brings it down with a loud cracking sound. Joshua falls to the ground in front of him. Old Man stands silently nearby and watches Joshua struggle to rise. The man steps toward Joshua and raises his sword. The Great Black War Horse comes into the scene at full gallop and stops between the man and

Joshua, rearing up on his hind legs, pawing the air with his hooves that are flashing silver flames. The man drops his whip and sword in front of the horse and slowly backs away. Then he falls to his knees and weeps. The man and The Great Black War Horse suddenly disappear and Joshua, now on his feet, stands alone.

Joshua awakens from his dream and sits up.

"Old Man! Old Man!"

Old Man doesn't awaken.

Joshua lays back down and immediately falls into a deep sleep. And in his sleep, he knows there is one of like spirit in Randall's Bow who will take him safely home, and they will know each other when first they meet.

*   *   *   *

Old Man and Joshua awaken before dawn and go to the back of the cave to fetch fresh water from the spring. They sit at the water's edge and look at their reflections. It seems as if two little old men are sitting beneath the water's surface, looking back at them. Old Man reaches down into the water and the images disappear into a series of small ripples.

Joshua looks into the water as their reflections slowly return. "What's Randall's Bow really like, Old Man," he asks

"It has a warrior's heart. The people there are good people and very brave." He pauses, then continues. "But it's hard for them to be gentle with each other." He reaches down and disturbs the pond's surface once again. "And they drive away what frightens them. Or they kill it."

The golden rays of the morning sun streak through the forest as Old Man and Joshua walk from the cave. The strain of yesterday isn't forgotten, but its pain is short-lived, like a memory from long ago. They walk side-by-side in silence toward Goat, sensing a new purpose in their day. But, as yet, what the experience of it will be is a mystery. One day soon, Randall's Bow will be within their sight as they approach it on the river, and their work there will begin. For now, however, Goat must be milked and breakfast prepared. Then the two of them will talk and each will open his heart to the other. Together they will learn to live within the mystery.

After they finished breakfast, they entered the forest in silence. The time for words had not yet come. Though unspoken, it was agreed. They would walk and they would wait.

Their lives were about to change and there was nothing Old Man could do to prevent it. It was predestined, if there was such a thing. Predestined by whom or what he didn't know, but he knew they would soon go to Randall's Bow and that their time there would be longer than he would like. He knew no more than that. That, and the foreboding he felt, a heaviness and dread that this time there would be more than just himself at the mercy of the forces in that place along the banks of Cold River, whose people were no better nor worse than those of any other place beyond the forest.

Old Man was the first to speak. "I had a dream upon the ledge." He spoke in a soft and gentle way, but the sudden intrusion of his voice came as a violation of the silence of the forest. The wildlife around them disappeared and they were left alone with whatever it was they would face together for the first time, beginning with this moment.

"I know." Joshua's voice was as soft and gentle as Old Man's.

Old Man seemed not to hear what Joshua said. "We are on a journey, you and I," he continued, "and I don't know where we are going. I speak of more than going to Randall's Bow. Let me tell you my dream, and then we'll talk. Perhaps together we can find its meaning."

"I know," Joshua said once more. This time, Old man heard him and knew what he meant. Joshua knew. And he knew what Old Man did not. The terror he had felt upon the ledge came to him again, and he asked his question, knowing that the answer would be the same two words he had just heard.

"Joshua." Old Man's voice trembled as he searched for words. "Joshua," he began again. Joshua looked up at Old Man, his expression clearly focused and unafraid. His smile was gone, replaced with a look of peace and acceptance. Old Man realized that Joshua knew what his question would be.

"Joshua, I hear a voice that comes from deep within me. It guides me to the truth of things, though sometimes it takes a very long time for me to grasp that truth. You hear it too, don't you?"

"Yes."

"And Joshua. The gift of seeing the future—of knowing what is to come— you have it?" The answer came, as Old Man knew it would.

"Yes. I know what is to be. Sometimes I hear. Sometimes I see. It's very new to me and I have much to learn about it. I need your wisdom more than ever now. We have a little more time to learn together, but not much. Three or four cycles of the moon, perhaps. No more than that will be given us to remain here. Our solitude is nearly done."

"And when?" Old Man asked, the thunder of his pounding heart made his voice sound very far away to him, "When did you first begin to see so far? And do you know the content of my dream?"

"Yes. I, too, awoke to terror before yesterday's sun had risen. And the dreams we had, yes, they were the same. But the dreams weren't one dream. You looked at Randall's Bow through your eyes. And the horror that you felt for what you saw, and the sorrow that you felt when you looked at me and saw how close I was to death, those feelings were within your heart. They belonged to you. They weren't mine. Our dreams were the same, but were not one. What you saw and felt and did within that space of self and soul was yours and yours alone. But I was there in that very place and by your side. The difference was that, while my eyes, too, saw those streets and rotting bodies and creatures walking as in death, I saw through my own eyes what will happen when you return to the place from which you fled,

"I saw only strength and beauty in your words and deeds. You weren't devoured by the horror that surrounded you. Nor was I, although it may have seemed I was, or was about to be. You've taught me well, and will be given more to teach, and learn, in the time we have remaining here. Rest your heart with that. The dream was but a dream and wasn't real. It warns us of a time that we must face, not to fill us with fear, but to help us prepare ourselves and gain in strength, as we will do. It warns us, tells us of what is to come. But it doesn't tell us why. Only that the time must come. And will."

And so they talked throughout the day about their dreams as they walked along the riverbank, first south towards Randall's Bow, then north, back towards the cave. They were at peace as they walked back into the clearing, busy with life made fearless with the gentle love that had enfolded them both, too, within the forest.

Three or four cycles of the moon. Joshua had said that was the time they had left here in this place. Old Man suddenly felt cold despite the warmth of the sun. And more that he could not name. Why was he returning to Randall's Bow? In truth, he did not know.

* * * *

There was movement at the far edge of the clearing as the wolf came out of the forest, gently carrying an injured bird in his mouth. He trotted over to Joshua, who was working in the garden, and sat down in front of him. Joshua patted the wolf on his head. "What have you brought me?" he asked, and took the bird in the palm of his hand and raised it up to eye level. "An injured wing, I see." He cradled the unmoving bird in both hands and sat down on the grass. The wolf moved to the edge of the clearing, laid down and watched Joshua. As did Old Man, who sat unmoving near the entrance to the cave.

Joshua said something to the bird, but Old Man was too far away to hear his words. Joshua continued to talk to the bird, then laughed softly as the bird began to move its wings. He spoke again to the bird and laughed as he held it in front of him and raised his hands above his head. The bird hesitated for a moment, then fluttered its wings and, with a graceful swoop across the clearing and back again in front of Joshua, soared above the treetops. Old Man, the wolf, and Joshua watched until the bird was out of sight.

The wolf trotted back into the forest while Joshua returned his attention to the garden. Old Man stood and began to walk towards Joshua, changed his mind and retreated into the cave. He had no words, no question to ask that would not belittle what he had just seen.

Who is this child who looks so old and heals the wounds of those he touches, he wondered. Who is this strange little boy who makes the bitterness in my heart disappear? A gentle breeze moved over Old Man and all became quiet and still. Even the birds seemed to have ceased their song.

The breeze died down and Old Man heard the birds take up their song once more, as if they had never ceased. He looked at Joshua working in the garden and marveled at the mystery—and the beauty—of their lives.

Chapter 12

"Please," Eleanor spoke softly to the frightened voice behind the door. "We'll do what we can do to help, and then we'll leave."

"I don't want your help!"

The door opened just a crack, then a little wider. Then a little wider, giving Eleanor and Leyla just enough room to squeeze inside, the door slamming shut behind them. The woman pointed to a narrow cot where a boy lay twisted and still under a filthy blanket. Eleanor hurried to the cot and looked at the woman who had let them in. "How long has he been like this?"

The woman avoided her Eleanor's accusing eyes and looked at the wall. "Yes. I know. He's dead."

Leyla put her arm around the woman's thin shoulders. "Are you alone here?" she asked.

"Yes. My husband died three days ago. This is my son. He died yesterday."

Leyla went to the cot and looked closely at the dead boy, gently brushing a lock of hair from his eyes. She looked up at her mother. "There have been more than a dozen like this in the last few days," she whispered.

The woman behind them began to cough, covering her mouth with a blood-stained rag. As Eleanor stepped towards her, the woman put her hands up.

"No! Stay back! There's nothing you can do. Go home, or you'll catch it yourself, if you haven't already!"

Eleanor came closer. "I'll get you some water."

"We have no water," the woman said through her coughing, now increasing in frequency and intensity. "Please. I'm dying, too. It's what I want. Please. Go."

Eleanor looked at her and nodded, The woman spoke the truth. She would be dead by morning. She took Leyla by the arm and pulled her toward the door. "Come," she said. "There's nothing we can do here."

Many died in Randall's Bow that year. The ragman had done his job well. There hadn't been a part of Randall's Bow that he had left untouched. As he traveled through the town that day, he stopped before each cabin that had left a pile of unwanted rags at their door and took them away—along with death.

Even the rats stayed away. The lucky ones had been able to escape to the safety of the riverbank and make their burrows there until some secret inward urging from nature told them that it was safe to return to their nests and scavenge in the town again. But even some of the rats weren't so lucky. Some of them caught the fever, too, and then went throughout the town, just as the ragman had done, the fever in their brains and leavings. Some only brushed against other rats in their nests. Some sank their teeth deeply into their own kind. Some bit humans. Others lay bloated and dying in the streets, untouched. It made no matter. All were carriers of death, and the fever fed and flourished where they lay or where they ran.

There were those in Randall's Bow who had been gifted by a natural immunity and worked among the sick without fear of the fever. As the months wore on, it became obvious who these gifted ones were and it was to them that caring for the sick was entrusted. A natural selection that grew smaller as one fell and then another, not from the fever, but from exhaustion.

Randall found that he had been given the gift when he had cared for the men who fought for him in the days when war was his work. And he found that he had been given the gift a second time when the fever raged in those early days in Randall's Bow. He and Eleanor worked fearlessly and unceasingly side-by-side among the sick. For many months they labored, seeing that all who needed help were cared for and that no on lacked for food or companionship. Or a speedy yet respectful burial.

Leyla, too, worked with them. A beautiful woman now in her mid-twenties, she was known as a healer, like her mother. The two women gathered herbs in the forest and mixed their medicines at the table in the kitchen of the manor. But they had found no cure. At best, they were able to mix concoctions that eased the pain of swollen joints for a little while.

The fever was so strong that the mixtures soon lost their power over pain and new mixtures had to be devised.

Randall was obsessed with defeating the fever, an enemy stronger than any he had ever faced before. And he was losing battle after battle. Each death brought him closer to losing this deadliest of wars. He had a large infirmary built on the outskirts of the settlement where he could concentrate his efforts by bringing all the afflicted together in one place. But his enemy relentlessly continued to claim its victims, and, in Randall's mind, the fault lay with him. As each day passed, his sense of failure increased. Until the fever stopped spreading of its own accord, until somehow it ran its course, there would be no hope for an end to this misery. Randall drove himself even harder. Sleep became a friend he seldom saw, and all who tried to help him were ignored. In his mind, the battle was his, and his alone. Merrill and Leyla gave up trying to communicate with him, much less help him, because he saw their attempts as interference with what he had to do. Even Eleanor was forced to step aside because she could no longer keep up with him.

And then what everyone feared, but hoped to be impossible, happened.

Randall awoke one morning to find the fever had taken him prisoner, too. He forced himself to dress, ate his breakfast and left the manor before Eleanor came into the kitchen. It was the first time he had begun his day without her presence since Judith's death and Eleanor sensed at once that something was terribly wrong.

When Rashan went to the stables to saddle The Great Black War Horse for Randall's morning ride, he found Randall already there. He lay half-conscious and delirious in the horse's stall, the saddle clutched tightly in his arms. The horse stood beside him like a statue, not moving until Rashan had pulled Randall to a soft pile of straw outside the stall. Rashan touched Randall's hot, dry forehead and saw his chest heaving as he struggled to breathe. The rasping sound of his tortured gasps seemed to fill the stables. A thin yellow crust had hardened from an oozing beneath his closed eyelids.

Rashan needed no one to tell him that Randall had not escaped from his worst enemy. Not this time. The fever, at last, had claimed him as its own.

PART TWO

Chapter 13

The raft drifted slowly downstream with the pull of the river's gentle current. Old Man sat at the stern holding the tiller loosely as he watched Goat feasting on the mixture of grass and grain in the rectangular wooden trough in the center of the raft. He envied Goat her calmness. He turned his attention to Joshua, sitting at the front of their raft of tightly lashed logs. His concentration seemed to be on the lush green banks of Cold River passing by on either side of them, but Old Man knew the true focus of his concentration was otherwise. Joshua felt as if his heart would burst, it was pounding so hard and so fast. He looked at Old Man, whose attention seemed to be on the river ahead, keeping their course steady and straight. Now that they were underway, his eagerness to take this journey had become more and more tempered with fear the closer they got to their destination. And now they were almost there. They would be in Randall's Bow before the sun had set.

"Soon now," Old Man called, trying to convey a lightness in his voice.

Joshua nodded and looked downriver without turning back. He hadn't spoken to Old Man during the several hours it had taken to come this far. What he knew and what he didn't know about the journey and what they would face in Randall's Bow were all mixed up in his mind. He felt as if his thoughts were separated from him by a kind of veil, and he preferred it that way for just a little while longer. He needed rest from the intense mix of a twelve-year-old's curiosity and the sensitivity to something he couldn't name that had consumed him for the past year. He needed rest and a kind of inner regrouping—the kind Old Man pursued when he sought his solitude on the cliffs. He had learned to find his own solitude with Old Man's help, who taught him that solitude and silence were necessary from time-to-time if he were to discover his true purpose in life.

Old Man had also warned him that solitude could become avoidance if it was misused. It could become hiding rather than seeking, would dull any gifts he had, and ultimately destroy him. His perception would become distorted and he would deny what was true. He and Joshua must tell each other exactly what was in their hearts, he said. They must come to know one another as they really are, in truth and with love. That was the way they had lived in the forest and they must not change now. The last year in the forest before their journey to Randall's Bow had been spent in strengthening the bond between them and it must become even stronger in the coming days.

At first, the burden of what he had been given had seemed too much for Joshua to bear. The intensity and the clarity of the experience came in short bursts, with Old Man usually receiving the same thoughts and images. There were other times, however, when only one of them knew what had transpired. It was during these times that Joshua experienced the gift of knowing what the future held for them, and always with an admonition that he must not reveal what he had seen to Old Man. This gift was for Joshua alone.

These times were difficult for both of them. Joshua would feel that he was doing something wrong—that somehow he was deceiving Old Man. And Old Man would sense that their roles had been reversed and that Joshua was now the teacher and he was the student, and he didn't know why. Where had he failed? What was it in him that was contrary to the inner truth that he felt as strongly as ever? Why was Joshua concealing something from him, and what was it? When he tried to talk to Joshua about it, he seemed sadly lacking in something he couldn't define. He would wait for Joshua to enlighten him during these times, but his waiting was rewarded by silence.

As difficult as it was for Old Man, the role reversal was equally difficult for Joshua. Suddenly his teacher seemed to know nothing. And as he watched Old Man suffer in his ignorance, Joshua also suffered. And yet, he had been told that he was not, under any circumstances, to tell Old Man the full extent of what he had been given.

And so they continued to talk—and suffer—together. Time passed, as did their trials. They came to know that they were not so far apart after all. As Joshua learned to use his gift of knowing the future and not to be afraid, it became a useful, even practical, part of his life. As his fear diminished, he became more at ease with himself and with Old Man. The tension between them lessened and life settled down to what it had been before.

Their efforts were rewarded with pleasant days in the forest, their trust in themselves and each other reaching deeper and deeper levels. And the more they came to trust, the more they had to learn to live with mystery. Then, as the day that they would leave their beloved forest grew ever nearer, a new fear gripped Old Man—that returning to what he had once fled would thrust him back to the way he had been those many years ago. In some ways, even now, it was as if he had never changed. His perception sometimes became more confused, while Joshua's became more clear. To admit fear seemed at first to be a falsehood against himself. But he soon learned that the falsehood was hiding his fear, and as he brought it to the light it began to dissipate. Truth was what he wanted—what he sought so desperately—and truth demanded that his fear be honestly revealed to Joshua if trust was to take its place once more.

But Old Man didn't know the whole truth. He didn't know how often the future was revealed to Joshua.

A new sense of peace came over Joshua as he experienced his gifts more and more. It came to him in little day-to-day incidents that were foretold and then became realities. And with that peace, he sensed that Old Man, too, walked the same path with more faith and trust.

And yet, thoughts of death had been much in Old Man's thoughts of late. What it was and what it meant when we leave this life as we know it, and whether there was another place or state of being after this one. Questions. Never answers. At times, he was obsessed with it and the silence without an answer crushed him like a cruel and heavy weight. And then there were times when the knowledge that he shouldn't know the answer to this thing until it was his to experience enveloped him in a sense of peace that he knew was but a foretaste of what was yet to come beyond this life. But today was now, and there was much to do before his time upon this earth was done.

And along the riverbank, as the raft came ever closer to its destination, loped one unseen among the trees—one who was there on that long ago night when a babe was found on the forest floor beneath the heavens.

Chapter 14

Leyla stood beside the bed and watched Eleanor wipe the fever-sweat from Randall's face. Her mother softly crooned a lullabye she had sung to Leyla as a child when she couldn't sleep, to help her not be afraid of the shadows that danced upon the bedroom walls. And so Eleanor sang the same song to Randall as the shadows of death danced nearer and nearer to the fallen warrior.

Does he know, Leyla wondered? Can he see the shadows as I used to, and do they frighten him? Can he even hear my mother singing to him, and if he does, does he know it's her voice that he hears? And if he's afraid, does her singing make him not afraid anymore, as it did for me? He looks so strong lying there, as if he's resting until the next great battle. Sick almost to death, he still looks stronger than any one of us. It's his spirit that does that. It's not his spirit that's sick or full of fear. His spirit sings to me now—sings to all of us, so we won't be afraid of what's happening here in the place he loves so much. I feel him talking to us now, telling us not to be afraid, for we will win this battle raging here. I hear him talking to us through my mother's voice. It's Randall who is singing as the other side comes into view. And it does not frighten him, he tells us. No. It does not frighten him at all.

Eleanor looked up at Leyla and smiled. She took the bowl of hot broth Leyla had brought and held it in her lap for a moment, cupping it between her palms. The way she looked at the steaming, deliciously fragrant liquid, it could have been a living thing. "He must eat," she said quietly, more to herself than to Leyla. She handed the bowl back to her daughter. "Try to make him eat, even just a little. He might eat for you. Speak to him. Sing to him a little. You know how he loved to hear your voice. Hearing it might wake him long enough so he can take a little nourishment. He needs more than just water if he's going to get well again." She looked past Leyla as she said the last. Randall was not going to get well. He would not see another morning. She knew that. But she was not ready to accept it. Not yet. To hear her own voice saying that would be too much for her to bear. And so she kept her gaze upon the floor in front of her and left the room, allowing the tears to come only when she was alone and in the safety of her kitchen.

*　*　*　*

The stench of rotting corpses brought tears to Merrill's eyes. He watched a horse-drawn wagon loaded to overflowing with bodies roll up to the edge of a large pit near the river and stop with a lurch. The weight of the bodies shifted, nearly toppling the wagon into the pit. Two men jumped from the wagon and began to pull bodies off the open back one-by-one and throw them into the gaping hole, like the mouth of the earth welcoming her children home. When the wagon had been emptied, Merrill, on horseback with a cross-bow resting across the saddle in front of him, called to one of the men.

"Theo!"

"Sir?" The man answered before looking toward the caller. He recognized that voice well and dreaded it whenever it called his name. It was the messenger of harsh demands, usually difficult to carry out and little time to do it.

"I'll look to you to keep the men working, Theo." Flames crackled as the bodies in the pit began to burn. A dark, stinking smoke from the heaps of burning flesh rose into the sky, hesitated briefly, then was carried across the river by a gentle yet insistent breeze, rising in a feathery arc above the trees. "Be sure you carry the ashes far downstream before you throw them in the river. We'll be rid of the fever soon. The fire and the river will take care of that if you do your job well."

Theo looked toward the pit, now nearly hidden by the dark gray, almost black putrid smoke. He said nothing. There was no way to tell Merrill what he thought of all this without putting his very life in danger.

Merrill cradled his cross-bow in the crook of his arm, looked at the flaming pit for a moment, then abruptly wheeled his mount and headed upriver.

* * * *

Leyla sat on the bed next to Randall and held a spoonful of broth to his cracked lips, now bloody from their dryness. She began to sing a song her mother had taught her about little boys pretending to be brave soldiers, bending closer to him as his eyelids fluttered briefly. After a short pause, Randall opened his eyes and smiled at her, a tear running down his cheek. He took a few spoon-fulls of the broth and then shook his head. He would take no more. He closed his eyes and slept again.

Leyla sat looking at Randall and thought of the last few months when she had begun to join him and her mother in their morning ritual, sitting in the kitchen over mugs of hot tea before he left the manor to make his daily rounds. At first, she had felt like an intruder on these private meetings, but soon she believed them when they assured her that her presence was welcome. She added beauty to their meeting, they told her, laughing at her shyness. And if she could manage to absorb some of their wisdom, no matter how boring it might be, she would someday rule the world. Well, if not the world, they laughed, then perhaps Randall's Bow. And as for them, they said, if they could absorb even a little bit of her beauty in return, it would be more than a fair exchange. But they had no illusions about that, they said, so she should join their company simply because they loved her.

The three of them would sit at the table in Eleanor's kitchen, drinking the strong tea she concocted from her gatherings of herbs, eating freshly made bread with a thick blanket of jam made from the forest's berries. Leyla picked the berries herself, though she could have asked one of the other servants to do it. It was she who was in charge of the manor's operations now, with Eleanor taking her ease or doing only the work she chose to do, which was usually in the kitchen or in the embroidery room. These years were years of rest for her, with Randall's welfare of body, mind and spirit and her medicines from the forest her chief concerns.

Leyla chose to gather the berries by herself without anyone else there to help her. She was drawn to that place in the forest where the berries grew in the greatest abundance—she could not help but go there even though it frightened her so much. What she had done near there many years before seemed like only yesterday, and it was always on her mind. She never went to that exact place she had seen only once and only at night. But she went very near there, for that is where the plumpest berries grew. And she never told her mother how deep into the forest she went on her berry-picking forays, although Eleanor had guessed the truth of it. She could tell where Leyla had gone by the expression on her face, a frightened look mixed with sadness, and a little anger, too.

Leyla would not speak to Eleanor when she returned, but only look in her direction, never meeting her eyes with her own. Eleanor would fortify the silence between them with a stern look in return, and they wouldn't speak to each other for a while after that, even avoiding being in the same room together. Then, after a day or two at the most, they would break the impasse with a silly comment about some inconsequential thing they both could laugh about. Until the next time. But they never mentioned what they both knew.

The memory of the newborn infant in her arms was always in the back of her mind, no matter what she was occupied with at the moment. She could still feel the movement of its breathing through the blanket as she hurried through the night with the tiny bundle in her arms. And as she remembered, she wondered if she really had a choice that night—if she could have told her mother no, and declared that the child would live. She would care for it and raise it herself, and her mother need not be bothered at all. Or they should let the mother decide whether her child would live or die. They had no right to decide for her, even though she was so near death herself. But she had been so young, Leyla told herself, and Eleanor, being the strong woman that she was, held great power over her twelve-year-old daughter.

And so she had done as she had been told, and had left the infant alone in the forest to die—that strange little one with skin so dry, almost like a little old man though just newborn. Like Randall lying there now so close to death, his skin dry as parchment like that little one's had been.

Sometimes she would awaken with a start in the middle of the night, sure that someone or something was with her in the room, a presence she was unable to define. She would look into the darkness and listen to the silence of the night and realize that once again she had relived that moment in a dream, when she had left the infant in the forest to die.

The dream was always the same. She saw herself lay the bundle between a large rock and the trunk of a fallen tree, frantically pulling small bushes from the ground to cover it. She saw her hands become bloodier and bloodier with each bush she placed upon the small bundle, with little movements from within disturbing the blanket's surface. Then, just before she left that place, she parted the bushes and looked at the bundle one last time. And she did something in her dream she had not done on that night when it had really happened. In her dream, she parted the blanket and bloody rags, bending close to see the little winkled face within. She crooned the lullabye that her mother sang to her on nights when she was afraid of the dark and couldn't sleep. And when her song had ended, she kissed the little dry forehead. Suddenly, in the dream, sunlight filled the forest with its golden light and she saw again that tiny, wrinkled face. But the strangest thing of all was that now the face was the most beautiful she had ever seen, though its distorted features and parchment-like texture remained the same. The baby smiled at her with such a loving look, and she felt a bond of sameness between them—not as if the child was hers, but as if she was the child's. She removed the locket from around her neck and placed it around the neck of the baby, because now, somehow, Leyla belonged to him. Then she ran. And as she crossed the clearing, she watched her blood-smeared hands turn white as snow as the moon shone down upon her.

She would awaken with a start, afraid at first, and then, remembering that smiling face, peace would come over her and she would fall asleep again. Leyla wouldn't remember the dream until days later, and she wondered at that. And when she remembered, usually when she was doing something she loved to do, like tending the flowers around the manor, she felt again the peace that came with the dream. And then she would feel the fear that came before it. Yes. She would always feel that fear again.

And so she picked the berries for Randall's jam herself, drawn to the berrying places she had passed that night, but never going farther than that, although it was just a little way more to the clearing. Leyla never wanted to see that place again. She knew that nothing from that night could be there anymore,but there was a pulling inside her to go back and look between the rock and the fallen tree trunk, probably rotted by now, where she had left the baby. To go and bend close to that very place and look at it with her face so close it would almost touch the ground. To see with her own eyes that nothing was there anymore. That there was no frightened, crying, starving infant still alive, still holding a golden locket, and left to suffer alone. But she could not go to that place. Instead, she picked the berries for Randall's jam and felt her heart pound as it had on that long ago night.

And now Randall was dying. She and Eleanor had tried to keep this knowledge from the people of Randall's Bow, lest they lose hope when they learned the fever was claiming the strongest of them all. Merrill had kept his father's morning rounds, riding the big bay stallion Randall often rode instead of The Great Black War Horse, and for several days no one suspected the truth. They had seen Randall driving himself beyond his endurance for months, and they knew the day would come when he would have to change his ways and seek the help of those closest to him. And who was closer than Merrill? Since Jude had come into their lives, the two men had changed in their feelings toward each other, and it seemed only natural that Merrill would ride his father's rounds, at least for a little while.

In Randall's last hours, he called for his beloved Judith many times. He saw her in Leyla's presence, and felt Judith's touch as Leyla held his hand and bathed his forehead with cooling cloths. It was Judith's voice in Leyla's that soothed him and made him cease the struggle that only caused him more pain. When she was with him, he would lie quietly, almost smiling as he listened to her lullabyes.

And now the end was fast approaching. Eleanor had told Merrill to stay at the manor through the night and into the morning, forsaking his daily ride if he wished to be at his father's side when he breathed his last.

"It can't be true, Eleanor! Randall will not fall to such a cowardly enemy as the fever," Merrill said, holding back his tears. But Eleanor's silence told him that the fever had won. The time was almost here. Randall would soon be dead.

Merrill knelt at his father's bedside opposite Leyla and took Randall's hand in his. He watched Leyla dip a cloth into a bowl of broth and bring it to Randall's slightly parted lips. His eyelids fluttered, then opened slightly and he seemed to be looking at her. She leaned forward so he could see her and smiled, placing her hand lightly on his chest, then quickly pulled her hand back.

"Oh!" she cried as she realized that what she feared most, hoping against hope that her fear was unfounded, had just happened.

Randall's labored breathing came in harsh gasps while a dry, rattling sound emerged from deep inside his chest. It was a sound that Leyal had heard many times before when she and Eleanor had been called in the middle of the night to the cottage of a family sick with fear, and the two women had been asked to perform a miracle that could only come from beyond this earthly realm. When they heard the rattling sound that heralded death's arrival, they knew there would be no miracle that night and that death had already claimed Randall as its own. Death's dry rattle gave only the illusion that life was still there, He was already gone and was taking his first breath after death. He ceased his struggle and released one more long, slow breath. Then there was only silence. Randall's eyes were half open, but unseeing.

"Mother!"

By the sound of Leyla's voice, Eleanor knew what had happened or was about to happen. She rushed into the room and one look at Merrill's face told her all she needed to know. "Merrill," she said calmly, "he's at peace now. Let him go."

"I can't." Merrill's voice was low, yet full of struggle. "I can't," Merrill said again, touching Randall's hand that covered his in a vise-like death grip. He kissed Randall's lifeless fingers, now wet with his tears. "Father," he whispered through his sobs.

Eleanor and Leyla knelt next to Merrill, one on either side. Leyla grasped Randall's wrist while Eleanor gently caressed his fingers. When she felt them relax just a bit, she slipped her own fingers between Merrill's hand and Randall's death-grip, made a fist and pushed up, freeing Merrill. He looked at his hand as if it belonged to someone else who had invaded his life unwelcomed, then smiled.

"Even in death," Merrill said, "he held me as he willed." He stood and looked at Eleanor and Leyla, still kneeling at the bedside. "We came to love each other these last few years," he said. "We loved each other, knowing that we did." He bent and closed Randall's sightless eyes, then softly kissed his father's forehead, still warm from the fever that had claimed his life, but slowly growing cold. "Take care of him," he said to the two women. "You know what has to be done. He would like that, I know, to have the hands of you two upon him, preparing him for this last journey. He loved you deeply, as you know. He will rest in the Great Hall beneath the portrait of him and his bride. He will rest there tomorrow and through the night."

"Perhaps longer," Eleanor said. "There will be many...."

"No." Merrill's voice was flat now, without emotion, but with a strength that spoke more than his words. What he would say now is what would be. There would be no discussion about it. "I will be alone with my father during that time. Then eight of his horses will take him through Randall's Bow to the village green. He will be buried there next to Judith and among his people. Tell Rashan to choose the horses and to dig the grave himself. I would have no other touch the ground but him, until the burial. He loved the manor, but he would not want to be a prisoner behind its walls after his death. He will be near the very spot where he felled the first tree that marked the birth of this place that bears his name. Send a crier through the village with the news before you begin to prepare him for the Great Hall. Then work carefully and thoroughly, but work quickly. When you have finished, come to me at once, for I would be alone with my father. We still have much to say to each other. I have much to learn from him before he goes into the ground beside his Judith."

Chapter 15

Old Man looked downriver, and there it was on the right bank only a few hundred yards in front of him. Randall's Bow. Twenty-five years before he had sworn that he would never return to this place. Seeing it appear so suddenly left him cold with dread. No. Fear was the word for the feeling that gripped him now. Even terror. He had miscalculated and thought that it would be a little while longer before the village would come into view. He wanted time to prepare himself for that. But now there it was, coming closer and closer. A lazy drift around a riverbank and his life would be changed forever once again.

"Old Man! Old Man! Look! There it is!" Joshua's voice, full of excitement at his first sight of what was called civilization, interrupted his thoughts.

There was no one to blame for this. Blame and accusations were not proper here. In his heart, Old Man knew his guiding voice was right, and he felt the coldness that covered him subside a little and a knowing began to take its place. He focused on the knowing and felt it spread throughout his body like a healing balm. He looked at Joshua and smiled. "Don't stand too close to the edge of the raft, Joshua. If you fall in the river, I'll have to ask Goat to rescue you and I'm not sure how willing she would be to do that. As for myself, I intend to enter Randall's Bow as dry as when I left our forest."

As they approached the shore, Old Man tried to remember what it had been like to live in Randall's Bow and to accept that way of life. Or perhaps he had been alone in his own distorted imaginings and had been living in a world of just one, a misfit unable to function in what was in the good and natural scheme of things for others. Many of those who stayed, if not most, had prospered. Yet, he had fled. And as he fled, he knew somehow that he was right to do so, and that there were better ways to learn in the solitude of the forest. Even then, his inner voice had spoken to him through the wall of fear that held him prisoner. Then, twelve years later, on a full-moon night, he had found the one who would have died that very night if left to fate's first dictate.

If he had stayed in Randall's Bow, he would have taken his own life. He was sure of that. And this little one he loved so much would have been long gone from this earth, as well. And now he was just as sure that to have stayed within the isolation of his beloved forest would have meant destruction, too, but of a kind that he must ponder a little more before he would know what this slowly growing realization was. His hand was strong and steady now as he worked the tiller and guided the raft to a place a little downstream from Randall's Bow. He felt no hesitation, and was grateful for the guidance that had brought him here.

Joshua turned and looked at Old Man. And as they looked at each other in silence, they knew that sorrow would be a part of what they were about to experience along with the joy. But that was alright now and they knew they had no choice—that they never really had a choice from the instant they met on that moonlit night upon the forest floor. And from that night, they had journeyed together here.

The raft gently touched the softness of the riverbank. They had arrived in Randall's Bow.

Chapter 16

Randall lay in state in the Great Hall, alone except for his son, who had sat alone beside his father's bier throughout the day and into the night. He refused Eleanor's and Leyla's efforts to eat even just a little, taking only a water from time-to-time from the pitcher they had quietly placed beside him. He had forbade them to enter the Great Hall after that, and bolted the heavy oaken doors from the inside so that even Jude, despite his pleas, could not pay his respects to the grandfather he loved so much.

Merrill looked at the body laid out before him, dressed in a suit of armor as if for war, his red-plumed helmet cradled in his arm beside him. What is it, father? What is it I feel? he silently asked himself. What is it that I sense but cannot fathom, yet I know it belongs to both of us? We believe in a world we can touch, you and I. A world where we can fight, and build, and do the things we wish to do. And if we do not do these things, you and I, we have none to blame but ourselves, for none other can hold us back. To blame other men, or some unseen force within us or without is for the weak. That is not the way for us. And yet it seems that something or someone other than himself dwells within Merrill's breast. You are my child, this presence says. As Jude is yours. The answer is with you and Jude—and another whose presence will soon grace this place.

But father, what of us? I am afraid I have lost you.

So it oftentimes is with men, my son. Until sometimes through circumstances that we can't understand at first and can't control, we find that which we could not find before. And then we know that it was always there, but we could not see it. It was not time.

But I long to see it, father. I long to see it, whatever it is, and I cannot.

The answer is in Jude. And in you. That is where you will find it.

But what of us, father? What of us?

The answer is the same.

Merrill slept at last, slumped in his chair, dreaming of his struggle with the question. What of us? He awakened with a start, anger with a father who would answer him no more filling his broken heart.

Merrill looked up at the painting of Randall and Judith above the fireplace. "What do you see, father, when you look down upon yourself in death?" he asked the portrait. There was neither love nor longing in Merrill's voice now. Only anger that would soon become rage. He leaned close to Randall, their faces almost touching. "Well?" He brushed Randall's hand lightly with his fingertips, then quickly pulled his hand back as if he had touched a hot flame. He looked at Randall for a moment, then rested both hands on his father's chest. Weeping softly, Merrill raised both hands over his head, then brought them down full-force on Randall's chest. He lowered his head and covered his face with his hands, still on Randall's chest. "Father," he moaned, as the sounds of The Great Black War Horse kicking against the walls of his stall thundered through the night.

Merrill stepped back from Randall and walked to the window of the Great Hall. The sounds of The Great Black War Horse echoed loudly over the cobblestones of the courtyard. He turned from the window, walked over to Randall's body and pulled his sword from its scabbard. "We'll see who is master of this house now," he whispered.

*　　*　　*　　*

The Great Black War Horse suddenly stopped kicking in his stall, whinnied and snorted, then stood motionless as a gentle breeze moved through the stables. He raised his head and sniffed the air, ears pointed forward in the direction of the river.

Merrill stopped at the stable door, his whip in one hand and Randall's sword in the other, and looked into the semi-darkness. All was quiet now as Rashan approached Merrill from the back of the stable, coming to a stop an arm's length in front of him. Merrill raised Randall's sword and pointed it at Rashan. "Hail to the loyal soldier," he said, his voice full of disdain. Rashan said nothing as Merrill stepped closer and rested the point of the sword on Rashan's chest.

"Get out of my way, Rashan."

"You won't get near the horse. I gave Randall my word."

"You'd give your life for a horse?"

Rashan was unyielding. "I'd give my life to keep my vow to Randall."

Merrill slowly uncoiled the whip, letting the long lash hit the ground, and handed the sword to Rashan. "Then it seems only fitting that you use his sword to keep your promise." Rashan took the sword. Merrill swung the whip's long lash over Rashan's head and backed out into the courtyard. "Step out here, brave soldier, so I can better see my target." He cracked the whip again, just missing Rashan's face.

Rashan laid the sword down on the cobblestones in front of Merrill. "I loved Randall in life, Merrill, and I love him now in death. I will not use his sword against his son." Rashan turned and walked back into the stable.

"Rashan!"

Rashan turned and faced Merrill again, but came no closer.

"Put his sword in with him when you nail down his coffin," Merrill said, pointing to the sword still laying on the cobblestones where Rashan put it. "Who knows? He may need it." Merrill coiled his whip, turned and walked back towards the manor.

* * * *

Merrill stood at his father's side for the last time in the Great Hall. *Randall is a warrior no more,* he thought. *This is how it ends for all of us. He won every battle he ever fought, but what is his battle like now, if there is one? And if there is one, has he won that, too? Or has he lost? Is there such a thing where he is now, or is there nothing?*

Merrill took Randall's lifeless hand in his and bowed his head. "Father," he whispered, "I feel as if I am losing my soul." He laid his head on Randall's chest and wept.

* * * *

The sun was coming up over Cold River as Merrill, Randall's sword in hand, returned from the stables and entered the manor as silently as he had left it a few hours before. He went into The Great hall, bolted the door and walked over to where Randall lay. Merrill looked at his father's body for a few moments, lost in the thought of what he had done in the hours before this day's dawn, then returned the sword to Randall's side, leaving the blood of The Great Black War Horse on its blade to dry in the darkness of it's scabbard. Rashan had not surrendered the sword easily, but in the end, he had no choice.

In the stables, The Great Black War Horse stood trembling in his stall. Blood streamed down his flanks and withers, and his muzzle brushed the straw between his forelegs. This was the stallion that Randall would never try to gentle, or force him to accept a rider. His spirit was too great for that, he had said. This horse was the greatest in body and spirit he had ever seen in any living thing. Man or beast. It should be left like that, Randall had said, with no man tampering with such strength lest he misuse it and destroy a sacred thing. A spirit such as that should be observed by men, to try to emulate—not to break in an attempt to to catch the fire this one too magnificent to be named possessed. This one to be known only as The Great Black War Horse.

Randall was the only rider this one had ever known because it was meant to be. They both knew that.

Merrill, consumed by hatred and rage against something or someone he couldn't name, sat in the Great Hall where Randall lay in his last few hours above the ground,. And from the painting above the fireplace, his father and mother looked down upon their son, their expressions hard and unforgiving.

*　　*　　*　　*

The workers on the riverbank paused as two diminutive old men passed by, with a snow-white nanny goat following closely behind. Some had seen the raft as it approached Randall's Bow and had called attention to it, so a small group of curious onlookers were there to greet them as they stepped on shore. Old Man looked straight ahead without expression. But Joshua, walking at Old Man's side, couldn't hide his excitement and wonder at the new surroundings.

The onlookers could hardly be blamed for their curiosity about two little old men and a goat appearing from nowhere, it seemed, on a crudely constructed raft. One of them was average in appearance for his age, except for his height. He was barely five feet tall, but the obvious strength and slimness of his body made him look considerably taller. He had long white hair that flowed to his shoulders from a fringe around his bald head, A white beard covered his chest.

The second of the two was a different story. There was nothing about him that could be called average. Appearing to be approximately the same age as his companion, perhaps a little older, the similarity ended there. Barely four feet tall, he was very thin and fragile looking, giving an appearance that was almost bird-like. His limbs had ball-like protrusions for joints, and he had a lurching, almost stumbling gait, as if he was unfamiliar with walking. His head was too large in proportion to his body, with veins clearly visible on his hairless scalp. His ears seemed larger than they really were because he had no hair. But the most prominent of his features were his dark brown eyes, very large and round with a clarity and directness about them that none in Randall's Bow had seen before, except perhaps in the deer that lived in the forest.

And oh, how those eyes did shine! And when he spoke, it was with a voice that could only be described as piping, almost flute-like, with a melody of words that came from a joyous heart. "Old Man! You have told me about all of this, but to see it is quite another thing!" Joshua looked up and down the riverbank, where men were loading and unloading boats with supplies to be bought or sold. Groups of women stood apart at a small distance, watching the activity. They laughed and talked with each other, shouting words of encouragement to their men, while children ran and played around them.

"People! So many of them, and how different they are from each other. And from us. Old Man—I don't see anyone who looks like me." Joshua fell silent then, as they walked along the riverbank for a bit, aware that they were being followed by curious eyes.

After a few moments, Joshua spoke again. "Why is that, Old Man? Why aren't there any others that look like me?"

Old Man gave Joshua a reassuring smile, though far from feeling reassured himself. It was beginning now, he knew that, and wondered why they had ever come here. Joshua was a frightened child surrounded by a strangeness that he couldn't comprehend, a newness that was so enormous and all-encompassing that it was beyond any explanation he could offer.

It had to be experienced. Yes, he had told Joshua much about this world, but his experience existed only in abstract imaginings, not reality. Just the visual impact of all of this was overwhelming. Old Man looked at a group of children playing nearby, and saw them as threats to the very life of this little one who walked so clumsily—so innocently—beside him. Those children were innocent too, but in a way much different from Joshua, although they had obtained their innocence in the same way Joshua had. As Joshua had absorbed and imitated the thoughts and actions of Old Man, so had those children playing on the riverbank absorbed the thoughts and actions of those around them. Their moral code had not been formed from an intuitive sense of right and wrong, but from a system of reward and punishment. Their stance toward Joshua if they knew he was a child would be vicious. And Old man could not judge them harshly, because they had been taught to fear what was different from themselves and to protect themselves from it.

Despite his curiosity, Joshua feared differences, too. That was what was happening to him as they walked. A primal instinct perhaps but, as a way of life, it made change experienced as growth impossible. Old Man knew ignorance as a death-dealing instrument, as lethal as the sword or crossbow, separating the mind and its intelligence and power of reason from the heart and its capacity to love.

"Joshua." Old Man's voice held a sense of urgency that Joshua hadn't heard before. He turned his attention from the activity on the riverbank and looked at Old Man.

Old Man spoke quietly, his voice barely more than a whisper. "Joshua, we must agree on something, and neither one of us must break our agreement in the days to come, no matter what happens. No matter how justified or necessary it may seem for us to reveal the details of our lives to those around us, neither of us can make that decision without the consent of the other."

Joshua didn't understand what Old Man meant and began to ask him a question, but Old Man held up his hand to silence him. "No, Joshua. Give me your attention now. All of it. Listen, and don't speak until I am finished. Our safety, and perhaps even our lives, depends on it. You know why I left this place and went into the forest." Old Man placed his hand over his heart. "I've told you of the pain I suffered, living here and conducting my affairs according to their ways until I could bear the deceit and hypocrisy no longer. To stay would have meant that I would continue to endure a living death. This place and the people in it violated the truth that I felt to such an extent that I had no choice. I had to leave or die in some fashion, even if it meant taking my own life. Whether Randall's Bow is still the same kind of place for me, I don't know. And I don't know how it will be for you. But I know this. Ones such as you and I are in danger here. We are different in many ways from those you see around us now. And though we intend no harm, there are those who will fear us because we are different from them. You can understand this a little if you listen to the fear you feel yourself because you see how much they are different from you. It's the same for them, but with an important difference. You would not do harm to them to protect yourself from what you fear, because you trust. They would do harm of some kind if they knew you were so different from them. If they knew you are a child. That is their way. They haven't learned what you have learned. Theirs is the way of fear, and it will cause them to destroy what they fear, even when destruction, or even protection, isn't necessary. Where we would love, they would first become afraid and their fear would turn to hate. So we will not tell them who we are or where we came from. And we will not tell them that I once lived among them, and that you are not an old one, as they think.

"They see us as two who are alike and we will treat it like a game between us not to enlighten them otherwise," Old Man continued. "At least not for a little while, until we see that such enlightenment would serve a good purpose. They will ask us where we come from, and we will tell them only that we have lived in the forest for many years. We will tell them that it is our curiosity that has brought us here, to stay awhile among our fellow men a while, and that is all. We'll make it like a game and try to make our lie—and that's what it is, so we must call it that—more palatable. Will you agree to do what I have said, Joshua? Differences in years don't meant the same to us as they do to those who live here. I need to be assured that you agree without question to what I have said. We will talk more about it in the days to come, to give us both more understanding. I, too, need to understand it more. But no questions now. Do you agree to what I have said?"

Joshua nodded in assent, but said nothing. He accepted on faith what Old Man had told him. although he didn't really understand. Old Man nodded in return and smiled, satisfied that Joshua would do as he asked.

"When questions come to us," Old Man continued, "keep silent for awhile. I will answer for us. And from my answers you will learn a language that is new to you. It will seem strange simply because it is being used in a place with which you are not familiar, where what is said is not always what is meant. Listen to the others, too. They will teach you much. But your questions must be asked only of me and only when we are alone.

"Already, you see what Randall's Bow is bringing back in me—how easy it is for me to justify my old ways of evasion. This is the part of me I thought had gone away forever. But we'll live this way for a little while, and see if I'm right. We'll see if we need to protect ourselves, as I have said."

The village market place was crowded with animals that were being herded to their destinations, to be sold or bartered for other goods. Despite their unusual appearance, Old Man, Joshua and Goat didn't attract much attention as they made their way through the crowd. To all outward appearances, they were simply two oddly dressed little old men and a goat.

Old Man wondered if he would see a familiar face, or if anyone would recognize him. Time had greatly changed his appearance, as the passing years have a habit of doing, and he hadn't worn a beard during his time here, so in all likelihood, he would go unnoticed. But the fear that someone would recognize him lingered.

Suddenly, Old Man stopped and stood unmoving. Joshua followed Old Man's eyes with his own to a wooden structure in the middle of the village green.

"It's called a stock," Old Man whispered, "It's used as an instrument of punishment and torture for those who have broken the laws or offended someone in power in some way. The prisoner is left imprisoned until those who have put him there proclaim that he—or sometimes she—have paid for their crime. Presumably, when the transgressor is released, he has been chastened and even sanctified in some way. The stocks are placed here so those who pass by may pause to humiliate and ridicule the one who is in its embrace. I had forgotten about this. I have never experienced it, but I have seen those who have. It's a cruel and humiliating punishment, and a change comes upon its victim that never goes away. A part of the spirit dies, it seems, and a broken heart is all that is left."

Old Man continued to stare at the stocks as if they were about to speak to him. Joshua gently touched his hand. Old Man looked at him as if without recognition, so deep was he back in the time where the stocks had taken his memory. Joshua smiled at him. "Don't keep yourself from me," he said. "Not now. Not ever. But I speak of now, here in this place that's so strange to me despite all you've told me and taught me and shown me. At the center of it all is our honesty with each other—our truth—that keeps our hearts connected to each other so we can come to know each other as well as we know ourselves. You've told me of the things that happen here and the nature of the ones who live here. Don't leave me alone today. Now is not the time. Perhaps the time will come for that, but that time is not now."

Old Man began to speak, but this time it was Joshua who raised his hand for silence. "No, Old Man," he said. "Now it is for me to tell you to keep your silence and listen to what I say. Today we have the choice to be together. So show your heart to me again, as you did for all that time in our beloved forest. Remember how we both rejoiced in the recognition of the fruits of that. How we felt a power of awareness of something greater than anything we had ever known before and couldn't put a name to.

"And remember how we knew that it required the two of us. Such a thing could not come from one alone. The seeds for that were truth and honesty and love between us, though our fear would sometimes block it for a little while. But we would not accept that for long. We would not tolerate that way of life—the way of life from which you had fled. A life of lies, sometimes spoken, sometimes committed in silence when words were needed but went unspoken."

Old Man's expression softened as Joshua spoke to him. Such wisdom and such strength in this little one, this innocent of innocents, he thought. And he is right. "Come," he said. "Enough of my foolishness. It's a reaction to the memories of a life that's no longer mine. We must return to the raft now and let it float downriver, away from Randall's Bow. Then we must find a place to stay. A place with rich, green grass where Goat can eat at her heart's content and give us her sweet milk. Come. We'll go now."

Joshua, without Old Man noticing, looked back at the stocks. They would play an important part in his life before he left Randall's Bow. He didn't know how he knew that, but he knew.

Chapter 17

Old Man led Joshua and Goat down a narrow dirt road off the main thoroughfare. He considered his choice of this street among several others that led away from the village green, trying to recall an incident from his past that might have called to him, but he remembered nothing. Perhaps it was simply the abundance of lush, green trees that lined both sides of the narrow road, their branches joining overhead to form a protective canopy. It reminded him of the safety of the forest. There are no memories for me here anymore, he thought. I'm a different man now. There's nothing to fear.

"This is a good road, isn't it," he said after a pause, smiling at Joshua, trying to reassure himself. "It's almost like we're back in our forest for a little while." He felt the fear slowly leave him as he and Joshua walked down the center of the road—a wide path, really—its dirt packed hard from horses' hooves, wagons, and feet. Children played in small groups in the neatly kept yards of log cabins along each side. Joshua looked in wonder as the children ran about in a way he had never seen before, and was unknown to him because he wasn't physically capable of that kind of uninhibited movement himself. For him, the joy and spontaneity of childhood play had been mostly an inner experience. Even his play with the animals of the forest had been limited to feeding and petting. He knew that those children running and playing were in fact his own age or near it, and that he was lacking in the things that enabled them to play as they were doing. He knew, too, that some of their laughter was directed at him. When they reached the end of the road near a narrow path that led into the forest, Joshua suddenly stopped, his eyes locked on the remains of a cabin that had once stood nearby. The walls had collapsed and what was left of the roof lay in shambles on top of the rubble. Staves of what had once been a rain barrel were scattered on the grass beside it. Old Man turned to Joshua and saw tears running down his cheeks.

"Joshua. What is it?"

"I don't know. Please, Old Man. Let's leave this place."

Old Man took Joshua's hand and started to walk toward the path that led into the forest.

"No!" Joshua was almost shouting now. "No! Let's go back. Please, Old Man, let's go back the way we came!" Joshua was sobbing now, pulling Old Man back toward the village green.

"Of course, Joshua. We'll go back right now. Can you tell me what's upset you so?"

"No. I don't know. I just know I have to leave this place."

Old Man brushed the tears from Joshua's cheeks. "We're hungry and we're tired," he said, "and not only in the physical sense, aren't we, Joshua? We have much love between us, do we not?"

"Yes."

"And that is all we need. That doesn't relieve us of the burden of what we experience here, whatever that might be. Nor does it always make us feel as if everything is alright and that we are safe from harm. But we will gain strength and, as we learn more, we will understand more about what it is that we are here for. And know this—despite the bad things I've told you about Randall's Bow, there is good here, too. I fear that I've not told you very much about that. Somehow, this street has something bad about it that has touched you deeply. Perhaps we'll learn more about that in time. Or perhaps not." Old Man reached out and softly touched Joshua on the shoulder. "But there's more to what you feel than just this street, isn't there, Joshua?""

"Yes. But I don't know what it is, Old Man. I don't know."

*   *   *   *

Old Man started down another street off the main thoroughfare. "Come, Joshua. Let's see what this one has to offer us. I'm beginning to remember now some things that were good here that I didn't want to leave. Somehow, I feel this street has some of them. Let's knock on this door and see what awaits us." The door opened before Old Man knocked. He looked into the smiling face of a very large man who immediately began to speak to them, but it was almost impossible to understand what he was saying. He had never heard anyone talk so fast.

"Hello. My name is Shannon. Loose your goat in the yard out back, and then come in. I'll leave the back door open. I don't know why I said that. It's always open anyway. So is the front door, so you could have come right in and helped yourselves to the tea I've just brewed and the cakes I've just made and I'd have never known you were here except I'm sure that everything would have been eaten. The two of you look very hungry. Very hungry indeed. Or if I came in while you were eating, why, I'd just sit right down and join you. Pour myself a cup of tea and ask you to pass the cakes please they look so good I think I'll have one. More like three or four if you judge the amount I eat by my size, which would give you a fairly accurate approximation, if I do say so myself. And I do. Yes. I certainly do. And with no amount of embarrassment on my part, I can assure you. No. None at all. None whatsoever. No. Absolutely not. And if you could eat words, you'd be full already and on your way again, wouldn't you? Yes. And I've so much as told you that there are tea and cakes here for you if you would like to join me. I've not said so directly, I know, but it's obvious to you two gentlemen, I'm sure, that I'm a kind and generous person, and probably a fine baker, to boot, if you were to judge the quality of my baking by my size, which would give you a fairly accurate approximation, if I do say so myself. And I do. I—oh my. Am I repeating myself? Some of this sounds very familiar to me. Does it to you? I do that sometimes, you know. Repeat myself. So be forewarned. And if you decide to stay awhile, which you are very welcome to do, well, you'll simply have to put up with it. That's just the way I am. Yes, it is. So. Hurry up now. Put your lovely goat in back. Then come in through the back door. I'll be waiting. Don't be long. The cakes are best when they're hot, right out of the oven like they are now. Jam, too. I have plenty of that. This is your lucky day. Yes, it is. It most surely is."

Shannon turned in a billowing swirl of bright blue robe, smiling red face, eyes of sky blue that twinkled every bit as much as the eyes of his guests were capable of doing on their happiest days, and thick, curly blonde hair, neither short nor long, neatly trimmed to just below his ears.

Joshua, being used only to Old Man's measured cadence of speech, had been struggling to understand what sounded to him at first like a strange, new language. He looked at Old Man, who stood staring in silence at the door that had closed as quickly as it had opened. The only sound was that of Goat methodically pulling and chewing the front yard grass. They looked at each other, not knowing what to say or how to react. The verbal outpour, combined with Shannon's generosity, unusual demeanor, and commanding presence, left them speechless.

Suddenly, they were laughing the way they had laughed together in their beloved forest. The laughter of joy and happiness and love. Love for each other and for this man named Shannon. Yes, they loved this person whom they didn't know at all, but somehow did because now his energy was theirs, too. They felt renewed as they laughed in the fading sunlight of late afternoon. Home didn't seem so far away anymore.

They led Goat through the gate of the wooden fence that surrounded the small clearing in back of the cabin. She was immediately contented to graze in the lush, green grass that carpeted its surface. Joshua removed the tether from around her neck and took Old Man's hand as they walked toward the back door.

As they neared the door, Old Man paused and drew Joshua to a stop. "Joshua, listen closely," he said. "For now, it will be known only to ourselves that the years between us are as great as they are. We agreed to do this before, and we must keep to our agreement. Our safety may depend on it. I don't know why, but I sense this most strongly. You must no longer take my hand when we walk. It is a gesture of love, I know. But from this moment, when we walk together we will walk as separate ones. I will miss this closeness because it is as comforting to me as I think it is to you. But for now, no more. Come. Let's see what awaits us. It seems that we have a new friend. And a place to stay if we wish, if I understand him correctly. But let's sit awhile and enjoy the tea and cakes with Shannon. After we've eaten, we'll tend to Goat. It will give us a chance to talk privately, and decide what we will do. In any event, let's plan to stay at least the night. I'm sure Shannon will enjoy Goat's contribution of sweet milk to the evening meal."

Old Man let go of Joshua's hand and they continued toward the door, not noticing the sky-blue eyes that had been watching them intently all the while from behind the curtained window.

"Well! Come in! Come in! Sit down! Sit down! Yes. Yes. I must be nervous. I must be nervous. I say everything twice when I'm nervous. Yes. Yes. I do. I do. Have you noticed? Have you noticed? Oh, dear. Oh, dear. How disconcerting. How disconcerting. And I can't seem to stop. I just can't seem to stop. What shall I do? Whatever shall I do? How terribly boring it must be for you. How terribly boring. It is for me, too, if that's any consolation. Yes, it is for me, too."

Shannon stopped speaking and suddenly there was silence. Then a wide, wonderful smile spread across his beaming face. "There," he said. "I've stopped. What a relief. What a relief. Don't worry, I'm not starting in again. That last repetition was for emphasis, not because I'm nervous. I'm not, anymore. What I am is happy. And most curious. You see, I've been watching you since you arrived on your raft at the riverbank this morning."

Chapter 18

Old Man hadn't felt suspicion toward another human being in many years. As he felt the weight of it fill his heart and claw at his stomach, he went cold with dread and remembering. Was this what he had come back to? Had the part of him he thought had died been waiting patiently all this time for him to return to this place so it could crawl inside him once again and feed upon the spirit he thought was so rich with love for life? Was this the horror his dream had foretold? Perhaps Joshua's words about the strength and grace he would demonstrate here were nothing but a child's wishful dream, concocted to give him courage as he faltered in his fear. Perhaps it was all a lie. Or was this a dream from which he would soon awaken and feel his strength again as sleep fell from him in the morning's welcoming light?

Old Man looked at Shannon, who was seemingly without guile or deceit. There was no malice in his look—no undercurrent of intent to do them harm that he could fathom. Old Man knew himself well enough to know that if those things were in this man, he couldn't hide them from his sight. But he sensed only good coming from him. Old Man looked at Joshua and his attention, too, was on this one who had said that he had been watching them since they had arrived in Randall's Bow.

"Are you hungry?" Shannon asked, his voice as gentle as his look. "You can stay here, too, if you like. You are safe here."

"We've traveled far," Old Man said. "We are very tired, and we feel as if we are at the mercy of strangers. You are new to us, and we are hesitant because of that. Let us start there, with the truth stated between us. Tell me of your interest in two old men and a goat. And forgive me if I am offending you in the face of the kindness you are offering, because I have no doubt that it's sincere. It's only kindness you are offering, yet I must voice my fear. We are defenseless here. Please, spare me from offending you further and answer any questions I might have, but for now will leave unasked. You know my concern now. I ask only that you tell us the truth."

Shannon had neither moved nor changed his expression while Old Man spoke. But now his smile was gone. The twinkle of merriment was in the sky-blue eyes no more. They seemed to pale in color as merriment was replaced by an intensity that asked a question of its own that had to do with the truth and the telling of it now. "It's best we talk after we have put the child tobed," Shannon said.

Old Man held his silence and waited for what Shannon would say next. And as he waited, he listened for his inner voice to guide him. But there was only silence. Joshua stood quietly by his side and seemed not to be concerned and Old Man wondered whether he had heard Shannon call him a child.

"He needs rest," Shannon said softly, brushing Joshua's cheek with the tips of his fingers. They smiled at each other and Old Man realized that Joshua had heard and understood what Shannon had said. There were no secrets between them, and Joshua wasn't afraid. "But first a little supper," Shannon continued, returning to his cheerful self. "Then sleep for Joshua." Shannon looked at Old Man. "Then the two of us will talk with the truth you spoke of—the truth you said you need. I, too, need the truth."

*   *   *   *

Old Man sat in front of the fire, enjoying the gentle warmth of the flames. It reminded him of the cave and he sorely missed its safety now. From today on, everything was new, Nothing was known. There would be no predictability in the days to come.

During supper, Old Man and Joshua had spoken to Shannon of the forest and had told him something of their day-to-day life there, hoping to give him some understanding of who they were without divulging too much. Shannon knew what they were doing and carefully crafted his questions in a harmless, almost innocent way, so they could feel safe in answering him. Despite an undercurrent of caution, it was a pleasant time for all of them.

After Joshua had been put to bed, Old Man could hear Shannon humming to himself in the kitchen as he brewed another pot of tea. He rose from his chair and walked over to a rack of several long-stemmed clay pipes on the mantle over the fireplace. He had left the comfort of his pipe and tobacco behind when he had gone into the forest, as a kind of penance for what he perceived as a cowardly act. He would leave the pleasures of civilization behind, as well as its evils. He had always regretted including his pipes among the sacrifices. Old Man took one of the pipes from the rack and held the stem so that it was almost touching his lips, then he smelled the bowl and breathed in the sweet aroma of tobacco for the first time in many years. He knew that this was a pleasure from the past that he would resume again and smiled at the anticipation of it.

"Go ahead. Fill it up," Shannon said as he came from the kitchen with two large mugs of steaming tea.

"I haven't enjoyed a pipe in years," Old Man said.

Shannon pointed to a canister next to the pipes. "It's full of tobacco—a very fine mixture if I do say so myself. And I do. Yes, I do. I mixed it myself. Yes, I did. Help yourself." Shannon was smiling and cheerful again, talking so fast that Old Man once again had difficulty understanding him.

Old Man smiled. This will be an easy one to decipher, he thought as he took one of the mugs of tea Shannon offered him. As he is, so he speaks. He felt some of his fear returning. It was one thing to discuss how the world should be and how to conduct oneself in it when considered from the lofty confines of a peaceful forest. It is quite another to do it among one's fellow human beings. It was from that he had fled.

"Thank you, " Old Man said, taking a sip of the tea and nodding his approval. "I haven't felt the comfort of a pipe in many years. And truthfully, I haven't really missed it until now." Old Man removed the cover from the canister, breathed deeply as the delicious aroma escaped from the open top, and slowly began to fill the pipe, tapping gently as each little pinch went into its bowl. "There is much that I want to tell you," Old Man continued, looking from the pipe to Shannon, then back at the pipe. "But I must proceed slowly, to become accustomed to the trust that I feel for you. That's new for me—to trust another human being as I am beginning to trust you. You see, I'm not a stranger to Randall's Bow. And memories have returned today that I had forgotten for a very long time.

Let us enjoy your wonderful tobacco together for a little while. That will bring back memories of contentment—memories of other evenings after a comforting meal and a warm fire, much like this one. To me, it seems like a previous life not connected with the life I am living now. It seems as if as it was lived by another person and not by me. Though, in the scope of time, it was only yesterday. The pipe and the fire will bring it closer in my mind."

"Yes," Shannon said, quietly, softly, almost as if to himself. "We must go slowly, my friend. I call you my friend from my heart though our acquaintance is very new. At your pace, my friend. We will go as slowly as you wish. I'm an impetuous man, I know, and can sorely test another's patience with my questions. But let me say, I had a question for which I divined the answer myself. But not entirely without your help. Your demeanor toward Joshua when the two of you are together says much about your love for him. And to one who is observant of such things, it's plain the years between you are not at all what they appear to be. You look upon him as a loving father looks upon his son. But more about that as you will, and only if you will. That is your decision, my friend, and I will pry no further."

Shannon sat by the fire and motioned to Old Man to do the same. "I feel a purpose in this room between the two of us, and hesitate to express it to you," Shannon continued. "It sounds strange to me and obscure, for want of a better word. But I think you sense it too, and are as confused by it as I. Let me fill a pipe and join you. And as we enjoy our pipes and sip our tea, perhaps we will be led to speak the things we long to say and hear the things we long to hear."

Old Man sat in shocked silence as Shannon went to the mantle, selected a pipe, and filled the bowl with tobacco, tamping it down gently as Old Man had done. He lifted a burning twig from the fire and lit the pipe, then returned to his chair, a slight smile on his lips.

"You know this place, you say," Shannon continued after a few thoughtful draws on his pipe. "So do I, my friend. So do I. I think sometimes of taking my own life. That is my darkest secret." He smoked in silence for a few moments, not taking his eyes off Old Man, who had looked away, into the flames. "Have you ever thought that? To take your own life? To look at me, one would never think that I might be so inclined.

And, in reality, I'm not. I don't think I'd ever do it. But sometimes, when I feel so intensely alone, I think those thoughts." Shannon laughed. "Perhaps I will flee into the forest and leave not so much as a note."

"There are those who would be sad, I'm sure," Old Man said. "They would why."

Shannon drew long on his pipe. He blew the smoke into the air and watched it disappear. "In truth, no one would wonder. Or be sad. No. No one would ever be sad. Curious, perhaps, but never sad. No more than we are sad about the disappearance of that smoke. No one would care at all. There are others who would quickly take my place, whatever my place is. Yes, there would be some who would notice my absence and who would miss my eccentricities for a few days or even weeks perhaps. And who would wonder why the grass had grown so tall in a yard that had always been kept so clean and orderly. And a few would knock on the door to see why things had changed. Then, finding no one home, they would wonder who had lived here after all. I exaggerate a little my friend," Shannon said laughingly. "Such is my way, I guess. What does Joshua call you? Old Man? Fitting." They both laughed now. "I will call you that, with your permission, of course. Alright? Old Man?"

Old Man nodded his assent, and his smile disappeared as Shannon continued.

"I am well-liked, even respected by some, in Randall's Bow, Old Man," Shannon continued without waiting for a reply. "There is no one who is really close to me, but when help is needed of any kind, I'm like as not the one to whom they come. And yet, I am a lonely man and that is of my own creation. I'm sure of that. I keep my distance, even from those who have come under my care for one reason or another. I tell myself that I'm misunderstood in some way, and that the differences are great between myself and others. And I know that's not true. We are all so very much alike below the surface—below the false selves we present to the world. The distance and separation that I create sometimes produces ignorance in me, Old Man. And I fear ignorance more than anything else. That's what breeds the fear we feel. For all of us. I think you understand. I think you know much of what I say, if not all of it. It was the pain of separation from your fellowman—born of ignorance on both your parts and then the fear and then the cycle created by them both—that drove you into the forest. But slowly. Let's go slowly. Let's drink our tea and smoke our pipes and look into the fire awhile. And then we'll talk some more. I have need of silence now. Like you, I'm sure. Old Man."

Old Man sat in silence while Shannon spoke. He thought about his flight into the forest and his years of solitude before that night when Joshua came into his life. He had felt separation, yes. A painful kind of resistance that he couldn't name—a part of himself he couldn't reach alone. It had taken the arrival of Joshua and the gift he brought to bring him closer to that. Another human being to love and to respond to in truth. And he felt that same stirring as Shannon spoke. And resistance, too.

The two of them turned their attention to the fire, their pipes, and to their thoughts. Old Man wondered how much he would reveal to Shannon that night. He felt that somehow their lives were connected now, and couldn't fathom why, nor judge it good or bad. And he felt that Joshua, though fast asleep, was with them now, and was the force around which their union and their very lives were being brought.

"Mystery," Shannon whispered at last, almost to himself but loud enough for Old Man to hear.

"Yes." Old Man's voice was barely audible.

"We must live with mystery," Shannon said to Old Man. "We must embrace it without fear."

Old Man watched Shannon as he spoke. Filled with fear, he did not reply.

Shannon rose slowly from his chair. "I'm very tired," he said, "and somust you be, too. Let's not discuss anything more tonight. Tomorrow. Tomorrow we will talk again."

"Yes. I'm very tired too," said Old Man.

"Come," said Shannon, taking Old Man gently by the arm and leading him out of the room. "Let's escape into sleep. A dreamless sleep would be a gift we would appreciate, would it not? It has been a long day, my friend. A very long day, indeed.

*   *   *   *

In Randall's Manor, a young woman weeps, trapped in a dream of that long-ago night when she left a newborn babe on the forest floor to die alone.

105

Chapter 19

Joshua awoke to Old Man's murmurings to Goat in the backyard outside his window, telling her what a beautiful goat she was—as beautiful as the new morning, he told her. He thanked her for her patience with him because of the lateness of his visit, and assured her that her discomfort would soon be alleviated.

Tears welled up in Joshua's eyes from the pain. Pain of spirit, yes, but he wasn't afraid of that because he knew what it would bring. He and Old Man would talk about the pain—what it was and where it was taking him. Old Man would tell him that he would know himself more deeply and live his truth more completely. And he would warm in the light of that reward. That would be enough. And Joshua believed that—he knew it to be true. He believed that a deeper knowledge of himself would be enough for him, as Old Man said. Old Man was far ahead of him on that point, though sometimes now, and more and more, Joshua saw a look in Old Man's eyes that said Joshua had experienced something that Old Man had not.

Joshua felt as if he was doing something wrong during these times— that he had erred in some way—until Old Man began to question him. And from the questions, Joshua knew that he had gone beyond Old Man in their journey, and that now he was the teacher. Old Man was amazed and yes, even a little frightened, at what he heard emanating from this child who looked as if he had been born directly from the ancients.

But spirit pain was not the only pain Joshua felt this morning. His body hurt as well, Sometime in the last few cycles of the moon that he and Old Man spent in the forest was when the pain had begun. He hadn't told Old Man about it—he didn't know why—but he hadn't. When the pain came, his joints burned as if they were on fire. He would lie among his pile of soft furs, pretending to be asleep until Old Man had left the cave to visit Goat. After he had left, Joshua would slowly crawl on his hands and knees to the warmth of the fire and lay next to it until he was able to sit and finally stand as if nothing was wrong when Old Man returned with the morning's milk. Old Man would pause and look closely at him, and then go on to prepare their breakfast.

Dreams, Old Man would think. His dreams came deeply last night and he feels them still. Sometimes they teach with harshness, but he must learn to bear that and to keep his heart open to the lessons he must learn. In time, Old Man came to learn the truth, when it could no longer be hidden or denied.

But now, here with Shannon, was not the time. Joshua heard Old Man bring the bucket of milk into the kitchen and exclaim to Shannon how deliciously rich it was. "You have never tasted milk as sweet as this," he said.

Joshua struggled to get out of bed, his body caught in an intensity of suffering he hadn't felt before. He was so afraid. What had he done wrong? Was there something Old Man hadn't told him about their journey, to spare him fear and keep him on their path? Was there something that, if he knew what it was, he would go no further? Perhaps he had strayed in secret and was unaware of it and now was being punished.. What was this thing that burned inside his hands and knees and feet—no joint was spared this torture. The pain even hurt his head, and made his heart pound so fast it felt as if it would burst inside him. He could hardly bear it now in silence. He hadn't felt this way since the full moon before this last one, and he had hoped this thing was gone forever. But this time was the worst it had ever been. If it was like the other times, it would be like this for several days and nights, made easier only if he moved about almost unceasingly. If he stopped and rested for more than a few moments, the pain and stiffness would come back so that he could hardly walk at all.

He had been able to hide his pain from Old Man when they were in the forest, because he could go off by himself for fairly long periods of time. When he was out of sight, he would curl up beneath the low hanging boughs of a tree and wait until the pain went away. But what could he do now? How could he hide it any longer?

Joshua dressed and slowly made his way downstairs. As he warmed himself before the fire, he looked at the pitcher of Goat's milk on the table. It made him feel safe, somehow. It helped him remember the cave and the quiet of the forest as if he was there now, and not in this place of strangers where he had wanted to be, not so very long ago. He longed for the familiarity of the forest and wondered at the strangeness of Old Man's and Shannon's behavior toward him, talking to each other as if he wasn't even there. As if he didn't exist for them at all.

"You remember Randall," Shannon said to Old Man. It was not a question.

"Yes. I remember him well. He gave me hope. I remember him as a good man, despite the wealth and power he held. And the blood on his hands. And he confused me. He made me think that I was wrong, somehow, although I don't know why. He had everything that I considered to be corrupting, though I didn't feel he was corrupt. The values that his possessions and position stood for were contemptible to me. Yet Randall, the richest and most powerful of all, was neither corrupt nor was he weak. Far from it. He was loved by most, and respected by all. Those who feared him had their good reasons, because it was Randall who would set right their wrongs, and not always gently or agreeably. He had a justice of his own, I'll grant you that, but his was a justice that also knew mercy. It was because of him that this place prospered."

"He'll be laid to rest today," Shannon said. "He died two days ago. Taken by the fever. He thought he was invincible against this enemy as he had been against so many others. But he was not invincible against this one. Even Randall, great as he was, couldn't encounter the fever as he did each day—breathed it in each day—to bring hope to all of us that it was just another enemy that he would bring to its knees. Randall thought It was only a matter of time.. And it was. But it was only a matter of time until he would fall, not the fever, and we didn't believe that would ever happen. And now he's gone, like so many before him. He'll be buried in the village green this morning. When we hear the drum, you can go there with me and pay your last respects, if you like."

"This fever that you speak of—how long has it been here?" Old Man asked.

"For many months. And still it rages as strongly as it did when it first hit us. Sometimes even stronger. There is no respite from its attacks. And it seems there is no remedy, except to wait until it has satisfied its hunger here and moves on somewhere else to create another Hell in another place."

Old Man looked at Joshua now, for the first time since he had come into the room. "The forest and its many healing herbs may hold the answer...." he began, but Shannon motioned him to silence. The sound of a distant drum could be heard through the open window.

Shannon stood and started for the door. "Come," he said. "It's time to lay Randall to his final rest."

* * * *

The cortège moved slowly down the empty street toward the village green, a steady, heart-like beat of a single drum marking cadence as the horse drawn carriage that held Randall's coffin, with Rashan holding the reins, came into view. Merrill, mounted on The Great Black War Horse, was in the lead, with Eleanor and Leyla walking just behind the carriage, each holding Jude's hand as he walked between them. The servants of the manor followed behind.

As the cortège neared the green, the people began to talk among themselves, surprised at what they saw, for it was not what they had expected. The carriage was drawn by the bay war horse that had been Randall's favorite mount next to The Great Black War Horse, and seven others. These horses, all bred for war, had never felt a carriage harness upon their backs. Saddle, bridle, and warrior had been the only weight they had carried until this day. The people knew that the black stallion was the one Randall prized the most, the one who would allow only one man, ever, upon his mighty back, and that man was Randall. Until now. The Great Black War Horse had a new master now, a master cut from a different kind of cloth than his father. The bloody stripes from whip and sword upon his midnight hide gave witness to that.

The sound of the drum was very close now as Shannon, Old Man, and Joshua made their way through the crowd. Joshua pulled back from Old Man and stopped. "There are so many people," he said.

"It's all right, Joshua. Just stay close to me."

109

The drumbeat suddenly stopped and the people fell silent as Merrill and his blood-streaked mount crossed the village green. The wagon bearing Randall's coffin followed, with the others walking slowly behind. Some gasped in disbelief. Others wept. Some spoke in angry whispers, while others looked away and kept their silence. Shannon, Old Man and Joshua reached the inner edge of the crowd, near the freshly dug grave.

"What's the hole for, Old Man?"

"Quiet, Joshua. Remember your promise."

A man standing next to Joshua heard his question. "Where have you been, old one," he said, leaning close. "We bury Randall today. And you may be next. Or me. We can only wait and see which one of us the fever chooses as its next victim."

Near the center of the green and next to Judith's grave was a mound of dirt that would follow Randall's coffin into the freshly dug grave. The Great Black War Horse walked slowly toward the grave, his head bowed low in submission to the will of his rider, or so it seemed. As Rashan guided carriage to the head of the grave, Merrill reined his mount to face the people, then waited as the rest of the grim cortège made its way across the green to the place where Randall would be laid to his final rest.

There was no grief in Merrill's eyes as he sat astride his bloody mount and surveyed the shocked and pleading faces that looked up at him. He saw their fear that a new day had come to Randall's Bow—a day they would not gladly welcome—and he hated them for their weakness though he knew it would serve him well. They knew that their lives had suddenly changed, but they didn't know how or why. They knew, too, that they would have nothing to say about it. And if they thought there was something they could do to change the course their lives were about to take—and if they voiced these thoughts—the whip and sword would find them too, and make their marks upon their backs—and hearts and souls. Like The Great Black War Horse, they would bow in submission to Merrill's will. They would do as he commanded. They would have no choice.

The procession stopped and the circle closed tighter around the grave. The plain wooden coffin with the red plume from Randall's armor that had been placed on the coffin over the place where his heart would be beneath the cover was lifted from the carriage by six of the manor's servants, carried to the edge of the open grave and laid upon the ropes that would be used to lower it into the ground after tribute had been paid. Flowers from the manor's garden that Randall loved so much, though it was laughingly said he was never tempted to tend, were placed one-by-one by each of the servants upon the coffin's top next to the red plume.

When the last flower had been placed on the coffin, Merrill reined The Great Black War Horse to the head of the grave. He looked at the wooden box that held his father's body, then at the circle of people that crowded around him, keeping his eyes on some for a moment before moving on to the next. There would be no churchman to read from a sacred book to plead for divine mercy for Randall, to provide a safe journey into the unknown or to bless him with much-deserved rewards when he reached his final destination. No. There would be only Merrill's words to send Randall to his final rest. Or battle, as some believed would be the case. And with Merrill's words, the new order would be established in this place upon the river that bore his father's name. There would be no doubt in anyone's mind that when they departed from the village green today, the hope they had been given by the man who had been returned to dust meant nothing. The son had inherited his father's capacity for greatness, and that was plain for all to see. It was indefinable, but strength of will was evident in Merrill's face and the way he carried himself now. But the son would neither welcome counsel nor forget differences, which were just two of his father's many strengths. This was a different day. The bloody flanks and withers of Merrill's mount gave proof of that. Yes. This was indeed a different day.

Merrill looked at Old Man and Joshua, who had unwillingly been pushed to the edge of the foot of the grave opposite him, with Shannon standing close behind and in plain sight of all. Then he brought his attention back to the others who gathered closely around him. All was silent now as the people waited to hear what their new leader would say to them.

Merrill's voice was cold, flat—and deadly. There would be no words of comfort this day.

"Randall is dead," Merrill began, looking around at the people and pausing for a moment. "My father is dead." He paused again, as if there were some who had not yet come to grips with what had happened. And was about to happen. "There is nothing left of him now, except what you see here before you. A dead man in a coffin. Nothing more. Soon he will be given to the ground of Randall's Bow, at the center of this place upon the river that he made his own many years ago. You mourn him now. And you grieve his absence now, and that is right. But he is gone. Randall is no more. I stand here in his place. What was Randall's place is now mine. Yes, I see you look at one another and wonder where my sadness is. You search my face for anguish. You see none and wonder why. That is because you fear for yourselves, not because you mourn my father. For you do not. You care only for yourselves. You fear for yourselves and you judge me to be cruel and cold of heart because you care only for yourselves.

"I have shed my tears. Be sure of that. I was with my father when he breathed his last breath upon this earth, and I was with him as he lay lifeless in the Great Hall. I, and I alone, was there. Neither sleep nor food could take me from his side. So judge me not by what you see before you now. Unless you judge my strength. I am Merrill, son of Randall, and that is who you see before you.

"My father was the kind of man the storytellers make in legends and myths, because his kind is rarely found upon this earth. But my mother's death when I was born changed him. I am told this by those who were with him in that time of sorrow, and who knew him before, when Judith was by his side. Some of you were witness to the time of which I speak, and so you know that what I say is true. The Randall of later years—the man he was after Judith's death—could not have taken this place from the forest and made it his own. No. He would not have had the strength of mind and spirit—or the passion that he needed—to wrest this place upon the river from nature's hands and place it in yours.

"It was Randall who raised me from the moment I was born. He was mother and father to me, with Eleanor by his side to help and guide him in ways about which he knew nothing without her help. Under her guidance, he fed me and he bathed me, and he wrapped me warm and held me for that first year of my life. After that first year, Eleanor took my father's place because, when he looked at me, he could only think that if I had not been born, his beloved Judith would still be alive. Eleanor loved me like a mother would, and she loves me still in that way. I know that. But I really had no mother. And in truth, I was without a father, too. Randall left me and he gave himself to you. You took the place of Judith. And of me

"But he was not the same as he had been before my mother's death. A part of him had died with her. And when the fever took him, he wanted that, I think, for it was not compassion for you that had driven him during his last year here. No. It was his wish for death, and he chose the nearest battlefield to find it. And he won that battle, as he had won all others. Randall had lost but once in his life, and that was when his beloved Judith died. Now he is with her—and in this final defeat, victory is his.

Merrill's voice rose. "If you choose to fight me, you will lose," he said, almost shouting now. "You have already lost, and you know that by the sight of me. You look at me as I stand before you now, and you know that the heart of the man who built this place upon the river now beats inside of me. You cannot stand against me. You are not able. I rule now, as Randall ruled before me. This place that bears my father's name is mine, as it was once his. I say again—and hear me well—I rule now in Randall's Bow."

Merrill glanced quickly at Old Man, Joshua, and Shannon. His expression at first was one of questioning, and then his eyes lingered on Joshua and his expression changed to fear. He suddenly turned and motioned to the six men who had placed Randall's coffin on the ropes at the edge of the grave. They walked to the graveside and slowly lowered the coffin to its resting place.

Merrill waited until the coffin was resting at the bottom, then he dismounted and threw a shovel-full of dirt into the grave. The dirt landed on the coffin with a loud thud, as if to emphasize what Merrill had said. Then, keeping his eyes on Joshua and Old Man, he handed the shovel to Rashan. "Finish it," he said. "It's what he would have wanted."

Merrill mounted The Great Black War Horse and turned him away from the grave. The horse stumbled and stopped directly in front of Joshua. A gentle breeze moved across the green and all became silent and still. The Great Black War Horse raised his head and looked at Joshua.

And Joshua knew The Great Black War Horse was the one who would carry him to the place he truly belonged. He stepped forward and put his hand on one of the stallion's wounds. The horse nuzzled Joshua and whinnied softly. Merrill abruptly pulled the horse's head up and rode to the edge of the green, then turned the horse around and rode back, stopping in front of Old Man and Joshua. His eyes passed quickly over Old Man and came to rest on Joshua, studying him as if he had seen him someplace else before this. He turned the horse again, stopped next to a man standing at the edge of the green, leaned from his saddle and whispered something to him. Merrill looked at Joshua once more, then kicked The Great Black War Horse into a full gallop toward the manor, digging his spurs into the horse's sides.

No one moved. Every eye was fastened upon Merrill's back as he rode away. Some knew of what Merrill had spoken, some did not. But all who stood in silence on the village green that day knew that life as they had known it now belonged to yesterday. Randall's was not the only death that had befallen them. A new force ruled them now, and only time would reveal what it was and what it would bring into their lives. And what it would demand and take from them.

Shannon and Old Man left the village green, walking in the opposite direction from Merrill's course, with Joshua following closely behind them.

Chapter 20

Shannon stood unmoving in front of the fireplace, looking down at the cold, gray ashes in a scattered pile beneath the iron grate. The fire had gone out while Randall was being lowered into the ground he loved so much, and now the room was without warmth. Like my heart, Shannon thought, as he slowly rubbed his hands together. Like my heart. Oh, Randall, how could you have died? How could you have left us like that? Death was not possible for you. That's what we believed. We thought you would live forever. Yes. That is what we thought, we fools of hope. We thought you couldn't die—that you were beyond death and that somehow you would never fall into that black night that will someday claim us all. But not you. We wouldn't accept that. We knew you would outlive us all and walk the earth forever. And now you're gone. We are at the mercy of Merrill now, and madness has consumed him in the few short days since you left this earth. Once again, Randall, you have abandoned your son. This time, forever.

Shannon's hand shook as he reached into a pocket in his robe and curled his fingers around the small wooden object he kept hidden there. The smooth wood warmed him a little in a room which seemed not to want him within its walls. Find your comfort somewhere else, it seemed to say. I have only coldness to give you now, and fear won't make it go away. So leave this place and leave me to my emptiness.

He felt the presence of Old Man and Joshua sitting in silence behind him, waiting for him to tell them the meaning of what they had witnessed less than an hour before on the village green, and he wished with all the coldness in his heart that they would go away—that they would disappear back up the river where they came from. He didn't know why he felt that way, but he did. There was something happening here that was far beyond his control, and he didn't like it. He didn't like it at all.

He wished he could withdraw his offer of hospitality of the day before and send them on their way, whatever that might be. Not to stay with someone else, but away from Randall's Bow. He wanted them far away now, never to return. He didn't want them here. Their presence here with him now would mean that Merrill's wrath, and it would be great, would be upon them all with a devil's fury. He had seen it before, and he would be at its vortex because he had given them sanctuary. Of that, he had no doubt. He didn't know the reason for it, but he remembered well the look in Merrill's eyes when he first saw those two across from him on the opposite side of his father's grave, and him standing with them. It had been the look of fear—no, it was terror that was in Merrill's eyes when he had first seen Old Man and Joshua. And then his eyes had moved to Shannon and he knew that, in that instant, Merrill held him accountable for some unforgivable deed or debt, and that his life could very well be the price demanded in payment.

Shannon turned and faced Old Man and Joshua. They had questions, and their faces were as gray as the ashes lying cold in the fireplace. They sat in silence. Waiting. Looking at Shannon for some sign of the friendship he had so generously shown them the day before. They looked to him for answers to the violence that was gathering around them like a living thing—like some kind of monster crouched to spring upon them and destroy them because of something they had done—something grotesque but, as yet, unknown to them. They found no friendship in Shannon's face as he looked down upon them now. It was accusation they saw there, and for what they did not know. They saw their own fear and confusion reflected back to them in Shannon's face. And they saw the avoidance in his eyes as he looked at them and then at the darkness now descending outside the windows of the cabin. And they saw anger, too, but they saw no answer in his eyes, and heard none in his silence.

Old Man and Joshua were a part of Shannon's life now, and he didn't want them to be. He wanted them gone. Now. Gone as far away as they could go from this place. Now. Tonight. He wanted it to be as if they had never come to Randall's Bow. He wished they were at the bottom of Cold River or in the ground now, beneath the village green, instead of Randall.

Shannon took his hand from the pocket of his robe and held it out before him. He slowly uncurled his fingers and lowered his hand so Old Man and Joshua could see the small black wooden horse that lay there in his palm. The three of them looked at the figure for a moment without speaking. The horse was so lifelike despite its size that it looked as if it could rear up from where it was cradled in Shannon's palm and gallop into the darkening sky that was covering Randall's Bow.

A strong wind was beginning to blow and leaves were falling from the branches that scraped noisily against the rooftop. Storm colors raced across the sky, dancing in time to the lightning's flash and thunder's drums. Rain clouds rolled in from across the river where they had crossed the mountains and were sweeping down upon Randall's Bow to empty their burden. A fitting sky for this day, Shannon thought, as lightning made its mark on the heart of Randall's Bow—if it had a heart—now that its master was dead.

Shannon curled his fingers around the carving and stared at the fist he had made. He opened his hand again and looked at the horse as if he hadn't known it was there. They could hear the branches moving in the wind like long, brittle, insistent fingers scratching on the windows, urging him to begin. He closed his eyes, remembering, then began to speak.. Slowly now, and with deliberation.

"When Randall came to this place for the first time, he knew he had found his home. He felled a tree with his battle ax, using his weapon in a labor of peace for the first time. It was a sign to himself, he told me, and to the forest that surrounded him, of what he intended to do here upon the river's bow. With the blade's first bite into the thick trunk of that ancient tree from which he would fashion the first home he had known in many years—only a crude shelter at first—he felt as if he had wiped the blood from his hands and he had been forgiven, if there was anyone or any force to forgive him—and if there was anything for which he had to be forgiven. He would make war upon this earth no more, except to defend himself and this place he would call home. That was the vow he took beside that first-fallen tree. It was his intention to live in solitude from that day forward until his life ended in whatever way fate would decree.

Shannon turned away from Old Man and Joshua and looked out the window at the gathering storm. Dark clouds were still sweeping in over

Cold River and the wind made the treetops sway in a worshipful dance. He looked at the little wooden horse still cradled in his hand and then continued speaking. His voice was stronger now, and his hand was no longer trembling.

"Randall kept a part of that first-felled tree to feed an urging in his heart. It was an urging that he had felt many times before when resting in his camp between battles. He told me that he would sit before his war table, looking at the maps spread out before him, and he would think of the battle that had just been won and of the one that was certain to follow. An emptiness would come over him at those times that sometimes brought him to the ground, and he would be consumed with the need to create in the wake of his destruction. It was a need he could not refuse to answer, for the pain would be so great that he felt he would die from it if he didn't do as he was called to do."

Shannon held the small wooden horse in front of him, reaching out to Old Man and Joshua. "Randall loved to carve in wood, you see," he said. There was tenderness in his voice now. "But for him to pass the time that way, for all to see, would have been unseemly for a warrior such as he. Idle time was meant to be used for sharpening the skills of war and weapons with those who followed him. But sometimes this urge to create became too great to be ignored. Unreleased, he said, this creative force caused him pain so great that he would feel as if his very ribs were about to be rent from him as his heart beat within his chest like a drum with a madman pounding on its skin.

"Randall would carve in secret, at night when the others were asleep and the campfires were burning low. The soft glow of a single small candle was his only light, lest someone should discover him in the weakness of his act. Yes, weakness, for that is what he imagined it to be."

Shannon held the small wooden horse closer to Old Man, as if asking him to take it in his own hand and hold it. "It's almost perfect, is it not?" he asked.

Old Man took the carving from Shannon's outstretched hand as if he had been given a sacred object. Yes. Yes, he thought. It is perfection. He moved his hand slowly across the dark, intricately carved wood as if he was stroking a living beast in miniature. It almost seemed as if the horse's muscles leaped to his touch, alive beneath its black, wooden hide.

"Yes," Old Man said, looking closely at the horse. "I sense the spirit in the horse that stood before him as he carved it. It is in the wood. And I feel the spirit of the one who carved it. I can feel Randall's love for the horse in the wood. It is truly remarkable." He handed the carving to Joshua. "Can you feel the life in it, Joshua?"

Joshua caressed the smooth wood with his stiff fingers. He looked at Shannon and then at Old Man. "It's the one that Merrill rode today," he said.

Shannon took the carving from Joshua and looked at it closely. "Why yes, yes it is," he said. He stepped closer to Joshua and bent down to look at him, their faces almost touching. "I didn't know," he said. "Yes. It is the very same horse. Randall didn't tell me it was The Great Black War Horse that he had carved. He gave it to me the day before he died. He told me it was the last thing he would carve from wood that he had kept from that first-felled tree on the banks of Cold River, and that he knew he would carve no more. He knew his days were numbered very few. He didn't tell me it was The Great Black War Horse that he had chosen to be his very last carving. He carved this upon his death bed, you see. He knew that we all knew the end for him was very near, and he knew we would not believe—could not believe—that one such as he could die in this way and in this time when we needed him the most. Oh yes, we knew. We knew, yet we hoped we were wrong." He turned away from Old Man and Joshua to face the fireplace and stared at the ashes. In time—and unbeknownst to him—his grief, and the strange turn it would take—would bring a sadness upon all who lived in Randall's Bow. A sadness as great as Randall's death had brought upon them—and there would be some who would say even greater.

"Yes," Shannon said through his tears. The effort it took for him to speak was almost too great for him to continue. "Yes, Randall knew his end was near. We all knew. Only our eyes confirmed it to each other when we could bear to hold another's gaze and see that knowledge there. We couldn't speak of it, but with our eyes we told each other that we knew. Until the end—until the very end when he was but moments from his death—it was until then that we pretended. We pretended that this warrior who had never known defeat of any kind except for Judith's death, which only he counted as defeat because he could not save her, would emerge victorious now. His strength of will couldn't rescue her from death. And so it was his belief that he had failed. But we believed—or hoped—that he could somehow save himself."

"This same foe would be victorious over Randall once again. But as the battle waned and Randall's banner lowered in defeat, he seemed not to mind nor be afraid. There was acceptance for his own impending death. He tried to speak of it to us, but we refused to listen. We turned away from him and denied him the comfort of friends who would hear his truth without fear. But acceptance of Judith's death? Never. Never did he bend in his defiance of that loss and its injustice to him and to the son she bore—the life she gave as she gave up her own."

Shannon stopped talking then, his eyes unseeing, lost in another time and another place, back on the banks of Cold River long ago when Randall and Judith were alive and the birth of their son was an event that was yet to come.

At last, Shannon spoke again. "Yes." he said, his eyes resting on Joshua. "This is The Great Black War Horse—the horse that Merrill rode today. This is the one whose armor was the blood not yet dry from the beating he had taken. He has no name. Randall would not name him. There was no name, he said, to fit a spirit such as that one has. Nor would he break him to be ridden—if he could be broken. No one knew, for no one ever tried. A man would have to be a god to tame that spirit well enough to sit astride him, Randall said. And then, one day, the horse spoke to him, Randall said. Spirit to spirit, Randall said. In the deepest silence Randall had ever experienced, the horse called to him from the stables. He left the Great Hall and went to the stallion, who told him he was Randall's to mount and ride. And no other has ridden him until this day, when the great beast that Randall loved so much, who had never felt even the gentle prick of spur to urge him on, bowed his head under whip and blade."

Shannon gently placed the carving on the mantle over the fireplace and stood for a moment with his head bowed as if in prayer before the little figure. "I'll build a fire," he said at last, drawing a breath that was deep and long. "A storm is not far off, and the chill of the night is upon us." He bent to gather wood from a stack of neatly cut logs next to the fireplace. "The man astride The Great Black War Horse today was a stranger to me," he whispered, almost to himself, but loud enough for Old Man and Joshua to hear. "I knew him not." He knelt to prepare the kindling beneath the logs as Old Man and Joshua sat shivering in their chairs, conscious of the cold now that Shannon no longer held their attention.

"It won't be long now," Shannon said, setting fire to the tiny sticks and chips of dry wood. When the logs had caught the kindling's flames, he filled his pipe and joined Old Man and Joshua in front of the fire. They sat together in silence for a while, each joined with his own thoughts, staring into the flames and feeling the cold ease gently from the room.

After a time, Old Man stood and motioned to Joshua to follow him. "Come," he said. "Let's tend to Goat. She has been without us all day and she must feel neglected and forgotten. We must tell her that we care about her and that we know she is most important to our survival, because she is, is she not?" The twinkle had returned to Old Man's eyes and Joshua felt better about their situation. He felt safer now, just seeing Old Man's gently reassuring smile.

"We'll leave our friend in the solitude he needs," Old Man said. "We know that need ourselves, don't we, Joshua?"

"Thank you, my friend," Shannon said, staring at the flames now dancing in the fireplace. Exhaustion had claimed his mind and body for its own and he had no more to give.

Old Man and Joshua sat together in the twilight and watched Goat as she enjoyed the sweetness of the grass. The wind had become a gentle, almost soothing breeze and the early evening had suddenly become a peaceful time, although gathering clouds foretold the storm that would soon be upon them.

Sounds of activity came into the yard through the open kitchen window. Joshua watched Shannon through the window as he worked, then shivered in the sudden dampness of the evening.

"Joshua." Old Man spoke quietly, almost in a whisper, as if he was afraid that Shannon would hear what he was about to say. "Joshua." Old Man spoke again as Joshua continued to watch Shannon. It seemed as if he hadn't heard Old Man's voice. "What is it, Joshua? Are you not feeling well? Tell me." It had been an exhausting time for both of them, especially for one as frail as Joshua.

"The horse, Old Man," Joshua said. "The one they call The Great Black War Horse. He spoke to me. His heart is broken, Old Man. And

121

his spirit is in great pain. The man named Randall was right. That one is more than others of his kind."

"Spoke to you, Joshua? In what way did the horse speak to you? Are you sure you didn't imagine it?"

Joshua's voice broke in little sobs as he tried to tell Old Man of his pain. "No, Old Man. No. You know what I mean. Like when our guiding voice speaks to us. Inside us. We hear it, but it's inside us and around us. It was like that with the horse. I felt it inside me, Old Man. I knew it. And I knew the horse knew it. His spirit is so strong, and he is more than the other ones that are called horses that I have seen in Randall's Bow. It was as if he was part of the voice that guides us or it was speaking to me through him. When he stood next to Randall's grave, all bloody, and when Merrill was talking—Merrill was speaking to us, Old Man, and not to the others. I know that. And The Great Black War Horse was speaking to me, making me know that we are alike somehow. We are part of the same thing, somehow. I don't know what any of this means, but I know the horse is my friend. I know it. And I know that the pain he feels is great. Merrill thinks that the horse's body is where he feels the pain, but the pain is deeper. Merrill has done a terrible thing, Old Man. He doesn't know how terrible is the thing that he has done. But he will, Old Man. He will."

Yes. The horse had spoken to him—Old Man had no doubt about that. He had felt it when he looked across the grave and saw the two of them covering each other with their eyes. It had been with great effort that the horse had arched his neck and had fought the bit and reins that kept pulling him the other way. But he had persisted, his eyes searching for something or someone nearby, and he would not be denied.

"The Great Black War Horse, Old Man—he told me that when the time comes, he will fly me home. What did he mean by that?"

Old Man was stunned by Joshua's words, but said nothing.

Joshua suddenly smiled and stood up. "I'm hungry," he said.

Old Man watched Joshua as he walked toward the back door of the cabin, his steps halting and stiff from the dampness of the night air. He rose from the grass now wet from a light rain, walked to Joshua's side and took his hand. "Yes, Joshua, I know," he said. "I know the horse spoke to you. And in time, you will know the meaning of what he told you. I know it not, for he didn't speak to me. It is to you alone that this gift is given, and its meaning will be given to you when the time for that has come. But now it's time for us to eat. Shannon has regained his humor, it seems, so let's go in and see what his kitchen has to offer us. I doubt that we'll be disappointed."

Shannon opened the door. "Come in. Come in," he said cheerfully. "I think you will enjoy what awaits you."

* * * *

Shannon lifted the top off a huge kettle that was boiling over a fireplace in the kitchen, filling the room with a delicious cloud they could almost taste. "Sit sit sit at the table and take it all in," Shannon commanded, pushing them toward chairs made from the curling roots of two ancient trees that had been blown down in a storm many years before. They were much like the chairs Old Man had fashioned for the cave in the forest, and Joshua looked at them and smiled. In truth, he longed for the comfort and safety of the cave.

""Tonight we feast," Shannon exclaimed! Yes, feast! it's been a day it surely has and now we eat. Let's sit in front of the fire and eat our soup and while we do there are some things I'd like to tell you things about Randall and Merrill, things I want to hear myself say, I think, as much as I want you to hear them."

Shannon became very serious, his words coming in a softer, slower cadence, as if an unwanted guest was listening. "We have not seen the last of Merrill, you and I," he said. And as He continued to speak, he let his eyes rest on Joshua, as if he was addressing only him. "Somehow, your lives are connected with Merrill's now. I don't know why, but I know the truth of what I say. You are in his life and he is in yours. He did not miss your presence on the village green this morning, and it was more than merely a passing notice. He saw you there and he didn't like it. And it wasn't because you are strangers here. It was something more than that. Come. Let's take our comfort before the fire, eat our soup and talk about today. Perhaps we can come to know the source of Merrill's fear, because that's what it was. That's what I saw in his eyes. Fear. For some reason, Merrill fears you." Shannon kept his eyes on Joshua. "And that is dangerous. If we can discover the reason why, then perhaps we can escape his wrath, for it is his wrath that will be upon us. Soon. I am sure of that because that is Merrill's way."

The sight of he flames gave them as much comfort as their warmth, familiarity being something they very much needed. Shannon followed them, pausing at the mantle to take the small wooden horse that Randall had carved and carried it with him to his chair. They sat for a time in silence enjoying their soup, the reassuringly warm nourishment in their bellies mingling with the snapping of the logs in the fireplace.

Shannon was the first to finish eating. He set the empty bowl on the floor beside him and looked at the carving in his hand. "Do you remember Merrill from your time here?" he asked Old Man.

"Yes."

Joshua continued to eat, but kept his attention on the two beside him.

"And how do you remember him? What was he like?"

"I remember him only vaguely. He was known as a mean-tempered child. I remember that. He fought and quarreled with the other children without apparent reason or provocation. I don't remember ever having seen him, although I might have. But my attention on gathering herbs and roots from the forest for my potions preoccupied me to the exclusion of almost everything else. I was acquainted with very few in Randall's Bow, and those I knew I didn't know well. In the end, I was alone, isolated even from myself, if you've ever experienced that. I told myself it was because I was different from the others—above them and better. But, in truth, it was because I was afraid. Of what? Even now, I don't know. I won't speak of my time in the forest yet. Do you agree, Joshua? Our new friend might drive us off into the unfriendly night if we told our story now, might he not?" He smiled at Shannon, but there was a question in his look, and Shannon saw it.

Shannon didn't evade Old Man's unasked question. "Yes, I had thought of that. When we returned from Randall's grave and I had seen Merrill's reaction to you, and my being in your company, I wanted to send you away from here. I wanted you gone from Randall's Bow. But I won't ask you to leave. You can rest here. I had thought of it because of what I saw in Merrill as I watched him looking at you. There is something that consumes him—possesses him. What it is I don't know. But you and

Joshua are part of it, of that I'm sure. We shall see. We shall surely see. We know not what times are upon us now.

Again, Shannon spoke directly to Joshua now, as if Old Man was not in the room. "Randall possessed a clarity about himself and those he met that he passed on to his son, for better or for worse. He sees something in you, Joshua, that declares you as his enemy. At least, in his mind. And he will fight you. He will fight you to the death. I know the truth of that, though I do not know the reason. And it bewilders me. You seem so frail, and yet there is great power in your presence."

"I'm not afraid of Merrill." Joshua's voice was strong and clear, and carried through the room like piping music. The sound of his voice lingered in the room as if someone had struck a bell from a mountain top, and the sound was still echoing in the valleys below long after the bell had been struck.

"I'm not afraid of Merrill," Joshua said again. He sat quietly in his chair, looking at Old Man and Shannon without expression while they returned his stare in shocked but silent disbelief.

Shannon hesitated, then held out his hand. The horse stood in his palm as if ready to charge into battle, a warrior astride his back with glory as his goal and immortality his dream.

"The one that Merrill rode today," said Joshua.

"Yes. The words that Merrill spoke today had great power, but the bloody stripes held more. Merrill left the horse's hide unwashed for all to see, and his blood was eloquent in its pronouncement that the course of events—whatever that course may be—will be at Merrill's whim. And anyone who is foolish enough to defy him will feel the whip and sword just as the stallion did. And it wlll be only by an act of mercy that the one who chooses to fight him will survive."

A sudden scratching on the windowpane broke the silence and Shannon strode quickly in the direction of the sound. His face was frozen in the way that only terror could evoke. The three of them held their breaths and listened, but the sound of the wind in the trees was all they heard.

"It's only the wind, Shannon," Old Man said after a moment. He paused and listened again. "And from what you have told us, it seems like a storm of another kind will soon be upon Randall's Bow."

Shannon looked out the window into the darkness once more before he spoke. It was as if he sensed Merrill's presence nearby, listening to what he was saying and planning the form his vengeance would take against this one who dared to slander him. Finally, Shannon returned his attention to Old Man and Joshua. "I don't know what Merrill intends to do, or what course his deeds will take to bring the reality of Randall's Bow to meet the image he holds in his mind. Even before Randall's death, Merrill knew his father was on his deathbed and admitted that fact to himself, though the rest of us could not. Perhaps he even welcomed it, although I don't say that is true. They had become very close in recent years because of Jude, Merrill's illegitimate son by a barmaid in the village."

"Randall loved Judith very much. Yes. I remember that," Old Man said. "Randall condemned his son—it is his responsibility, at least in part, for the madman who stands in his place this very night. Merrill was innocent, of course. He hadn't murdered Judith by his birth. But in his heart, Randall laid that judgment upon his son even though he might not have been aware of it. As he had vowed to Judith before she died, Randall devoted himself to Merrill for the first year of his life. To the hour, he honored his deathbed promise to her. It was as Merrill said at his father's grave this morning. It was as if two men had emerged from the one who was with his son for almost every waking hour.

There was the man who had condemned his son—that man was there and his presence was deeply felt. But there emerged another man as well—a man who stepped out from the darkness into the light and was reborn. Randall told me that in that first year of Merrill's life there occurred a shift in his perception of what his own life meant and how he wished to spend what remained of it. He had taken enough from the world, he told me. He had continued to take even when he had put his sword and battle ax to peaceful tasks. He had taken lessons from the world around him—all new to his experience—to somehow make him whole again. To help him wash the blood of war from his hands. But in that year with Merrill, the direction of his energies underwent a shift. He could name the day and hour that he felt the change, and he knew that he had become a new and different man. He couldn't name the nature of it, nor could I aid in that though we discussed it through many sleepless nights, drinking ale before the fire in the Great Hall."

Shannon looked out the window into the darkness and listened for a moment to the silence of the night outside. There was sadness in his voice as he continued with his story. "Merrill had his father for a year and then his father left him. How could a small child know the reason? What must he have felt, to have had his father suddenly go away—to be there no more? As young as he was, he must have still felt the absence of the familiar touch, his smell, the sound of Randall's voice—that absence surely must have struck terror into one so young and unknowing. What horrible thing must he have thought he had done to have caused his father to suddenly abandon him? Merrill's sadness soon turned to anger that was released upon those around him. For many years this was so. Eleanor was like a loving mother to him but she couldn't take his mother's or his father's place no matter how hard she tried.

"And then, when Merrill had become a man, a baby was left on the steps of the manor in the early morning dawn. That child was Jude. You saw him this morning at Randall's grave. Merrill named him Jude, after Judith, Merrill's mother."

"He was standing between the two women behind Merrill," Joshua said, interrupting Shannon. "We were looking at each other and he smiled at me. And I smiled back at him. It was as if we recognized each other. I don't think he thought that I'm older than I am. I think he knew that we are alike."

Old Man turned to Shannon in alarm. "Is it possible? Is it possible that he could have guessed the truth about Joshua? As you have guessed it?"

Shannon looked at Joshua for a moment before he answered. "Jude is a perceptive child. He has the eye of his grandfather when it comes to that. And although Joshua looks far older than his years, there is a quality about him that belies what his appearance would have you believe. And Joshua, I feel your warmth. You are a delight. But we must be careful. There is much superstition here in Randall's Bow. Differences are feared, and their sources are ultimately destroyed because they aren't understood."

Old Man nodded in agreement, but said nothing. Joshua looked into the fire, his eyes focused on some far away place beyond the flames. Shannon and Old Man observed Joshua in his silence. It was as if he had left them and gone away to another world.

Shannon walked to the window and looked again into the darkness, listening closely to the rising wind as if he was expecting someone to walk from the forest uninvited and knock on his door. He hesitated for a moment than returned to his chair and looked at the small carving in his hand.

"Merrill contrived a situation whereby he took his rightful place beside his father in the seat of power," he said. "He, in fact, made them equals, astonishing as that may seem. The place next to Randall had been appointed as mine, not as an equal, but as a trusted friend and confidant. Randall wanted Merrill by his side, but only as an observer to sometimes contribute when Randall decided it was appropriate. Merrill's day would surely come, but it had not, as yet. That did not suit Merrill. He became a braggart and a drunkard. Abusing horses and women were all that seemed to matter to him, with no regard for the damage that his so-called sporting in either direction inevitably inflicted.

"He ruined women and horses alike. He used them for his own selfish purposes, and then he left them to whatever came their way. He accepted no responsibility for his deeds, and moved on to the next in line when his present company or mount bored him or was no longer useful to him. Then, in an instant, Merrill changed. Randall had thought Merrill's son would be a burden to him. A punishment for the life he was living. But such was not to be the case. In the instant that he first held him in his arms, Merrill became the father to Jude that he had never had himself. Randall couldn't bear it. When he saw Merrill and Jude together, he was witness to all of the things he hadn't done for his own son. And he knew he had failed Judith too, for this was precisely what she had sought to avoid when she exacted the promise from him before she died.

"Randall kept a distance between him and his grandson. His days were spent on horseback, in the fields, or in the stables. Evenings found him alone or with me in the Great Hall, planning the next day's activities. It continued like this until one day when Jude would have no more of it. He stood beside his grandfather in the courtyard, looking up at him astride The Great Black War Horse, His hand was on Randall's stirruped boot as if to say, 'Stop! This will be no more." Jude was magnificent. He told Randall that he had decided to be like him. He told Randall that Merrill had told him that it would be a good thing to aspire to be such a man as

Randall, because Randall was truly a great man. And so the wounds were healed. For good, we thought.

"And so it did appear. The years from then until now were filled with a growing love for each other. Their lives together appeared to be rich and full, the past between them forgiven and forgotten. Merrill was at Randall's bedside through all his illness—he would leave the room, only to quickly return and take his father's hand to comfort him and to make his presence known even as Randall slept. Merrill was with Randall when he died. But something happened…."

Shannon paused and listened, then walked quickly to the window, his face suddenly grown pale. He held his hand up to order Old Man to be silent as he started to speak—and then they heard it—the sound of a horse coming at full gallop toward the cabin. The sound of pounding hooves ceased and there was only silence. The silence was broken by someone pounding his fist upon the door. Old Man and Joshua watched as Shannon went to the door and unbolted the latch. There was no need to ask the visitor to identify himself.

They knew who it was.

Chapter 21

Shannon pushed the bolt on the latch and the door slammed against his chest, pinning him against the wall as Merrill strode past him into the room where Old Man and Joshua were sitting. He stood in the middle of the room without speaking, glaring at them and slapping his coiled whip against his boot-tops. Leather against leather was the only sound in the room. His face was white and his dark eyes burned against the paleness of his skin, His coal-black hair was wet from the rain and matted around his face, giving him the look of a dog that was sick and gone mad. Merrill's free hand, a fist at his side, was gloved in black leather and his chest heaved from the exertion of his ride and the rage that possessed him.

Shannon followed Merrill into the room and stood at his back by the opposite wall without making a sound. He folded his hands in an attitude of prayer, a mixture of fear and anger written across his flushed face. He had known that Merrill would come tonight.

Old Man and Joshua sat unmoving as Merrill looked from one to the other and then back again as if to determine who would be the first to feel the cut of his lash. He stilled the whip, raised it slightly, the only sound now his labored breathing. His eyes came to rest on Joshua, who smiled, his eyes unblinking and with a question as yet unasked.

Merrill walked to the fireplace, put his whip on the mantle, and pulled the glove from his hand. As he warmed his hands before the fire, the others watched his back and the heaving of his shoulders as he took in air in long deep breaths. After a few moments, he turned and faced Old Man and Joshua again, this time including Shannon as he glanced quickly around the room. His expression was a curious mixture of cold calculation, rage, and amusement.

"When my father died," he said to Shannon, "you pledged your loyalty and your service to me." He voice was level and cold, the voice that Shannon had heard at other times when Merrill was at his most vengeful. "You made this vow at Randall's deathbed, when his last breath had left his body and was still in the air around us. You swore your loyalty to me upon your honor and, whether you know it or not, your life."

They waited. No one moved or made a sound. Shannon looked furtively at Old Man and Joshua, then turned his attention back to the silent and unmoving form of Merrill, standing like a statue with his back to the fire. It was as if Shannon was rooted to the spot where he stood, doomed to live or die according to Merrill's whim. Whatever the verdict, he would accept it without resistance.

There was madness in Merrill's eyes when he turned and faced Shannon. He took a step toward him, then smiled and stopped. "I need the loyalty that you pledged to me on that sad day. Do I have it? Do I have your loyalty without question or condition?"

Shannon was sick with fear now as he struggled to look directly at Merrill. But he could not. His eyes sought the mantle behind Merrill, and fell upon the carving of The Great Black War Horse. He wanted no part of whatever it was that Merrill had planned for Randall's Bow. There would be no good in it, no matter how cleverly Merrill tried to disguise his true intentions.

When Shannon gave him no answer, Merrill took another step forward. This time, there was no smile. "My father's death was proof enough that one man's efforts are not enough to do what must be done if this sickness that devours us is to be conquered. It must be defeated soon or it will eat away at us until the last one here is gone. Have you forgotten, Shannon? Starvation bowed its head to us because we fought together, side by side, to defeat the famine. When the crops failed, we found new ways to coax nourishment from this sometimes stubborn soil. And we will win again, you and I, side by side."

Merrill came close to Shannon and placed his hand firmly upon his shoulder. It was not a gesture of friendship or alliance. Rather, his pressing grip said do as I say, or suffer the consequences. Shannon felt only the trembling hand of a madman upon him. He hadn't missed the obvious threat in what Merrill had said—the tone behind the words that said agree to everything I say or I will count you against me. And if that is so, then you will remember this night with sorrow and regret, and you will wish to all the powers that be that you had chosen differently.

Shannon, paralyzed with fear, stared at Merrill's whip and kept silent.

"I have no illusions about you, Shannon," Merrill said. His voice was soft now, but the edge was hard and threatening. "Your pledge was to me, yes, but it was meant for my father. Nonetheless, I hold you to it. Your oath is binding to me—as binding as if my father was still alive and standing with us now. I want your help. And you will give it to me, will you not?"

Shannon nodded his assent, his eyes fixed upon the small wooden horse that seemed alive and prancing on the mantle. Still, he could not speak. He looked down at the floor, his face crimson with his shame.

"I know where your loyalty lies, Shannon," Merrill continued in the same cold, quiet voice. His hand, still trembling from the effort of containing his rage, remained on Shannon's shoulder. "Your loyalty lies with yourself—yourself and no other. And so we are somewhat alike after all, you and I."

Shannon still did not respond.

"Are we not?" Merrill said, increasing the pressure of his grip upon Shannon's shoulder. It was clear his patience with Shannon's silence was growing very thin.

Shannon finally looked at his inquisitor. This would be an alliance between the two of them. That was what Merrill wanted him to believe. But this would be no alliance. Merrill would discard him as quickly as he discarded one of his horses when he had outgrown his usefulness.

"Yes," Merrill said, and smiled. "Yes. You understand. As do I. And if each of us understands our agreement, then we have a chance to win. We are strong men, you and I. If we were not, we could not have known Randall as we did. He would not have let us close to him. And between the two of us, we are strong enough to do what must be done to chase the fever from Randall's Bow."

Shannon smiled at Merrill, but it was not a smile of friendship. It was a smile of duplicity that said yes, we know what is best. Not only for Randall's Bow, but most importantly, for ourselves. He waited for Merrill to tell him more. Merrill was not finished yet, and Shannon knew it.

"The others cannot think for themselves," Merrill said. "They need our guidance, or they will die. They know they cannot make their own way through this and survive. They need someone to show them the way. Without someone to show them, they are helpless. And they will follow us. We will make sure of that. And we will not be challenged. Yes, without us they will die." Merrill paused, thought about what he had just said and laughed. "And perhaps there will be some among them who will live yet wish they had joined the others in death. There are some in Randall's Bow, my friend, who do not wish me well. There are those who are plotting at this very moment how they will profit from my father's death, and they see me as an obstacle who must be removed." He brought his face so close to Shannon that he felt the heat of Merrill's breath on his cheek. "At this very moment," Merrill whispered, "we may be certain, you and I, that there are those who are putting their schemes in motion to take back what they had gained then lost during the hunger. These same ones listened to you in the past because you had Randall's trust and friendship. And they have listened to me because I am Randall's son. That will be enough for them for a little longer. They will buy time with the deceit of appearing to join us. And in so doing, they will buy us time in the bargain. We will win them to our ways, Shannon. If we do not win it one way, we will win it with another. Make no mistake of that."

Shannon's fear sent a strange weariness though his body. He felt as if he could stand no longer—that he would faint if Merrill didn't step back from him and give him room to breathe. He couldn't bear to have this man so close to him. He felt as if he was suffocating from Merrill's closeness and the smell of drink on his breath.

Shannon sat down next to Old Man and Joshua. He looked at them in surprise, as if he had forgotten they were in the room. Merrill sat across from them and crossed one leg over the other. Dried blood was streaked across his black boots, and the sharp points of his spurs were caked with it.

"I'd like some brandy," he said pleasantly, as if talking to long-time friends. "I won't miss this day when it ends. I won't grieve its passing."

Shannon rose from his chair, grateful to be released from the madness of Merrill's relentless stare. He went to a cabinet and took out a large decanter of amber-colored liquid, looked at Old Man who shook his head, then brought the decanter and two glasses back to his chair. He poured the brandy into one of the glasses and handed it to Merrill, then filled the second glass for himself, looking at the liquid as if it was medicine that would save his life.

Merrill drained his glass with one long swallow, and Shannon followed suit, relieved not to be alone in his need for escape from whatever it was that had happened only a few moments ago.

Merrill held out his empty glass and waited for Shannon to fill it. He leaned back in his chair, cupping the full glass in his hands, content to feel the warmth of the brandy move slowly through him. He stared into the fire then closed his eyes, and for a moment it looked as if he had fallen asleep. After a few moments, he opened his eyes and began to speak as if he was unaware of anyone else in the room and was addressing only the dancing flames.

"I will summon the council to the Great Hall tomorrow night. Together, you and I shall fulfill our ambitions. The others will benefit as well, although they might not agree with us in the early stages of what I have planned. And Shannon—hear me well. Do not attempt to betray me. I will find you out if you do, and you will pay a price most dear." Merrill looked at the full glass of brandy as if he was surprised to see it there, then raised it to his lips and drank deeply, once more emptying his glass in one long swallow. He stood up, knocking his chair to the floor in the process, and staggered to the door, putting his hand on the latch to steady himself. "We have no time to lose," he said, his back to the room. His words were barely understandable now, slurred and running together. He slid the bolt from the latch.

"Wait!" Shannon's voice shot through the room. Merrill stopped, almost falling to the floor. Shannon quickly walked to him and put his arm around his shoulders to steady him. "Surely, you must be curious about my guests, Merrill," he said, guiding him back into the room where Old Man and Joshua were sitting, and helping him back into his chair.

Merrill looked at Old Man and Joshua through narrowed, bloodshot eyes.

"Perhaps the wisdom of their years could be of use to us in these difficult times," Shannon said, his voice gaining confidence when he saw Merrill was attentive to what he was saying. At least, he was remaining in his chair, and it appeared to be more than the brandy that was keeping him there. He looked at Old Man and Joshua in recognition, as if he was seeing them after a very long separation.

Now that Shannon had Merrill's attention and a little of his own courage had returned, he knew that if he hesitated he would lose what little advantage he had. "Merrill, may I introduce one to you who is known as Old Man. Most apt, is it not? He was called by another name in another place—in another life, perhaps—but now he is Old Man. It is by his choosing, and so it is respected." Scarcely pausing, Shannon continued, "And this is Joshua."

Merrill rubbed his eyes as if he was brushing away a cobweb that was clouding his vision. He looked briefly at Old Man, then turned his attention to Joshua, who smiled and returned Merrill's confused stare with his own. There was a look of fear on Merrill's face, as if he saw some grave threat in the frail little one who appeared as if he had risen from the ancients to visit once more the earth upon which he had once walked.

"I'm not afraid of you." The silence was broken by the sound of innocence. There was neither challenge nor insult in Joshua's voice, but a kind of neutrality, as if he was presenting Merrill with a fact that he thought should have been obvious before he brought it to his attention. In a way, there was understanding and even reassurance in his tone too, much as a friend would give another to indicate their closeness, even in the heat of argument. "Have you tried the forest?" Joshua asked.

"What?" Even in Merrill's slurred words, his surprise was evident.

"Have you tried the forest? The answer is there." Joshua smiled at Merrill as he spoke.

Merrill shook his head. He looked at Shannon as if for an explanation, then back at Joshua. This old one confused him. He appeared to be of advanced years and quite fragile, and yet his voice said something else about him. It was like music somehow, with the strength of youth in it. He wished now that he had not had so much to drink. The brandy was making him sick to his stomach as well as blurring his senses and it was difficult for him to make sense of what he was hearing. He wished that he was back at the manor now, asleep. A pain was starting at the back of his head and he feared that one of the pounding headaches that sometimes came upon him and drove him into darkness and his bed was descending upon him now. But he must hear this old one out and understand what he meant before he returned to the manor. He must hold out somehow for just a little while longer.

"What do you mean?" Merrill asked. It was a challenge more than a question. "And do not let your lack of fear—if indeed you do not fear me—give lightness to your words. You are in more peril than you know when you anger me. There is no shortage of those in Randall's Bow who will attest to that." Merrill looked at Shannon, his eyes passing quickly over Old Man.

"There is an answer for the fever among the roots and herbs in the forest," Joshua said. "I am sure of that."

"You are sure of that?" Merrill's voice was full of contempt. "You are sure? The only thing to be sure of old one, is that the fever quickly kills the very old and the very young. To them, it is merciful. To the others, it shows no such kindness, bestowing upon them a lingering and painful death that, indeed, is a hell upon this earth. So you may take some comfort in that. If the fever should choose you to be among its victims, you will not be long among us. You see, old one, you have more to fear than me, of whom you say you have no fear. Do you have no fear of this mysterious adversary that I have just described?"

Joshua gave no answer, He sat quietly, watching Merrill.

"Hear me when I say you are in danger here," Merrill said, then abruptly turned his back on them and walked to the door. He put his hand upon the latch, hesitated, then turned and faced them again. "Bring these two with you when the council meets tomorrow night," he said to Shannon. "I'm sure they will be most interested to hear what I propose. As will you." Then he looked at Joshua. "Proceed with care, old one. Proceed with great care lest you offend me more than you already have."

With that, Merrill left, closing the door quietly behind him.

Shannon looked out the window at Merrill's dark form bent over his mount's neck, his face almost touching the flowing mane, whip raised high and poised to strike.

"It is not The Great Black War Horse he rides this night," Shannon whispered into the darkness.

*   *   *   *

Shannon bustled about his kitchen as if nothing had happened, preparing tea for the three of them before they retired for the night. No one spoke. Old Man and Joshua sat at the large oak table and watched him as he moved about as if they weren't there. He seemed to be completely absorbed in preparing the tea as if all was well.

Old Man was greatly disturbed about what had happened, and it wasn't only Merrill who concerned him. He had seen behavior like that before in others and knew that usually nothing—or at least, not as much as he feared—came of it. Merrill had been drinking even before he arrived and was very distraught about the loss of his father and what had happened between them long ago. His was a painfully wounded heart. He bore deep scars and for the first time in his life he was feeling a pain deeper than he had ever allowed himself to feel. For Joshua to have incurred the wrath of this madman—for that is what he was now—was unthinkable. He had endangered their safety and placed this kind stranger, who had taken them in when they had no place to go, in danger, too.

Old Man held his silence until Shannon came to the table with their tea before he spoke. "I offer you our apology, my friend. We have offended your hospitality, and put you in danger with a man who is buried in his madness." Then he turned to Joshua. "You surprise me, Joshua," he said, with no attempt to hide his anger. "You gave me your word that you would hold your tongue unless we were in agreement about what you wanted to say."

"Our agreement didn't demand my silence," Joshua said with a boldness that took Old Man and Shannon by surprise. There was neither anger nor hurt because he had been scolded in front of Shannon, as Old Man had expected. And certainly, no contrition. Old Man had purposely held his words until Shannon was seated at the table because he wanted to chastise Joshua for his rashness. In a way, he had sought to educate Joshua by letting him experience anger aimed at him in the presence of someone other than the only human being he had ever known before coming to Randall's Bow.

"Our agreement was that I wouldn't reveal that we're not the same in years, Old Man," Joshua said. "We had agreed on nothing else. You speak from your fear and fear has nothing to do with our safety. There is an answer for the fever. You know there is. And you know that the answer lies in the forest. You know the truth of that, because it was from you that I have learned such truths."

"You know nothing of this world, Joshua," Old Man replied, kindly now, despite the urgency of his message and his fear that Joshua wouldn't hear it. Or, if he did hear it, he would ignore it. Joshua began to answer, but Old Man put his finger tips upon Joshua's lips. "You are to hold your silence now," he said, "and listen well to what I have to tell you. You will not speak until I have finished. Then, and only then, will I allow you to reply."

Old Man took his hand from Joshua's lips and continued. "It was from this world, Joshua, that I fled to the safety of the forest. This world was killing me. And it will kill you too, though you don't know that yet. It will kill you if you try to deal with it on your own terms—if you confront it and challenge it in the way you learned to live in our time together in the forest. This world does not understand our way, Joshua. This is a dangerous world. A destructive world. Can you not see that? Have you forgotten yesterday's laughing children or The Great Black War Horse this morning, covered in his own blood? And for what? For being what he is, and no more than that. Only men such as Randall recognize the value of something such as that one is, whether it be man or beast. And men like him are very few. This is a world that is full of danger for those like us and The Great Black War Horse. You must never forget that. Never."

Once again, Joshua began to speak, and Old Man raised his hand as if to strike him. Old Man looked at his raised hand as if it belonged to someone else, then let it drop limply to his side. "There," he said. "There. You see how much I fear this place? Listen to me. Please hear my words and try to understand. Understand, for I know you can if you will. My meaning is not beyond your comprehension. We both know that."

Old Man touched Joshua gently on his cheek and then took his hand in his. "You are innocent of the dangers here," he said softly. "and you have transgressed as grievously as it is possible to transgress in this world by what you have done. You have told the one who holds the power here that you do not fear him, and the one in power lives and survives by the fear in those he dominates. You have not only endangered us, but also the only one here who has given us his friendship. He has given us his time and trust, at high risk to himself. That would have been so even if you had said nothing. This is a place of superstition, Joshua. They won't understand our differences. Not how we look, nor how we think and live. As for our appearance—how similar we look, but how vast the difference in our years—not even we can understand that, or how such a thing could ever be. And what of those who left you in the forest to die that night so long ago? What if they should discover that you are here now, and know you are the one they left to die? Understand, Joshua—the essence of our agreement was that we not draw attention to ourselves. You know that—of that I am sure. And you have violated it. Why?"

Old Man was finished talking now—he would listen to whatever Joshua had to say without interruption. There was nothing more he could do. If Joshua didn't understand, they would leave Randall's Bow tomorrow and return to the forest. To remain in this dangerous place would be foolishness, and he wouldn't permit it. And yet, in his heart, he knew that Joshua had much to justify what he had done. So he would listen now to what this little one had to say. He leaned back in his chair, for he was weary, and looked at Joshua in silence, waiting for him to reveal what was in his heart.

There was only strength and clarity in this little one now as he spoke. And, yes, joy. Old Man and Shannon saw him standing above them somehow, and they felt their own fear all the more because of it.

"There is no difficulty of choice," Joshua said the them, "because there is no choice. There are many who are very sick. Many, maybe most, of them are dying. We can help. We know how. You and I can go into the homes of some of the sick ones, Old Man, and we can see for ourselves what the sickness is like. Then we can go into the forest and find the roots and herbs that we know will help. There is fever burning here, and we can help that. What is the danger in that? Merrill will welcome our help. He will be grateful because of it."

Old Man began to protest, but now it was Joshua who would not be stopped from saying what he had to say.

"No, Old Man. You must hear me out. After we have brought relief for the pains of the fever, and after we have been awhile with those who are sick, we will find the final remedy. I am sure of that. The answer will be given to us. It is given to us already. We need but to go into the forest and find it."

"Joshua…." Old Man was deeply moved by what Joshua had said. He kept his silence for a moment, listening, and then, suddenly, he knew the answer. And in that instant Joshua knew, too, that he was right. They would find the answer in the forest, as he had said. But the answer to what? More than the antidote for the fever. Much more than that. Old Man waited, straining to hear more, but his inner voice would take him no further. "Yes, Joshua," he said." We will find the answer in the forest."

Joshua's was silent. He no longer felt joy as he listened to Old Man. A sadness that seemed to come from far away, yet here in Randall's Bow, too, overtook him and would not loose its grip.

"But there is still danger here," Old Man continued. "We must proceed with great caution. Merrill is no friend of ours, no matter how right we may be in our actions, nor how much they may benefit him and the others here. And by his words, he is no friend of Shannon's nor, I suspect, of any man. Least of all, himself, though he knows it not. You have great power, little one. More than either us know. I feel it as we stand here together. Merrill felt it, too. He fears it and he will not forget it. Any power that isn't his own he sees as a grave threat to himself."

Old Man paused to make sure he had Joshua's full attention, then he continued. "Merrill will observe with great attention the one who made him feel such fear. His attention will be upon you, Joshua, and it will be unceasing. You may be sure of that. If not with his own eyes, then with the eyes of others. We know that what we sense is good, whatever the nature or the purpose for which it is intended. But it's a threat to Merrill, because it is his opposite. He looks upon you as his enemy now. He fears you because of what he felt, but can't define. The unknown brings out the greatest fear in men and causes them to destroy those whom they perceive as its source." Old Man smiled, then laughed softly, as if to himself. "And, if the truth be told, I, too, am a little afraid of it."

Old Man looked at Shannon, who had been standing quietly behind Joshua. His hands were folded in front of him and his head was bowed slightly in their direction. "You must find all of this confusing," Old Man said to him, laughing as he spoke. "If nothing else," he said, pointing at Joshua, "this one's brashness has forced us to be honest with you. Come. Let us sit before your friendly fire and we will tell you all."

It was well past midnight when Old Man finished telling Shannon his story. He had told everything there was to tell, some of which, much to his surprise, he had forgotten until the telling. He told Shannon of the years he had spent in Randall's Bow before he had sought the solitude of the forest, and of the despair that relentlessly held him in its grip until it nearly claimed his life. He had chosen the unknown of the forest instead, he said, and had lived alone until that night twelve years ago when he had, as chance or fate would have it, been present when an infant was left to die on the forest floor by a shadowed someone from Randall's Bow. He told how he had named the child Joshua and had raised him as his own, and why they had chosen to come to Randall's Bow.

When Old Man had finished his story, the three of them sat in silence, each with his own unspoken thoughts. They knew they were being swept along by new forces, that the direction of their lives had changed, and Merrill had a part to play in that change, for better or for worse.

Shannon was the first to break the silence. "I knew you were but a child," he said to Joshua. "But I would not have known it if I hadn't seen you on the riverbank when you first arrived in Randall's Bow. I followed you for a little while out of curiosity—otherwise, I would not have known. You hid your secret well."

Joshua struggled to understand what was happening. Yes. He was a child, whatever that meant in this new world he had come to. And he looked like one who had lived for many years, whatever that meant, too. Neither meant anything to him. The concept of differences wherever he turned was strange to him.

Child. Old man. He had heard these words many times today. They meant different things, and yet they had been said about him. What did they really mean? He was Joshua. That was all. Until only a few short days ago, neither child nor old man meant anything to him. Until only a few days ago, he had known only the forest. There was a natural working of things there, where comparisons such as those didn't exist, as far as he knew. There had been only the thing that his inner voice called love. That was what he knew.

But now he also knew that all along it had been different with Old Man. They had never been the same, and Old Man had known that. Old

Man had been comparing them all along while he, Joshua, did not even know what that meant.

Old Man had known from the night he had found him that he had not been in harmony with nature. And yet, Old Man had let him believe that he was. And he had been born in Randall's Bow. He was a child of this terrible place. Not of the forest. They had not wanted him, whoever they were. They had left him on the forest floor to die.

Joshua sat unmoving while he listened to Old Man tell his story. He was hearing for the first time—just as Shannon was—the truth about himself and his heart was filled with a greater pain than he had ever felt before.

Chapter 22

There was another in Randall's Bow who felt great pain that night.

It was after midnight when Merrill returned to the manor. Eleanor had been awakened from a deep sleep by the sound of hooves clashing against the cobblestones in the courtyard. But it was another sound that claimed her attention and she strained to identify it. The sounds were of an animal that was caught in a trap, it seemed, its pain and rage combining to produce a howling moan that sounded almost supernatural. The trap was grief, and clenched within its jaws was Merrill, howling into the night like the crazed animal he had become.

It's happening again, she thought, remembering the first time she had heard those howling sounds—it had been on the night before Randall's funeral. Could it have been only the night before? It seemed a generation ago when last she heard that terrible sound. Perhaps it had been just that, for a generation had surely passed from their midst when Randall died— and the one that claimed his place felt like evil to her heart.

Eleanor remembered what she had seen in the courtyard the night before, and she felt sick to her stomach at the memory of it. She would see it in her dreams until the day she died—she had no doubt of that. And in her waking hours, it would always be in her mind, to come into her remembering when she least expected it.

* * * *

It had happened during the night that brought them to the day when they put Randall's body into the ground. Eleanor was awakened from a fitful sleep that night and had risen from her bed. She left the manor through a side door that led into the courtyard and had looked toward the stables. As her eyes adjusted to the moonlight, she recoiled at the horror of what she saw. At first, she was unable to tell which of the two was the aggressor. Both of them were bathed in blood that glistened in the moonlight as it dripped upon the cobblestones, already smeared and red-slick. Whether it was the blood of both or only one she couldn't tell, there was so much of it. She had thought at first that Merrill had fallen beneath the hooves of The Great Black War Horse, and he was fighting for his life against the attack of the raging beast.

She had forced herself to remain hidden, the reason instinctive but unknown to her. She wanted to run to Merrill's side and care for him as she had so often done when he was a child and had fallen while playing in another one of his rough, made-up games. But something held her in the darkness to watch in secret. Something told her that this was different and if she revealed her presence she would be placing herself in grave danger. She would not be able to fight back, as she saw then that The Great Black War Horse was helpless despite his power. It was clear that the horse was not the aggressor and that Merrill was not defending himself.

There was a glint of metal and she saw the heavy chains that were wound around the stallion's neck that bound him tightly to the post in front of the stable doors. Each time the horse reared and pulled back from Merrill's blows, the chain pulled tighter and cut off his breath, forcing him back to the ground where he collapsed and then heaved up on all fours again to vainly attempt to defend himself. It was a murderous noose that Merrill had fashioned with skill and calculation, and the horse had no choice but to advance toward the source of the cutting blows. If he did not, he would die from suffocation.

Eleanor had watched as Merrill slowly circled around The Great Black War Horse, whip in one hand and Randall's sword in the other. As he raised the sword to strike, a deathlike cold swept through her. When she had placed the sword in its scabbard beside him, she had thought it would be there for all eternity, resting at the side of the one who had so carefully forged it and who had been the only one to wield it in war or peace. This was the sword that had been used only for honor and had only been drawn against a foe where the balance between them was as equal as it was possible for it to be. Now the blade had been turned against the one that Randall had loved as much as any living thing that ever walked the earth. Merrill and the stallion were at war, but this battle had no honor in it. Blood dripped from the blade as Merrill held it high above his head to strike again.

With all her heart, Eleanor wanted to wrest the sword from Merrill's grasp and replace it in its scabbard, bloodless and without the stain of dishonor. Despite herself, she cried out as Merrill cracked his whip above the horse's head. When the stallion wheeled toward his attacker, Merrill brought the sword down quickly upon his flank, opening yet another bloody stripe. He heard Eleanor's cry and turned in her direction. When Eleanor saw Merrill's ugliness full-face, she felt as if she would faint from fright. Somehow, she kept her feet under her and stood still, praying that Merrill would not see her in the darkness.

Merrill crouched in the middle of the courtyard, as if to spring upon his enemy, as yet unseen. He looked in Eleanor's direction, staring directly at where she stood, his chest heaving as he fought for breath. Whip and sword held in readiness, he was frozen in his crouch as The Great Black War Horse stood unmoving behind him, his eyes unblinking and shining as if on fire, victory still within his grasp.

Suddenly, as if aware of the stallion for the first time, Merrill returned to the cruel task he had set for himself.

Eleanor retreated to her room, walking carefully in the darkness, trying to block the grunts and screams of The Great Black War Horse from her ears. When she reached the top floor of the manor, she looked in on Leyla and Jude, who were still asleep in their rooms, then returned to her own bed. She lay awake then, frozen with terror at what she had witnessed. The shrill sounds of The Great Black War Horse continued, and she didn't know whether they were in her mind or if Merrill was still inflicting his bloody act of madness upon the horse.

When she could stay in bed no longer, Eleanor went to the Great Hall where Randall lay, quietly opened the door and, upon seeing that Merrill had not yet returned, knelt by the side of the bier. Placing her hand on Randall's, she looked at the empty scabbard by his side.

"Oh, Randall…." Eleanor's gentle sobs curled gently around them both. "What will we do? I don't know what's happening here. Help us, if you can. We need your guidance and your strength. Merrill is consumed by grief, and I fear for us all, even Jude. If you can hear me from wherever you have gone, come back to us for just a little while and tell us what to do. We need your wisdom so."

Eleanor rested her aching head upon the bier and listened for an answer that never came. Then, in the silence, she became aware that the sounds of the struggle in the courtyard had ceased. There was only the sound of Merrill's boots as he walked across the courtyard toward the manor. She rose and kissed Randall softly on his cold cheek and left the Great Hall, disappearing around the corner just as Merrill was sliding the heavy bolts in place on the front doors. Her heart pounded as she thought about what Merrill would have done had he discovered her with Randall. She suspected that she would have envied The Great Black War Horse his fate, in comparison to what her's would have been. When she reached her room and closed the door behind her, she laid on her bed without moving, as if Merrill would hear her very breath if he passed by.

*　*　*　*

And now, on the following night, Eleanor lay scarcely breathing once again when she heard Merrill return from Shannon's cottage and go directly into the room that had been Randall's. It was now the room that Merrill claimed as his own, to sleep in the bed in which his father had breathed his last.

Merrill did not defeat The Great Black War Horse last night, and it seems that he has left him alone tonight, Eleanor thought as she allowed her breathing to slowly return to normal. And she knew that Merrill would never ride the stallion again. Lash and blade would never again make that one bend to the will of any man. Eleanor knew, too, that it had not been because of Merrill's hand that he had been ridden. There was no earthly power that could force the stallion to accept a man upon his back if somewhere within his noble being there had not been consent. Eleanor knew, somehow, that it was because it was to be Randall's final journey in this lifetime that the horse had accepted bit and saddle and carried a man upon his back that was not Randall. He would be there when Randall was put to his final rest, and no amount of cruelty could prevent that. Merrill would never mount the horse again, though, as yet, he knew it not. But he would learn or he would die beneath the stallion's hooves. There were no chains on earth that could deny him that if Merrill chose to lock in combat with him once again. Merrill would not get close enough a second time to do what he had done the night before, and walk away with his life.

Eleanor fell into a deep sleep for the first time since Randall had been infected by the fever. She dreamed that a change had come to Randall's Bow that was terrible in its way—yet, something good had come to this place upon the river, too, but its nature was not revealed to her. That time would come, she dreamed, but she must have patience for just a little while longer.

Eleanor awoke just before dawn, when the sun was about to come up over Cold River. She felt a great peace and fell again into a sleep that was as deep but not as restful as the first. She dreamed of her farewell to Randall as she stood beside his grave, and she saw two men standing across from her. Their eyes were on her—they said nothing, yet seemed to be telling her something in their silence. Their years were many, or so it appeared, and their size was less than normal size, as if their years had taken their physical stature from them.

In her dream, Eleanor saw the smaller of the two men take his gaze from her and turn it upon The Great Black War Horse. The stallion looked back at the diminutive old one and softly whinnied through his pain. It was as if the two of them recognized their kinship as they stood together beside Randall's grave. She awoke then and rose from her bed. She walked to the window and looked out at the stables, her dream forgotten for the moment.

Chapter 23

After Joshua went upstairs to bed, Old Man and Shannon sat for a while in silence, each one alone with his thoughts until Shannon rose to place another small log on the fire. It was well past midnight now, and both of them were very tired. But they knew a night of half-sleep and disturbing dreams awaited, and neither of them was eager to enter that fitful place of unrest just yet.

Old Man glanced at the decanter of brandy on the small table next to the fireplace. "It has been a long time," he said.

"What?" Shannon asked, only vaguely aware of Old Man's presence. His mind was on what Merrill's next move might be.

"The brandy," said Old Man. "It has been a long time since I've tasted any kind of spirits.. It wasn't one of the luxuries that I took with me when I left. Nor did I try to make such a potion while I was there. I could have done so, of that I'm sure—at least after a fashion. I grew potatoes, and from those I could have concocted drink even stronger than what you have here. Have you ever had the drink of which I speak?"

"Not that I recall."

"Old Man smiled. "Then you may be sure you haven't. It's an experience that you wouldn't have forgotten."

"It's good to see you relax a little, my friend," Shannon said. "Your return to Randall's Bow hasn't been a happy one. Let's have a brandy, you and I—a celebration of sorts for just the two of us. We can celebrate this quiet time before the fire and be grateful that this day is done. Or yesterday, for it's already tomorrow. Come. Will you join me?"

"No. No thank you. But I will join you in a pipe-full, if I may."

Shannon took one of the pipes from the mantle and filled it from a wooden bowl that sat next to the horse Randall had carved. "Randall was a carver of pipes, too," he said, handing it to Old Man. He gently touched the pipes. "He made these for me over the years as tokens of our friendship. I have yet to see finer ones. He's all around us, isn't he?"

Old Man ran his finders over the exquisitely carved pipe Shannon had given him. Its stem was ebony, long and delicately curved, connected to a briar bowl carved into the likeness of a woman's head. Her long hair flowed as if caressed by a gentle breeze. Her face was finely featured with a delicate beauty that felt lifelike to his hand. It seemed as if the small mouth returned his smile as he looked at it, holding him in a kind of spell.

"She speaks to you, does she not?"

"Yes," Old Man whispered. "She is so lifelike, it startled me."

"And when the pipe is lit," Shannon said, "and you hold it in your hand for a moment, the heat gives the bowl the warmth of a woman's skin. Such was Randall's mastery in all that he did. Such was his love for Judith."

"Judith?" Old Man looked at Shannon in surprise, and then back at the pipe.

"It is her likeness that you hold," said Shannon. "The face on the bowl is Judith's."

Old Man looked at the pipe more closely. "Her beauty was truly one of a kind," he said.

"Yes. Judith was beautiful in every way. She had a light that shone from within her on all she encountered. It spoke to all, no matter what their station. All were equal in her eyes. Merrill's loss was great when he lost his mother. He never knew how great that loss really was. Randall did. And with Judith's death, a part of Randall died, too. It was as if a part of him had gone into the grave with her. He was never able to really love again." Shannon paused and looked out the window into the darkness. "Perhaps the stallion," he said. "Yes. The Great Black War Horse. And Jude. Tell me, what was it like to be a magician for the people of Randall's Bow. To cure their ills. Did you feel power from it?"

Old Man laughed. "My intellect is considerable, if I do say so myself. And do not think that I joke when I say that, my friend. I do not. As is yours. So you understand what I mean when I say that my feeling was more of contempt than of power, although sometimes the two are interchangeable—two elements of the same compound, so to speak."

Shannon persisted. "What was it like?"

"I have a natural and intuitive knowledge of human nature and its motives," said Old Man. "It sometimes leads me into error, I admit that, but most times I'm accurate in my judgment of others. I understand what you mean when you speak of this aspect of Randall—the power he held over others without saying a word. In the hands of a man such as he, this ability can lead to much good. In the hands of others, misfortune is the most common consequence. But in my hands, alas, it accomplished little of anything, good or bad. It revealed that most of the illnesses that were brought to me for miraculous cures were mostly in the minds of those who thought themselves afflicted. And I played to their imaginings by prescribing harmless mixtures with pleasant tastes and sometimes intoxicating effects. They expected miracles, and miracles they received. Or so they thought." "When their maladies were genuine, I recognized that, too, and prescribed as best I could a remedy that, if it wouldn't provide a real cure, at least it would alleviate the pain. I dealt with the symptoms rather than the illness itself, as men usually do in other areas of their lives that are stricken with malfunction of some sort." But I was only playing games—sometimes with people's lives. I became more and more bitter, and eventually people stopped coming to me.

Old Man stopped talking when he heard a creaking of the stairs. He and Shannon looked in the direction of the sound and there, in the soft glow of the firelight, they saw Joshua's silhouette standing at the foot of the stairs. He stood without speaking or moving, looking like a spirit from another world.

At last, Joshua spoke. "There is a sickness here, and there is something we can do about it, Old Man."

The power in Joshua's voice was the power they had heard when he had faced Merrill, unafraid. It was the power they had heard when he had faced them and told them that confronting Merrill had been right. They had known the truth of his words then and now, again, they knew that what Joshua was telling them was true.

Yes, Joshua knew what they should do and there was joy in his knowing. There was joy in knowing who he was. Abandoned? Yes. Different? Yes—in some respects but not all. Not in the ways that really mattered. Within himself, he was the same as others. The goodness and the strength he felt now he knew to be himself—and, so too, was the strength and goodness in others who they truly were, although they might not know it. That didn't matter. It needed only to be remembered and accepted to change them for the better. And perhaps even to save their lives. And Joshua could help them do that. He knew that now about himself. He could see others in their truth. He could see them as they really were. He could see them in their innocence. He was united with all that lived by that power that lived within himself. Even in the face of their ridicule and pulling back from him because of the way he looked—even then, he saw them in their innocence.

That is what his guiding inner voice told him. It kept him strong within himself. He knew that now. He knew that he was the teacher now, and that the others would learn from him. And so there was power in Joshua's own voice now. He heard it too, as he spoke, just as Old Man and Shannon heard it. It held the certainty that only truth can bring. Old Man would follow now—and he would learn. As would the others.

"Shannon, I want to speak with the woman called Eleanor. The one of whom Merrill spoke at Randall's grave. And I want to see the sick ones, to be with them a while and observe the nature of the sickness—to see what the fever does to them. I want to see what it does to their bodies and to their minds. Then we will go into the forest and find what we need to help the ones who can be helped. The answer is there. And the answer is in the ones who are sick, too. I know it is." Joshua turned away from them then, and slowly climbed back up the stairs to his bed. This day had been long and hard for him, and he was more tired than he had ever been before. He would rest now and, despite his pain, his heart was filled with joy.

* * * *

In the darkness of the stables, The Great Black War Horse standsunmoving in his stall, his powerful neck arched and head held high once more in the attitude of battle. His ears are pointed forward, straining toward something that he senses, brought to him, perhaps, upon the rays of a new day's sun. His eyes are clear, his breathing comes in deep, rhythmic intakes of the morning's air. It is as if the blows that had drawn his blood that was still upon his flanks and withers have been nothing but a distant dream. He listens to the morning sounds, and his spirit flies to a place beyond his sight.

And in another place in Randall's Bow, one of like spirit sleeps, though not in a body so perfectly made for war. It is another kind of battle this little one, this innocent of innocents, will fight. And though as yet he knows it not, he, too, is made for noble combat.

In the battle this little one will fight, he will be the champion of innocence. And in this battle, these two will be allies—The Great Black War Horse and the little one who sleeps so soundly in the night, withdrawing in the solitude of slumber from the previous day and its events. He is like a baby waiting to be born, curled like an infant in the warmth of his mother's womb. It was this that they had known as they looked upon each other across Randall's open grave.

Joshua stirs in his sleep, a sigh of contentment slipping from between his smiling lips. And in his stall, The Great Black War Horse whinnies softly as the wound that little one had touched at Randall's grave disappears and is no more.

Chapter 24

Torches set around the courtyard of the manor light the way for those who had been summoned for the meeting of the council. Shannon, Old Man, and Joshua arrived early, taking the well-worn path that wound around the village and along the edge of the forest, ending at the manor gates. As they walked across the courtyard toward the ornately carved oaken doors now swung open for all to enter, their shadows scurried along beside them, thrown there by the flames from the torches. Rashan stood by the steps that led into the manor. ready to take the reins of those who had arrived by horseback and to tether their mounts by the watering trough across the courtyard in front of the stables.

Eleanor stood in a large foyer just inside the open doors, giving council members unnecessary directions to the Great Hall where they would meet. They had been there many times before at the request of Randall. This meeting, however, was a different matter and they all knew it.

As they neared the bottom of the steps, Shannon saw Eleanor and stopped. He stepped quickly to the side of the steps and stood in the shadows out of Eleanor's sight, motioning to Old Man and Joshua to do the same. "Eleanor is standing just inside the doors," he whispered when they were well out of sight. "She saw you at Randall's funeral—I am sure of that—because that's her way. Nothing escapes her notice. I saw her carefully observing you, and you may be certain she has already reached some conclusions of her own about who you are and why you are here. Your company with me must surely be a point of curiosity with her. I'll introduce you to her when we go in and ask if we might visit her at her cabin sometime tomorrow. She spends most of her time here at the manor, while her daughter Leyla is usually at the cabin—especially now. Leyla's distrust of Merrill is great."

Shannon turned to Joshua. "Joshua, you must hold your silence tonight." Saying nothing more, he stepped from the shadows, nodded to Rashan and walked up the steps and through the open doors. with Old Man and Joshua following closely behind.

Eleanor greeted them with a smile and without much apparent interest. "Come in. come in. I've been expecting you," she said warmly. She exchanged a few cordial words with Shannon, who then introduced her to his two friends. "I look forward to seeing you tomorrow," she said, then turned her attention to greeting the rest of the council members who were just arriving.

They were a curious looking threesome as they entered the Great Hall, and their entrance did not go unnoticed. Shannon was wearing his customary billowing blue tunic that rippled like water as he walked. A thick leather belt from which dangled a leather pouch that held a small clay pipe and some tobacco was buckled around his large middle. He looked like a sky-blue friar who had come to spread his own special gospel.

The three of them stood off to one side of the Great Hall and watched as the men gathered into small groups. Their conversations were very animated, with much gesturing and movement from group to group. They looked and sounded angry and worried—they knew they had not been summoned to receive news that was good. The unknown purpose of tonight's meeting, which had been unexpected, was not a good sign. Merrill had proven himself to be unpredictable and uncompromising, and he had kept tonight's agenda to himself. He wanted no one other than himself to have the opportunity to prepare for what was about to transpire. This was not to be an evening in pleasant conversation and agreement. Merrill would tell them what was going to be done, and he would tell them to do it without question. They would have no choice, for he would give them none.

Merrill was nowhere to be seen as the council members looked anxiously around the Great Hall. They would wait and, when he was ready and at his own conniving pleasure, Merrill would appear.

Several of the council members approached Shannon to ask what he knew of Merrill's intentions, as his close association with Randall gave him a position of authority within their group that they respected—and envied. He told them nothing because he knew nothing. They did not believe him.

Suddenly, as if by command, there was silence throughout the Great Hall. Two enormous wolfhounds bounded through the doors and took their places near the fireplace, enjoying its warmth. Merrill would soon be with them. They stood unmoving and watched the open doors through which he would make his entrance.

The only sound in the Great Hall was a nervous cough or two and the scraping of a boot heel against the polished wooden floor until a shout rang out from just outside the doors—a kind of command—and another giant hound, larger even than the first two, ran into the Great Hall and took its place near, but slightly removed, from the others. Merrill followed closely behind. He walked to the fireplace, looking straight ahead and acknowledging no one, bent to touch the hounds affectionately and say a word to each of them. It was if he was alone with only his hounds for company.

Merrill stood with his back to the Great Hall and looked up at the portrait of Randall and Judith hanging just above him. Still silent, he turned and gestured toward the long table in the center of the room. When everyone was seated, Merrill walked to the empty chair at the head of the table and stood behind it. He looked at Shannon and nodded toward the empty chair at the end of the table opposite him. Shannon rose from where he had chosen to sit, midway down the table's length, and took his place where Merrill had indicated. Old Man and Joshua remained where they had been seated, halfway down the table on Merrill's left, with members of the council on either side of them.

Merrill glanced at Shannon after he was seated, then looked at Old Man and Joshua. His face was without expression. He nodded his acknowledgement to them, looked at Joshua for a moment longer, and then looked around the table at the others, one-by-one. His eyes circled the table slowly, stopping at each man to nod slightly before moving on to the next. There were few who were able to hold Merrill's steady gaze with their own, though each one tried. Those who succeeded then questioned their wisdom in doing so, fearful that Merrill would interpret their boldness as a challenge rather than the pledge of loyalty it was meant to be.

When Merrill sat down, one of the wolfhounds trotted to his side. He looked at the dog and pointed to the spot he had just left. They all watched the wolfhound return to his place with the others, his tail between his legs. We are like dogs, too, Shannon thought. We are like obedient dogs, and no better. We are like obedient animals without the will and courage to break free of our bonds. Fear and disgust swept through him him as he recognized his own willingness to obey almost any command from Merrill in order to protect himself.

Merrill began to address the council. "You have work to do and you must do it quickly and without question." His voice was at a level that could be heard, yet low enough to command complete attention lest a word be missed. "The fever will kill all of us if we let it. But I will not permit that. I will force it from our midst and it will not return. Hear this well— the work that I will order you to do tonight is the work that you will do. I did not summon you here to listen to your opinions. You will hear what I command you to do and then you will do it. To put yourself against me in any way will be a grave mistake. And to compare my way with what you conjecture would have been his," he pointed to the portrait above the fireplace, "is foolishness.. It would take a mind like his to know his ways, and there is not a mind like his among you. His place is mine now. That is done. Now hear what I will have you do."

Merrill rose from his chair and began to slowly walk around the table as he spoke. His voice was level, and he put his hand upon the shoulder of each of the councilmen as he passed behind him. It was clear that Randall's power and ability to lead men—even in something that was against their will—had been inherited by his son. And what they heard was indeed against their will. It offended them to their deepest hearts, yet not one of them spoke out against it.

"Downriver, and on the opposite bank from Randall's Bow, there is a large clearing. You all know the place of which I speak. You will build a structure there to house the sick. We will cut them off from us—all of them, be they young or old. It makes no difference. Each one who has been stricken with the fever will be taken there. It makes no difference what stage the fever is in—beginning or advanced and near death—it does not matter. They will be taken to that place across the river and there they will remain until they die or until they recover on their own and are well enough to return here under their own power—whichever is their fate. There will be no exceptions. Tomorrow, at your direction and under your supervision, the able-bodied men of Randall's Bow will go to the clearing and there they will build the structure. You have done this on a much smaller scale when you built your barns and stables. This is not a task that is beyond your capabilities. The ground is cleared and the forest is thick around that place. It is a simple task that I have set before you. Take great care not to complicate it."

A few of the councilmen followed Merrill with their eyes as he slowly circled around them like a devil circling their souls, but most stared at the surface of the table in front of them, listening in despair and disbelief at what he was ordering them to do. But they would do as Merrill commanded. There was not a man in the room who doubted that. And they knew they had not heard it all, that there was surely more to come.

"How long will you need? Five days? Six days? Certainly not more than that. Was not the world completed in that time?" Merrill laughed quietly, almost to himself. "Surely you can build a simple wooden structure in as long as it took to build the world. And when it's completed, you will go through the village. You will go into every cabin, one-by-one. Now hear me, every one of you, and hear me well. You will bring forth all who have the fever, be they infants or old ones—it does not matter. You will bring them to the—what shall be call it? The infirmary. Yes. The infirmary. It is for the infirm, is it not?" Merrill laughed quietly once more. "And there they will remain. The women, what healthy ones there are, will provide them with water and whatever food they can tolerate. And as they die, their bodies will be burned and their ashes will be thrown into the river and carried downstream, far away from us, until at last there is not a sick one—nor their remains—left in Randall's Bow. And when the infirmary is no longer needed, it too will be burned piece-by-piece and its ashes thrown into the river. Do not think to deceive me by concealing or attempting to spare anyone, for I will find you out.

And you will be put to death by my own hand. Now go and do as I have told you. I will be with you through each day and I will give you guidance as I see fit. Remember what I have said. If you deviate from my command, the price will be your life. I swear that upon my father's grave." Merrill looked directly at Shannon as he spoke his final words, glanced briefly at Old Man and Joshua, then left the Great Hall, his hounds following obediently behind him.

* * * *

All was silent in the Great Hall. Merrill's hounds could be heard barking in some far off part of the manor—and then a curse was heard, a yelp from one of the hounds, and all fell silent.

The councilmen sat without moving, with all eyes on Shannon. He was the one to whom they would turn. Shannon was not held in favor by every man who sat at the table, but he had no enemies of any consequence among them. And he had been their last link to Randall in the days before he died.

Many times in the past, in the midst of important consideration, they had seen Randall pause and turn to Shannon for his counsel. Randall would take him by the arm and lead him to a secluded place where the two of them could talk without interruption or being overheard. They had seen Randall stand silently, his eyes intently upon Shannon, concentrating on what Shannon had to say about the issue at hand. When he returned with his decision, he would speak with Shannon beside him, his hand upon his shoulder, acknowledging his influence in what he was about to say.

It was that same wise counsel that the men at the table needed now. They had been issued a directive that was grotesque, even to the most insensitive among them. Yes, there were times long ago when quarantine and fire had been used. But only when all else had failed, and no other course was known. There was another way now, too. There had to be. But what was it?

There was not a man among them who would not be directly affected by what Merrill had ordered them to do. Each one had a family member who lay at that very moment upon a pallet soaked in the fever's sweat. Some were sure to die. Others had a chance to survive if they were given the proper care. Few would live under the conditions Merrill had created.

And for those who would die, it would not be the beloved ground of Randall's Bow that would embrace them in their final rest. No. They would not go into the ground they had cared for with so much love—to nourish it with themselves for the next generation to till and cultivate in

158

their stead. No. They would be thrown first into the fires to be devoured and turned to ashes, and then thrown into the waters of Cold River to be carried from this place forevermore. There would be no place to go for those who remained, to know that there, in that very place, is where they rested, where memories of times now gone could be remembered and cherished.

And so they looked to Shannon to tell them what to do. It would be by his direction that they would be delivered from this madman who would tear the very foundations of their families from beneath them.

Shannon looked around the table, and he knew what they expected of him. His mind was frozen. He was unable to think, and his stomach churned with bitter juices from the terror that he felt. He rose from his chair at the foot of the table and stood beside it for a moment, saying nothing and looking at each man for a moment then passing on to the next. He felt only separation from them as he looked from one to the other. Sweat gathered at his temples and ran into his eyes, blurring his vision.

He motioned for Old Man and Joshua to follow him, turned and walked from the Great Hall, leaving the others in silence as they watched the one they hoped would save them walk away.

*   *   *   *

No one spoke on the way back to Shannon's. When they arrived at his cabin, each of them went to his bed with his thoughts unspoken. It was as if they had reached an agreement to let tomorrow tell them what it held.

Even Joshua was content to let the silence show them what their next course of action would be.

After breakfast the next morning, they took the path along the river once again. The talk so far had been sparse, Shannon saying only at breakfast that he wanted to talk to Eleanor about what had transpired at the council's meeting the night before. "Eleanor knows Merrill well," he said, "and she will be able to tell us what his motives really are." His hands trembled as he sipped his tea, and he ate nothing. Old Man and Joshua said nothing in reply.

Shannon led the way along the narrow path. Just before they reached the manor gates, they took another well-worn path that branched off from the one they were on, leading into the forest. They followed it for a short time as it wound among the trees and through a small, sunlit clearing until they reached the edge of a larger clearing that opened suddenly before them. It was covered by a thick carpet of grass that seemed to sparkle in the sunlight. The trees around its borders were straight and tall, growing close together as if forming a wall of protection around the small cabin that rested in its center like a lily floating in a quiet pond of green. A narrow, flower-lined path led to its door, now open to welcome their expected arrival. Freshly baked bread surrounded by small clay pots of several varieties of berry jams were on a table in the center of the room that greeted them as they entered.

Eleanor looked up from the fireplace where she was brewing a pot of tea as Shannon led them unannounced into the cabin. She smiled at Shannon, then turned her attention to Old Man and Joshua.

"So," she said, carefully examining the two of them, making no effort to conceal her curiosity. "We meet again. I saw you at Randall's grave yesterday morning. You were a welcome diversity for me on that sad occasion."

"Merrill paid you a visit, didn't he," Eleanor said, addressing Shannon. "I heard him when he returned to the manor, and I knew that it was you he had gone to see." She waited to see how Shannon would react to what she had just said. She was fond of Shannon for the most part, though she sometimes found him to be exasperating, concealing his real intentions in a swarm of words that assaulted her ears and left her a little confused. She knew that Randall had held Shannon in the highest regard, but there was something in the way he attempted to ingratiate himself with almost everyone he met that she found to be manipulating and self-serving. Her conclusions about such matters were usually correct and she had learned to trust the feeling that held her back from some people and urged her on with others.

There had been times when Shannon appeared to maintain a calmness that was remarkable when all else around him was a raging storm of emotions. And then a point would come when he could no longer contain the anger that was always buried just beneath the surface. With Merrill, at least, it was out in the open, bidding all who came near to beware lest they cross a boundary that they should not cross. But with Shannon his anger, at least at first, was cloaked in the disguise of openness and generosity.

"You saw his mount at the grave," said Eleanor.

"Yes. I saw. How could I not? It was meant to be seen by all of us. But what does it mean, Eleanor?" What are we to think? What does he want us to do?"

Shannon was pleading for an explanation, and Eleanor knew it. "I had presumed that you know more about it than I." Eleanor's own anger was coming to the surface and she made no effort to hide it. "He came to you. Not to me. And did he not reveal more about his intentions at council last night than what he told us at the grave? It was more than a visit of friendship that brought him to you. Am I correct? And what of the meeting of the council last night? Surely you know much more of what Merrill intends than I. He has scarcely spoken a word to me since Randall's death. And surely, you have an important part in his plans because of your close association with Randall." There was a bite in Eleanor's voice and she could see that Shannon was upset that this confrontation was happening in front of Old Man and Joshua.

"We will discuss these matters at another time, Eleanor." Shannon was angry and confused, his face flushed crimson as he fought to control this unexpectedly unpleasant situation. He had hoped that he and Eleanor would be allies, and he didn't know the reason for her hostility now that they could be of valuable help to each other. Shannon forced a smile and turned so that Old Man and Joshua could come closer to Eleanor. "But now," he said, "I would like you to meet my new friends. They will be my guests during their stay in Randall's Bow. Eleanor, I would like you to meet Old Man and Joshua."

"Have we met before?" Eleanor asked, looking directly at Old Man. "I mean before I saw you at Randall's grave. There is something about you that's familiar to me. Your eyes. I feel as if I have looked into your eyes before this day."

"No, We've never met before" Old Man replied, smiling.

Eleanor watched him carefully as he answered. If he was lying, she would know. He kept his smile, holding her eyes as she held his. Old Man didn't waver, and at last Eleanor looked away for a moment then returned her attention to him as he began to speak.

"We arrived in Randall's Bow only the day before Randall was buried." He held his hand out to Joshua, motioning him forward. "This is Joshua. And I am called Old Man, for reasons that are obvious."

Old Man laughed, but Eleanor did not share his laughter. Her stern expression didn't change. She nodded her certainty. "We have met before," she said, and then turned her attention to Joshua and smiled. "But we have not, have we? I am certain of that. I am very tired. We have been fighting the fever for a long time, and now the death of Randall—he meant much to me and to all of us here. It's an unrelenting enemy. And it is winning, I fear. But come. I've made tea and fresh bread. You can sample the jam I've made, too, from the berries in our beautiful forest. My jams are the sweetest in all of Randall's Bow—or so I'm told. They spent the rest of the morning sitting in Eleanor's kitchen discussing the recent events in Randall's Bow, carefully avoiding the council meeting of the night before until Eleanor abruptly stood to indicate that their visit had come to an end.

"I stood outside the Great Hall last night and listened to what Merrill ordered you to do. Do not oppose him on this, at least not now," she said to Shannon, putting her hand under his arm and guiding him out the door. "The raising of the structure—the infirmary—Merrill described began this morning. Merrill is convinced that his way is right. He has no doubt about that. He will tolerate no one who is opposed to him. He meant it, Shannon, when he said that those who are foolish enough to oppose him will pay with their lives. Believe him. There are things that have occurred at the manor since Randall's death that I have not spoken of—perhaps they will remain my secrets forever. I tell you this—Merrill is mad and he cannot be reasoned with. So don't try. It will mean your life. Yes, even yours. Do not doubt it. Perhaps especially yours, if you try to fight him. When the infirmary is complete and the sick have been brought there, come and see me there." Eleanor looked at Old Man and Joshua. "Then we will talk about another way. We will talk of healing—healing the sick with the help of our forest. We may find the answer there."

Eleanor became silent then, and suddenly stepped closer to Joshua. She bent and looked deeply, almost pleadingly, into his eyes. "I am so tired," she said to him. "So tired. My eyes are beginning to play tricks on me. For a moment, I thought you were a child." She backed into the cabin, keeping her attention focused on Joshua, then closed the door softly behind her.

Chapter 25

Old Man and Joshua walked along the riverbank beside Shannon until they came to a narrow bridge constructed of logs and rope. A wider bridge had been built next to the footbridge to hold the heavy, horse-drawn wagons that were transporting the sick to the newly-constructed infirmary across the river. They took the footbridge to the opposite bank of the river and made their way down a cleared area that had widened the old footpath into a crude road leading to an enormous, barn-like structure built from logs cut from trees felled around the perimeter. The stumps had been left standing like crude memorials to those who would soon die there.

Piled on both sides of the infirmary and circling around to the back were piles of brush and limbs that had been cut from the fallen trees. "For the fires," said Shannon, as he led them to the open doors of the infirmary. Several wagons, empty now except for small piles of filthy rags and straw, stood off to one side. The horses had been loosened from their heavy harnesses and were tethered nearby to graze at the edge of the clearing.

As they were about to enter the infirmary, Shannon stopped and looked at a section of the clearing nearest the river. "Wait here," he said, and went to the spot that had attracted his attention, following a narrow path into the forest. After several minutes, he reappeared, walking quickly, a look of agitation on his face.

He walked up to Old Man and Joshua, still standing where he had left them, and stood silently for a moment, his hands trembling beside him. He tried to speak but was unable to calm his breathing. He walked to one of the empty wagons and leaned heavily against the side, resting there until he could regain his composure. "He's had them dig pits by the river," he said, with one hand resting on a wagon wheel to steady himself.

"Deep pits like the one upriver, where the dead will be burned before their ashes are thrown into the river." Shannon looked in the direction of the pits and then back at Old Man and Joshua. "Let us go in now and find Eleanor." There was both anger and sadness in his voice. "Perhaps there is something we can do. Perhaps not. Perhaps we can only stand and watch while this terrible thing takes place, and then begin again when it's over."

They entered the infirmary and stopped just inside the door. The sights and smells that confronted them were appalling. "With so many sick in one place," said Shannon, "there's no hope of healing here. This is a place of death." He looked around the infirmary at several small windows that had been cut on each wall. "There's no air here. The smell of death is overpowering. This is where Eleanor and the other women will be spending their days, and many of their nights too, I fear. And for no good—no good at all."

They saw Eleanor nearby in a small open area near the door, about to begin her morning rounds. She had been there earlier, before the sun was up, to determine who had died during the night and then she had sent Leyla to notify their families. If they were lucky, they would be able to spend a few minutes with their departed loved ones before those who had been assigned to tend the pits that day came to carry them off and incinerate them.

Shannon had come upon the first pit in which the remains of several bodies were still smoldering when he left Old Man and Joshua.. The ashes were about to be shoveled into buckets by the pit's tenders then carried to the river and thrown into the water to be carried downstream. The men who tended the pits were changed each day and were personally selected by Merrill. At the end of the day, the men reported to Merrill the number of bodies that had been disposed of and the names of anyone who had caused trouble or even voiced their objections to what was happening. As yet, no one had spoken out, but everyone knew it was only a matter of time, and Merrill fully intended to carry out what he had threatened to do. The rebels would pay with their lives. Anyone who tried to stand in Merrill's way would die by his hand.

Old Man, Shannon, and Joshua watched as Eleanor, unaware of their presence, tried to force the contents of a small cup between the lips and down the constricted throat of a child who was lying motionless and unresponsive on a dirt-encrusted pallet. She had mixed a potion that would reduce somewhat the unrelenting thirst that gripped those with the fever—a thirst which no amount of water could slake. It was the best that she had been able to do. If permitted, they would drink water until their bellies were painfully swollen—but still, the thirst would consume them. Until Eleanor had discovered her potion only a few days before, the only relief had been the unconscious state that occurred intermittently during the several hours of suffering it took to die. At that point, death was a mercy.

Old Man and Joshua followed Shannon to the far wall beneath one of the small windows where Eleanor knelt over the child, whispering gently to her, urging her to drink. A small beam of light was coming through the window above her, falling across Eleanor's hair and face. She looked like an agent of heavenly mercy who had come to heal the child, or take her home to a place where there was no more pain for one so young and innocent.

"Come now, my sweet one. Only a little. Just a little," she crooned. "Just one small sip. It will make you feel so much better. You would like that, wouldn't you? To feel better? Now do as Eleanor says. Just a little drink to get it started, and then perhaps the rest. Come now. Please."

The child remained motionless on the pallet, unseeing through half-closed eyes. Her breathing was so slight and shallow that it seemed as if she wasn't breathing at all. Eleanor looked up at the three behind her, then returned her attention to the dying girl. Shannon leaned forward and touched her gently on the shoulder. "Eleanor," he whispered, "she's going. Eleanor. There is nothing you can do. Let her go in peace."

Eleanor looked up at Shannon. Anger swept across her face and she wept tears of sadness and frustration. "Let her go in peace?" she hissed. "What peace does this poor child know? She's being cooked alive, Shannon. The fever is cooking her alive. No amount of water or anything that any human being can do will put the fire out. So don't speak to me of peace. There is no peace here for this child." She looked around the infirmary at the others. "Nor is there peace for any of those you see lying here in this terrible place."

Eleanor looked at the dying child for a moment more, then slowly rose to her feet. "Her family must be summoned quickly," she breathed, motioning to one of the boys who had been appointed to carry buckets of water from the river to the infirmary, "Go to the cabin of this one. Quickly." Eleanor said to him. "You know which one it is. Tell them they must come here at once if they wish to see their daughter alive and make their final farewells—though I doubt she'll hear them. Quickly, now—be off. There's no time to spare if they want to be here when she departs this world. Run as fast as you can." Eleanor turned to Shannon, and smiled wearily. "I feel so helpless here," she said. "I could use some of that wonderful tea you brew, Shannon. And the day has just begun."

Eleanor looked down at the dying girl, then bent close to her face, her cheek next to the child's slightly parted lips. "Her breath is very faint," she said, looking toward the door. "If they're not here soon, they will have lost their chance. In a few minutes, she'll be gone. I'll stay here with her for a little longer. There are so many who need attention—but I can't let her die alone. So many do. There are so many to care for." Eleanor looked around the infirmary. "I just can't let her die alone. Most go with no one by their side to hold their hand or whisper a word of comfort and say a small prayer to send them on their way to whatever lies beyond this place. This one, at least, will have someone who cares by her side."

Eleanor sat on the straw-covered dirt floor beside the child and took her hand. The others watched in silence as her frail chest began to move in a faster rhythm for a moment—and then it stopped. There was no movement. Then one last, long and heavy sigh, as if from resignation to her fate, escaped through her lips, still slightly parted, then there was nothing. The child had died.

Eleanor sat holding the little hand, feeling it grow stiff and cold in hers. She leaned over and gently closed the eyes that were still half open, staring sightlessly at the crudely raftered ceiling high above her, then tenderly pressed under the girl's little chin until her mouth was closed. Her cracked and bloody lips seemed to form a prim little smile, almost in the shape of a heart. She looked like a child who was simply taking a little nap after an afternoon at play.

Eleanor drew back as a short gasp of air escaped from the girl's slowly deflating lungs. She looked closely to make sure there was no more life left in the still little body. There was none. She was sure of that. But her breath had seemed so real. No. There was no life there. She folded the child's arms until her hands were resting together on her bony chest, as if in a silent prayer of thanks that she was done with all of this. The presence of death and grief in the cavernous infirmary was overwhelming. It was as if all the air had left the structure as it had the child's body, and a wet and heavy mist had somehow taken its place. Eleanor sat next to the dead girl for a few moments more, than leaned down and gently kissed her cold cheek. She stood and looked at Old Man and Joshua, tears streaming down her strong yet saddened face. She wiped at the tears with the corner of her apron. "So," she said. "Shannon tells me you can help us. Or at least, you think you can." Her words hung in the air, waiting for their response.

Old Man and Joshua said nothing. Joshua's eyes were on the face of the lifeless body on the floor.

Shannon stood silently nearby, anxiously waiting for someone to say something. When he could no longer stand the silence, he decided to speak.

"Eleanor...."

Eleanor motioned to Shannon to keep silent. She kept her eyes on Old Man and Joshua, doubt clouding her face. At last, she spoke. "We cannot be afraid of this. This thing that is among us will claim the fearful as its own. The courageous are untouched, while those who fear the consequences of their closeness to the sick are soon stricken with the fever themselves. And yes, sometimes the brave among us are claimed, too. The bravest of us all you saw laid to rest on the village green." She looked around the infirmary. "There was no fear of this in him," she said. "There was only love and compassion for those who had been stricken. And now even he is gone. With Randall went much hope, you see. It seemed as if, as long as Randall was alive, then somewhere, somehow, we would find an answer for this terrible thing and chase it from our midst. But now...." Eleanor's voice trailed off and she looked again at the lifeless child lying at her feet. "But still we must not fear it. As long as at least some of us are not afraid, there is hope."

Joshua stepped forward until he was standing next to Eleanor. He looked at her, and then knelt beside the dead little girl, bending until his face almost touched her pale white face, and opened her closed eyelids. He looked into her sightless eyes, already cloudy now with death, then closed them once again. He gently touched her stiffened hands and touched the dry and slightly brittle skin of his own hands. Then he looked up at Eleanor.

"What does that do?" he asked, pointing to the cup from which Eleanor had been urging the child to drink.

"It's for the thirst." Eleanor's voice was soft and subdued, and could barely be heard by Shannon and Old Man. They had no understanding of what was happening now between those two, or the meaning of Joshua's actions. "Sometimes it relieves the terrible thirst that comes upon them in the hours before their death. It does nothing for their pain. Their joints swell terribly, as you can see, before they die. It's then that we know we've lost them. When the joints begin to swell, we know then that it's only a matter of time before death claims them. And then the thirst. The thirst tells us that the end is very near—only hours away. If we can manage somehow to do whatever is required to keep the swelling of the joints away, we know that they will live. But we never know. We don't know what it is that we do—if anything—that helps some survive. Perhaps we do nothing. Perhaps it's only good fortune—or perhaps they do it themselves."

Eleanor picked up the cup and held it out to Joshua. He took it from her, lifted it to his nose and smelled the contents. "What does it come from?" he asked, dipping his finger into the cup and licking the drops of yellowish liquid from his finger.

"It comes from the yellow root in the forest. When the root is boiled in water, it softens. Then I mash it into a paste that's boiled again in water until the paste dissolves. The root produces a potion that, when it's again mixed with water, but this time cool, reduces thirst and sometimes slows down the fever's fire." Eleanor stopped talking and waited for Joshua to respond to what she had said. She had a look of expectancy, as if she knew that here was one who knew what she would say before she said it—and whose knowledge of such things surpassed even her own.

"You are truly gifted," Joshua said with a smile. His piping voice carried throughout the infirmary, somehow overcoming the sounds of suffering with its clarity. "The yellow root is not easy to find. It seldom grows, and when it does, it grows deep into the ground and is usually hidden beneath rocks. How did you find it?"

"It found me," Eleanor laughed. "I never have to look for it. And I have discovered that when I do—when I try to search it out—I return home with my basket empty. If I look for other roots that I need, somehow this most elusive one of all mysteriously appears when I need it. When my supply is nearly gone, that's when I'm given more."

Eleanor looked intently at Joshua. Who is this one, she thought? He knows. He knows of what I speak because he has experienced it, too. "I've learned to trust that," she said, speaking only to Joshua now. It was as if the infirmary and all that it held didn't exist—except for the two of them. "I've learned to trust a voice I hear sometimes—it seems to come from inside me, from my heart—when I go into the forest to gather the things I need, I think only of the needs that I want filled, rather than the things that I think will fill them. The forest always gives me what I need. Sometimes it's a surprise—I get something that I didn't expect. You know that too, don't you."

Shannon was amazed at what was happening between Eleanor and Joshua. Eleanor was most cautious about revealing anything about herself, and he had never heard her discuss her healing methods with anyone except Leyla.

Eleanor wasn't a superstitious woman. It wasn't that. But she liked to know who it was she was really talking to so she could communicate with them on their terms without compromising her own. She had learned the importance of that from Randall. And from Merrill, too, in an odd, almost perverse, way, for there had been times when she had been hurt because she had been too candid about herself with him—or he hadn't understood her meaning because of the way she had addressed him, and he had retaliated with a cruel remark.

And now she had revealed a part of herself to Joshua that she hadn't shown to Shannon. When Eleanor had spoken about the voice she had heard or felt, Shannon remembered his experience with Old Man and Joshua before Merrill had burst in upon them. There was mystery here, and it frightened him. What was his role in all of this? What was he supposed to do, if anything? He felt as if he was being swept into uncharted waters, like the ashes of the dead, and he was powerless before them.

Joshua looked at the three of them and smiled. "May I give the rest of the cup to him?" he asked Eleanor, looking at a small boy who was lying on one of the straw pallets nearby. He was awake and was breathing in short little gasps, his thin chest heaving under the difficulty of his labor.

169

He had not been able to hold any food down for several days. And his body had barely enough strength for anything but to try to sustain his basic life functions at the lowest level.

Eleanor nodded her assent, although reluctantly. It was plain to her that the child had little time left to live. They watched as Joshua knelt close to the boy, put his face close to his flushed cheek and looked into his fever-glazed eyes. Joshua took the boy's hand in his and smiled. To their surprise, the boy, who had been in and out of consciousness for days and who had refused Eleanor's pleadings that he take at least a little nourishment, smiled back. Joshua bent closer to the boy and whispered in his ear. He spoke so softly that the others could barely hear what he was saying.

"Come now. Drink this. It will make you feel better. You feel the burning now, I know. You feel as if you are on fire now. I know. This will help some of that go away. Not all of it. Not all at once—but some of the fire will go away. And then you will be able to keep a little water in your stomach. And more of the fire will go away. You will still feel sick, but not as much. And you'll keep feeling better while Eleanor and my friend and I go into the forest to find the things we need to make the potion that will make the fever go away—from you and from everyone in Randall's Bow. Soon you will be all better. I know that. You must know it too. Know it with me."

As Joshua talked to the boy, he pulled slowly away from him until he was sitting up and talking in his normal voice and was no longer whispering. The boy's eyes opened slowly until they were fixed on the source of the music in the voice he heard. He smiled at Joshua and raised his hand to take the cup that Joshua offered him. With Joshua's help, he brought the cup to his parched lips. Joshua spoke to him while he drank from the cup in small, hesitant sips.

"It hurts, doesn't it?" Joshua said. His piping voice was lower now, but the music was still there, like a lullaby to comfort a frightened infant. "I know what hurt is like. I hurt sometimes, too, and all I want is for the hurt to go away. This helps it go away for me, and it will help you, too. Eleanor made it for you. Look. She is here."

Eleanor knelt next to Joshua so the boy could see her. "Come," Joshua said to him. "Drink everything that's in the cup and then you will sleep for a little while." Eleanor stroked the boy's hot forehead while Joshua held the cup to his lips. "And when you wake up," Joshua continued, "you will feel much better,"

When the cup was empty, Joshua set it on the floor beside him and put both of his hands on the boy's cheeks. He turned his head gently until they were looking directly at each other. ""I know." he said. "I am telling you that which is already true."

The suffering child reached for Joshua's hand and held on to it, trying to smile bravely. "It still hurts," he said. "But I believe you." He closed his eyes then and drifted into the sleep that Joshua had promised him, a smile slowly spreading across his thin, cracked lips.

Old Man and Shannon, watched intently as Joshua spoke with the boy. And they learned a truth as a they watched—Joshua was not afraid of the fever. It was as if he really didn't believe that it existed at all, and that the sick boy was rid of it already. All that needed to be done now, it seemed, was to accept whatever answer the forest gave them and then administer it to the sick. The power of what had just happened swept over them. It wasn't in what Joshua had said, really. His words had been simple—he had told the boy that he understood—that he knew. He knew the pain he was feeling and how much he was suffering. There was nothing extraordinary about that. Even when he had told the boy that he would get well, it was said as a simple statement of fact, without emotion, as if it had already happened. No. The power was not in what Joshua had said. It was not in the words he had used. The power was in his manner—the way he touched the boy—and in the tone of his voice, somehow. Concealed, yet revealed, in mystery.

And it was in his eyes—it was the way Joshua had looked at the boy. That was where the power lay, too.. Something had come through Joshua's eyes and had connected with the boy and he had believed that he would get well. That he was, somehow, already well. He had hope now where he had none before.

Eleanor looked at Old Man and Shannon with astonishment—and with certainty. This one knows, her look told them. This little old knows, and with his help we will come to the end of this terrible thing that is destroying us, and we will live in peace once more.

Eleanor returned her attention to the two on the floor. This time, she saw something else—something that had escaped her before. It had not been Joshua who had been the cause of her astonishment. After all, there had been nothing extraordinary about what he had said. There was power—yes, great power that she sensed in him—but there was something else. There was something more than that. It was the boy's response to Joshua that had given Eleanor hope. She was filled with so much hope that she thought she would burst from it. When Joshua had first knelt beside the boy, his eyes had been glazed and partly closed, with only their whites visible in the dim light of the infirmary. But as Joshua spoke to him, the boy's eyes opened wider and she could see he was trying to focus on the source of the music that he heard—the music that spoke to him of healing and relief from his pain.

And the child was urged toward something else, too. The music that he heard in Joshua's voice told him to reach for something deep inside himself. It told him to believe what Joshua was telling him. If he could know the truth of Joshua's words, it would be his own response to that truth that would make him well. In truth, he would heal himself.

At that moment, Eleanor knew that all was well. She felt her body chill with the realization of it, and then, for a brief moment, she herself feared the fever. She feared that it would somehow seek revenge and take away the hope that was soaring within her. And then she knew again that yes, all was well. She had never seen such a one as Joshua. Somehow, in the person of this one who looked so ancient and so frail, and yet who possessed such great power, were the answers they were searching for but had despaired of ever finding. Eleanor looked at Old Man and Joshua and smiled. "I'm glad you're here," she said. "We need your help."

* * * *

Old Man felt a stirring in the air when Joshua knelt close to the suffering child. What had just happened was part of the reason for their coming to Randall's Bow. He looked at Joshua, who was still kneeling on the floor holding his hand. "You have done so much here," Old Man said, touching Eleanor's hand gently as he spoke. "The miracle that we seek—a part of it—is already here among us."

Another wagon loaded with the sick arrived just outside the doors, and they were being carried one-by-one on crude stretchers to empty pallets that had been vacated by those who had died during the night. Shannon watched the last of the newly arrived sick being laid on the only empty pallet left and then looked anxiously toward the door. He felt strangely separated from what was happening. He didn't understand what Old Man had just said to Eleanor, and he felt threatened by the closeness that had suddenly emerged between Eleanor and Joshua.

This was not what he had planned. If, by chance, they found a cure for the fever, it would be a mercy on them all. He knew that. But such good fortune would not set well with Merrill, for it would prove him wrong and expose his cruelty upon the sick and their families more than it had already. Old Man and Joshua would feel Merrill's wrath—perhaps even Eleanor—for he didn't doubt for a moment that Merrill had the capacity for such extreme revenge. But it would be Shannon who would feel it the most, because Merrill would hold him responsible for bringing them together. Merrill had as much as told him that. Old Man and Joshua were Shannon's guests, and therefore within his control as far as Merrill was concerned. He didn't know what to do, if indeed, he should do anything.

Even that confused him, because he knew that Merrill was wrong in what he was doing. If only there was a way to make him see that destruction and tragedy were what he was bringing upon the people his father loved so much. Not survival.

Eleanor usually kept her distance from strangers, and Shannon sensed that Joshua held a kind of power over her—and over him, too—and it frightened him. He had lost control and he felt threatened by something he couldn't name and didn't understand. Until they had come to the infirmary, the control had been his, or so he thought, and now he had lost it to this strange little one who looked so old but was really a child. And he didn't know how or why it had happened.

At first, Shannon had perceived an alliance with Old Man and Joshua as an advantage over Merrill, and he wanted to bring Eleanor into that alliance. He had seen them as a shield against his inaction, and as scapegoats should there be trouble. Eleanor held great sway over Merrill at times, and her influence could direct Merrill's wrath upon the strangers if she could convince him that he had Shannon's full support, no matter what happened. Eleanor's influence in Randall's Bow was considerable, and Shannon knew he had much to gain from that. And much to lose if he lost her as an ally. He felt her slipping away. He had lost her to this frail, misshapen child, and there was nothing he could do to win her back.

There was another side to this—another way to proceed—but it held great risk. If Old Man and Joshua did, in fact, save Randall's Bow from the fever, Shannon could claim more than a little credit for it. After all, it was he who had given them the sanctuary of his home for as long as they wanted when they had nowhere else to go. Old Man and Joshua felt a debt of gratitude toward him and he knew it. In truth, Shannon could not deny a fondness for them, especially Old Man. It had been a long time since he had relished the company of another—except for Randall—as he did with this old one who possessed so much wisdom.

It was obvious to Shannon that Old Man was confused, too, at his sudden exclusion from the exchange between Joshua and Eleanor. His silence told Shannon that this was a new experience for him, too. It was only Eleanor and the peacefully sleeping child whose hand Joshua still held in his who didn't feel threatened. Eleanor and the boy seemed to have responded to Joshua in the same way, with some kind of energy flowing between them, and it hadn't lessened. It wasn't in anything that Joshua had said,. His words had been the ordinary words of comfort that anyone would offer to a sick and frightened child. The part about what Joshua knew—what was that but merely something for the child to hold on to and perhaps build a little hope where there had been none.

But something emanated from Joshua that had not been there before they had come to the infirmary, and Shannon felt that he could almost reach out and touch it. He felt an urge to reach out with his hands into the space in front of him and caress the air in an attempt to grasp the power that surrounded them. He had actually felt a kind of heat that manifested about them when the sick boy had accepted the cup. He decided that he would keep a close watch on this little one who was looking at him now, looking into his eyes as if he knew what he was thinking. He recalled what Eleanor had said to Joshua as they were leaving her cabin on the day she first met him. She had told Joshua that, for a moment, she had seen him as a child. Shannon knew that the answer was there. He would wait and he would watch, and more would be revealed if he was patient.

Shannon stepped forward and took the empty cup from Eleanor, brought it close to his nose and drew a quick breath. He pulled away quickly with a look of disgust, and handed the cup back to her, laughing. "My good woman, Is it indeed your plan to go into the forest to find more of this vile smelling concoction? It would be sufficient, it seems to me, if you would but walk slowly about the streets of Randall's Bow, putting the cup under the nose of everyone you meet and ask them to breathe deeply of it. Then you need only inform them that if they become ill, they will be forced to drink the concoction. There you will have your cure. The fever would disappear forever, because none would have anything to do with it after that, knowing the method of cure they would be forced to undergo. You would have no need to go into the forest at all."

Shannon's attempt to disrupt the spell that was in the air—and from which he was excluded as if an unseen wall cut him off from the power of the moment—went unnoticed. "Come with me today," Eleanor said to Old Man. "Both of you. Come with me while I make my rounds here. You will see them in all stages of deterioration. Those who have been recently afflicted and who have been brought in just a short while ago, as you have seen, and who may still have a chance to survive. And you will see those for whom it is too late. Death is certain for them and it is only a matter of time until they breathe their last. A week. A day. Perhaps only an hour or even minutes until death claims them. Like the dear one there." She pointed to a young girl who had just died and had yet to be removed to the pits by the river and burned. Her family had not yet arrived and she lay cold and alone now, as if abandoned forever.

"Or perhaps they have but another moment here with us," Eleanor continued. "You will know. There is something about them that speaks of death, even though it may be some time off—but death has already staked its claim on them. Or them on death. You can sense that, somehow. And you will see some here who will recover. For reasons that are unknown to us, they have been spared and death has decided to pass them by. It will visit them at another time—such as this one before us now."

Eleanor looked down at the boy, still sleeping peacefully, who had taken the cup from Joshua. "This little one will know a long life," she said. "But I will tell you this." Her eyes were shining as she spoke. "It was not so until you came to him this morning, Joshua. It was only yesterday that I had judged this child to be one of those who would not be with us much longer. And now I know that he will live."

"Yes," Joshua replied. He smiled at Eleanor, but said nothing more. Shannon and Old Man looked away, as if they would be intruding where they had no business to be.

"Observe, and talk to all you wish to talk to," Eleanor said to Joshua, ignoring the other two. "Later we'll go to the manor and talk about the thingsyou have seen here, and what you have been told, and how they seem to you. It will help us in what we are about to do."

"I have other things that I must do, my friend," Shannon said to Old man, avoiding Eleanor's amused look. It had been obvious to him that Eleanor would not welcome his company when they went into the forest, and he would not challenge that. He had no knowledge or interest, really, of what they intended to do. And he didn't want to be seen in their company as they conducted their search. He would leave them now, but he would be at the manor when they arrived there. There would be no mistake about that, for there would be no plan in Randall's Bow that would be without his knowledge and influence, no matter what the price. And if Merrill saw him in their company as they discussed the direction of their actions, then so be it. He would take that risk rather then be ignorant of what they intended to do. It would be the lesser of the dangers before this thing, whatever it was, had run its course.

He was not eager to count Eleanor as an adversary, for she would be most formidable, second only to Merrill. But he would not permit her to exclude him from anything he deemed important to his welfare and influence. New lines were being drawn, that was clear, and the lines would be his—not Eleanor's—whether it pleased her or not.

"Go with Eleanor," Shannon said to Old Man and Joshua, as if he was giving them needed permission. "It will be valuable to the success of your efforts." His voice was strained, and he felt as if he had lost a battle, though he didn't know what the battle was or what it was about. His voice sounded hollow to his ears and without the authority he was trying to project. "I'll meet you at the manor." He turned away quickly and left the infirmary before Eleanor could respond. He would be with them this evening whether they liked it or not, and there was nothing she could do to prevent it. He had served her notice on that, and it would not be disputed. He would not permit it.

Eleanor watched Shannon leave the infirmary, his full, blue tunic billowing behind him, and smiled. When he had disappeared out the open doors, she turned to Old Man and Joshua. The smile was still on her lips, but her eyes belied her true feelings. This was a new day. There had been a shift in her relationship with Shannon and it had occurred here among the sick and with Old Man and Joshua beside her. She and Shannon had held counsel together many times in the past. Not in friendship—they did not delude themselves or each other about that. Their's had been an alliance of convenience and protection, united in their roles of advisors to Randall and Merrill when called upon. Their closeness had culminated during those days of sadness and helplessness at Randall's deathbed, when they gave comfort to Randall and to each other.

That was only a few days ago. How could so much have changed between them in so short a time? It seemed that Shannon had taken on some of Merrill's madness, and Eleanor could not guess the reason why. He was keeping something to himself, and somehow she had gotten in the way of it. But she would not spend her energy on such things now. She could not, and do the things she and Joshua had to do.

Eleanor looked around the infirmary at the poor suffering ones lying on their filthy straw pallets. There was not enough room for even one more. Perhaps there was hope for some of them, but not many. If she couldn't save their lives, perhaps she could at least ease their pain until they breathed their last. She would concentrate on that and let others play their insane games of power. She handed the basket that held little pots of potion she had mixed the night before to Old Man. "Here," she said to him. "Take these and follow Joshua. Walk among the sick and give the potion to those whom Joshua thinks will accept it. I'm going to the manor and I'll bring my daughter with me when I return. She helps me in tending to the sick each day when she has finished her duties there. Leyla has great knowledge of the forest's healing gifts—a far greater knowledge than mine."

Eleanor turned her attention to Joshua. "My daughter has a way with the sick that I have seen in no other—until today. Sometimes I think it's only her presence that brings healing. Like you, old one. Like you. That is what I feel about you now, as I speak of Leyla. It's a rare gift. I think that you and my daughter will like each other. I think that you will have much to tell each other. Sometimes with words and sometimes, perhaps, through silence because there will be no words to express the things you know. Now go. Walk among them. I will find you when I return. I won't be long."

Chapter 26

Old Man stood at the front of the infirmary near the barn-like doors that were left open day and night to allow clean air to circulate in the dank interior by the occasional breeze that came in from the river. Over one arm, he held the basket that held Eleanor's clay pots of the potion. A feeling of helplessness came over him as he looked at the fever's victims crowded together on the floor. What could he and Joshua do against the power of this sickness that destroyed nearly everyone it touched? Were they deluding themselves when they spoke of finding the answer in the forest? He believed what Joshua had said—that the forest held the answer. But the misery that he saw now filled him with a fear that told him they were too late, there was nothing they could do except burn the dead and remove all traces of them from Randall's Bow. Perhaps Merrill's way held the answer, after all.

Straw pallets had been arranged in rows the length of the infirmary, with just enough room to carefully walk between them. There was no room at all between the pallets themselves. They had been laid end-to-end, with the foot of one pallet touching the head of the pallet that followed it. And there was not one empty pallet to be seen.

The bodies on the pallets were startlingly similar. The fever's fire had robbed each one of any semblance of individuality and dignity. Each poor figure was drenched in sweat, laying in his own filth that had mixed with the dirt from the earthen floor and the leavings of the ones who had lain there before them. It would have taken too long to construct a wooden floor, Merrill had told the workers. A wooden floor would take at least two days to complete, and it would be for no good purpose as far as he could see. This was only a temporary structure and they would burn it as soon as it had fulfilled its purpose.

Clothing clung to the sweating bodies that looked as if they were almost without any flesh at all, they were so wasted. They were contorted and twisted into positions of suffering that made their bones protrude beneath the skin at what seemed to be impossible angles, forming shapes that looked like pieces of a grotesque puzzle of humanity that had been laid out and hastily assembled on the infirmary floor.

Joshua approached a woman on a pallet near the door. Like the others, she was soaked in sweat from the battle she was waging against the fever-fire. Her head was thrown back on a thin pillow that had been left when her family had bought her to the infirmary, sparing her the ride in one of the wagons. She would die. They knew that. But concern for themselves was what drove them now, and her death would be a lonely one. Her loved ones would not be at her side when she passed from this earth. They would not return to the infirmary when they were told of her death, and her ashes would be thrown into the river with all the rest.

There was not one of them who had the courage to be with her as she wasted away, to finally die the painful death that would surely be her fate. And so she had been left alone and laid there with no one that she loved to hear her cries and give her comfort. A thin, dirty sheet had been thrown over her to conceal her almost totally naked body. It was her only protection against the cold night and the chill that would overtake her. The sheet, wet from her fluids, clung to her like a filthy burial shroud. Her mouth opened and closed spasmodically as she struggled in little gasps to bring air into her constricted throat. Her eyes were opened wide in terror as she fought for every breath.

The woman saw Old Man and looked at him in silent pleading. He knelt by her side, setting the basket on the floor beside him. She looked as if she was very near death, but it seemed as if her mind was alert as she examined this old one who had suddenly appeared from nowhere. Perhaps he is the ghost of my dear husband, she thought, dead for almost a decade now, and has come to take me home. Yes. He would take her home now, and she would be out of this place of misery, no longer tormented by the unceasing sounds of suffering that were all around her. She would find rest at last.

Joshua followed behind Old Man and knelt down beside him. Old Man watched Joshua bend close to her and look into her eyes. Smiling, he took her hand in his, but she gave no response except to look at him in confusion. Was this ancient one her husband? Was this the one with whom she had lived for more than forty years as wife to him and mother to their eight sons, the joys of their life? She looked at Joshua closer then, through half-closed eyes, but his features were not familiar to her no matter hard she struggled to convince herself they were. Perhaps their time together had been too long ago for her to remember. She had no idea how long she had been in this terrible place. Perhaps time had erased the memories she had thought would be with her forever. Theirs had been a great love—a magnificent love. She remembered that. Yes. She remembered that. So full of passion. And so full of tenderness, too.

Joshua wet his finger in the cup and gently rubbed it on her parched lips. The woman's eyes widened in surprise, and then she nodded her gratitude as she sucked on his wet finger. She stopped only to allow Joshua to wet his finger again and return it to her mouth.

As Old Man watched Joshua, he relived those times when the dreams in his mind and in his heart were more vivid than anything he had ever experienced in the outside world. And so it was now, except this time there was a difference—it wasn't a dream. It was real. It was there before him on the floor of the infirmary. And he knew that what he saw and what was really happening was far beyond his own understanding.

Joshua gently stroked the woman's hand for a few moments, then released her hand from his. He took a piece of cloth that was on the floor next to him and handed it to Old Man, who wet it in a bucket of water nearby and gave it back to Joshua. He folded the cloth and placed it on the woman's forehead. She seemed to have fallen asleep while he was stroking her hand, but now she slowly opened her eyes and looked at him. Old Man saw the same feverish glaze in her eyes that he had seen in the boy who had died a short time before. She looked at Joshua as if she didn't see him—that he was somehow beyond her sight. It was as if she saw only with the eyes of death now, and had given up her life. Joshua put his face very close to hers and smiled. He took her hand again and resumed his gentle stroking. Old Man watched in amazement as her glazed eyes began to clear and she became aware of the face that was so very close to hers, almost touching her cheek. She moved her lips as if trying to speak. Old Man stepped closer to be sure he was not imagining what he saw.

"Hello." The music of Joshua's voice was like the tinkling of glass chimes hanging in the wind. It was clear and strong in a way Old Man had not heard before. Not in Joshua, nor in any human voice within his memory. It seemed devoid of emotion, yet was neither flat nor without expression.

What was it that Joshua's voice made Old Man feel? And his sight was as sharp as it had been when he was a young man. It was Joshua's voice that was bringing this from within him. Old Man was sure of that. Joshua's voice possessed the command to be totally present in the moment. It was a command to him and to the woman lying sick and dying. Be here and only here, his voice commanded. Do not let your mind long for things gone by or enter into the fear of things to come. In that one word, "Hello," he had brought them to meet him where he was, and they had never been to that place before. They were there now, in that very instant, for the first time. Together.

She looked at Joshua and smiled. Old Man suddenly realized that Joshua had been telling her something, but he couldn't remember hearing what he had said. Her struggling and ceased, and she was lying quietly on her pallet, looking at Joshua with a peaceful, almost happy, smile.

"Hello." The woman was hesitant, as if she wasn't quite sure that she still could speak. She lay silent for a moment, savoring the sound of her voice. She had forgotten how it sounded and needed to be sure it really belonged to her. "Hello," she said again, more sure of herself now—her voice a little stronger.

"Who are you?" she said, with a little laugh. The fever's cloud had been lifted from her eyes, replaced by the light of life.

"Joshua."

"Joshua." She repeated his name, reaching out to take his hand. "Joshua," she said again tenderly, as if to recall a name that once meant much to her. "Joshua." She closed her eyes for a moment, her face free of pain as relief enfolded her body with a warmth and promise of rest at last. She opened her eyes. "Well, Joshua, what do you want with me? As you can see, I'm in sorry shape." She brushed her thin hands across her face, letting them come to rest on the wet and matted strands of hair that lay in the wrinkled curve of her neck.

Joshua took the cup that Old Man had set beside him and held it to the woman's lips. "Drink this," he said, brushing away some of the hair that had gathered at the corner of her mouth.

The old woman laughed. "Eleanor's evil tasting concoction from the woods? It helps a little. But not much—and not for long. The thirst goes away for a little while sometimes. And I can sleep a little then. But it comes back again. Stronger than ever, as if seeking payment for the little relief that I've had…." She paused and lifted her head a little and looked around the infirmary. "Although I do feel better now. It's strange." She lay her head back down on the pallet. "I feel no pain now. Only weakness. I feel so very weak." She looked closely at Joshua, as if seeing him for the first time. "Who are you?" she asked again, and this time there was no laughter in her voice, replaced by a demand that he answer her question.

Joshua held the cup to the woman's lips again. "Drink this. Drink it while you are without pain or thirst and it will help them stay away. Drink now."

She drank the contents of the cup, her eyes on Joshua all the while. When she was finished, she repeated her question. "Who are you?" she asked, this time softly, barely above a whisper. "Tell me who you are."

"Joshua. My name is Joshua." He took the empty cup from her hand and handed it to Old Man without looking at him. All of his attention was on the woman.

"Yes, yes. I know that," she said. She was growing impatient with what she interpreted as evasion. "I heard you before. But that's just your name and it doesn't answer my question, does ir?" Joshua remained silent. "Does it?" she repeated.

Joshua smiled. "I come from the forest." He said. "The forest is my home."

Old Man stepped forward so the woman could see him. "We live in the forest. As he says." She seemed satisfied by the explanation, at least for the present. She looked at Joshua and smiled. "I like your voice," she said. "It sounds like a kind of music that I have never heard before. It soothes me." She closed her eyes for a moment, and then looked at Joshua again. "Yes. I feel better. And I think it isn't just Eleanor's concoction that I have to thank for that." She squeezed Joshua's hand, as if she wanted to reassure him.

"I'm glad you're feeling better," Joshua said. He turned to Old Man. "This is my friend. His name is Old Man. We are waiting for Eleanor. When she comes back with Leyla, we will go into the forest together to look for something that will help us fight the fever and make everyone well. The forest will give us something that will help you, and soon you will be well again. And then you can help us make others well too, if you like. We will need your help. When the others see you, they will know that they can get well, too. And when they know that, it will help them get better faster."

"Yes, Joshua. I would like that. But perhaps you dream." She looked at Joshua one last time before falling into a deep and restful; sleep.

"Come," Old Man said, touching Joshua's arm, "there are more for us to see."

Joshua's attention came to rest on a child who was contorted in pain on a nearby pallet. The girl's tongue was swollen and protruded from her mouth like something foreign that had become lodged there and was infecting her body. He bent close to the girl, until his face was almost touching hers, took her clenched fist in his hand and lightly stroked it while Old Man watched. It seemed to him that Joshua had no fear of the fever and its fiercely contagious nature, and that closeness to this agent of death was something he actually desired.

Old Man handed a cup of the potion to Joshua and then stepped back. He guessed that the girl was close in age to Joshua, about twelve or thirteen years old. Their similarity was striking. The fever had ravaged her so much that she looked more like an old woman than a young girl. They looked like brother and sister—one giving his last farewell to the other. Joshua said noting as he gently stroked her hand. She tossed restlessly on her sweat-soaked pallet, moaning softly. Her lips were cracked and bloody from dehydration. Joshua wet a cloth from a nearby bucket of water and pressed it against the girl's lips, then wiped away the blood that had gathered and dried at the corners of her mouth. He wet the cloth again and put one of the dripping ends into her mouth. She sucked weakly at the rag until the end was almost dry and he repeated the process.. Then he wet the rag again, folded it and laid it on the girl's forehead. She lay quietly at last, as if in peaceful slumber.

"The water tasted good to her, even though it was very little," Joshua said to Old Man. He started to pull his hand away from hers, but the girl tightened her grip and opened her eyes. "Please," she said, "Please don't leave me. Stay with me just a little while longer before you go to the others." She closed her eyes again, a smile on her lips, and slept.

Old Man watched their hands join once more. It is strange, he thought. Those hands that are so often stiff and full of pain—those hands that are so young but are the source of more pain that even mine, the hands of one who is truly old—are now as supple as the hands of the boy that he is. It was as if Joshua had been transformed, even as the sick were being transformed by his presence. Their sickness seemed to have been lifted somewhat simply by his nearness to them. Like the boy and the old woman, this girl's eyes were sightless from the fever's cloud when he first knelt close to them. And now, like them, her eyes were clear and her focus sharp and steady when she looked at him. And now, like the other two, she was sleeping peacefully. Old Man could but stand and watch, at a loss to understand what was happening here.

The girl awakened and smiled at Joshua. "I was very thirsty."

"Would you like more water?"

"Yes."

Joshua took the cloth from her forehead to wet it in the bucket.

"No, a cup. I would like to drink from a cup."

Old Man took a cup from the basket, filled it with water, and gave it to Joshua. He put his hand under the girl's head and helped her lift it slightly from the pallet, then held the cup to her lips and watched as she drank. "You are getting well now," he told her. "Look at me. Look at me as you drink. It's as if we are drinking the water together. When you are finished with the water, I'll give you something that Eleanor made that will help keep the thirst from coming back. You'll sleep for a little while and when you wake up you'll feel much better. You'll know that soon you'll be well again. Tomorrow, I will come back with something new for you to drink. And for the others, too."

She emptied the cup of water and then laid back on the pallet and smiled. "Thank you," she said. "I was so thirsty."

"Here," said Joshua, putting a small, clay cup to her lips. "Drink this. Eleanor made it. It tastes bitter, I know, but it will help keep the thirst away."

She made a face, but emptied the cup, and then she laughed. "I hope what you bring tomorrow tastes better," she said. "Like the berries in the forest. This tasted so bitter thatI could barely swallow it. I drank it for you, whoever you are. I drank it because you told me to. Like the sweet berries in the forest—can you promise me that? What is your name?"

"Joshua."

"Joshua. I like your name, Joshua. I've never seen you before. What a beautiful voice you have. It sounds like you're singing a song when you talk. And you have a funny face." She laughed again and then stopped. "I'm sorry. I meant it in a nice way I like the way you look. It makes me feel better. It goes with your voice…." She stopped talking and closed her eyes. "I'm going to sleep now and I'm going to get well, just like you said I would. I know I will. Do you promise to come back tomorrow?"

"Yes."

"And do you promise to make your potion taste like the sweet berries from the forest?"

Joshua laughed. "I'll try, but I can't promise."

She gave Joshua one last, long look, closed her eyes with a contented sigh and fell asleep.

Joshua let go of the girl's hand and rose slowly, painfully, to his feet.

It was true. Old Man knew that beyond a doubt now. He was only an observer here, and the meaning of what was happening was not for him to know. He slowly followed Joshua, who was a few steps ahead of him, and could feel his power sweep over him. It seemed to him that Joshua walked straighter than he ever had, even in the forest in those days before the pain had come upon him.

Yes, Old Man knew he could only follow and watch now, He had neither the intellect nor the heart to tell what was happening in the infirmary. It was beyond anything he had ever experienced, He would wait and watch in silence. And he would listen for his guiding voice to come to him again. It hadn't failed him on the ledge above his cave, and it would not fail him here, for it had been the voice that had guided them here.

Old Man noticed that Joshua was quite selective about those he gave his attention to. There was a common bond—a connection, somehow—between him and those he knelt beside. It was always the same. He took their hand in his and smiled, even though some were not even aware of his presence at first. But, without fail, those whom Joshua had chosen—or perhaps, in some way they had chosen each other because they had come together in this place for a purpose—would open their eyes and their expression would change from one of suffering to one of peace.

The power of the experience enveloped Old Man and brought him into it as if he was being swept along by a river's undercurrent and had no control over the course he was taking. He had no choice, whatever the dangers ahead might be. He knew there was no escape from this thing he could not name.

The fear he had felt since he and Joshua had first set foot upon the banks of Cold River grew even colder now. He felt paralyzed as his fear was confronted by the power that Joshua now possessed. It was as if he had never left Randall's Bow, the peace of their beloved forest had never been, and his escape had been nothing but a dream. And oh, how he longed for that peace. How he longed to feel the forest's peace once more and to be rid of this dread and sadness that had come upon him and would not loose him from its grip. Perhaps they should take Goat and leave this place without a word to anyone and return to the safety of the forest.

But he knew that leaving wasn't the answer. It was fear that was talking now, and fear would destroy him if he let it rule his actions. He knew that without question as he watched Joshua kneel beside yet another of the sick, this time an old man like himself. He saw the transformation occur once more as Joshua bent close to him, held his hand, smiled, and spoke.

There. That was where the answer was—whatever it might be. Yes. The answer was in Joshua, and Old Man knew that he must learn the lesson that was being taught to all of them by this innocent of innocents. He must learn it, however long it might take. All would learn here, and Old Man trembled as he realized the certainty of that. Yes. They would all learn from this little one—and the lesson would be a hard one in the beginning.

Old Man knew there was no going back for them. If they returned to the forest, they would not find what they thought they had left there, for this was another day and they had come too far in their journey to turn back now. It would never be the same again, no matter where they were—Randall's Bow or the forest. In truth, they had no choice. They must stay in Randall's Bow. But, oh, how he wanted to feel the peace he had known in the forest once more—the peace he had felt among the cliffs above the cave. To know the peace he had felt as he watched Cold River make its way to the place they were now—and to know that never again would they have to return there.

And now he stood amidst the worst that Randall's Bow had ever known, and he knew that, somehow, he was part of the answer to the coming mercy that would surely descend upon them all and take their pain away. The answer was in Joshua and what he was doing here. Old Man was no longer the teacher, and he must embrace that.

He watched Joshua hold the old man's head as he sipped water from a cup that Joshua held to his parched lips. Peace. Yes. Peace was here. Joshua was overflowing with it. It was in his wrinkled little face. It was in his voice as he sang his healing song, ordinary words—spoken, really—but filled with the music of well-being. It was even in his halting walk as he moved through the infirmary in his hobbling clumsiness, where the sick of Randall's Bow lay separated from their loved ones—imprisoned by a madman.

Somehow, Joshua was a person of grace in this place of suffering and death. His walk was still the halting, clumsy one of the forest, his deformed body moving sideways sometimes, like a crab from the river, when his pain was at its worst. Yet, the deer in the forest did not surpass him in the grace that he was exhibiting now. Peace and, yes, power, were in his being now. Peace and power are his essence. And love. Above all else, love.

Merrill had seen that, though he could not name it, and he knew that he faced his better in this little one. And Shannon knew it, too. It was no wonder they were frightened. Such mysteries strike terror in the hearts of those to whom peace is a stranger.

The old man had fallen into a restful sleep like the others Joshua had touched. Old Man saw himself in his face, near death in this place if he hadn't fled those many years ago. And if he hadn't left, would some other one have found this innocent of innocents and raised him as his own? And would he have brought him here to Randall's Bow to snatch his life back from the fever as he lay soaking in his own fluids upon a filthy pallet?

They continued to walk through the infirmary, Old Man walking behind Joshua and filling a cup with Eleanor's potion when Joshua chose to stop and attend to one of the sick. He passed by many, most, if truth be told, and Old Man wondered why, though he did not ask. And there were others that he knelt beside and took their hand for a moment, and they gave no sign that they felt his touch or knew that he was near. Joshua would bend close and whisper something in their ear, then rise slowly and move on, not asking Old Man for a cup of the potion to give them.

*   *   *   *

There was one who stood in the shadows watching, whip slapping at his boot as Old Man and Joshua moved about the infirmary. His eyes were dark and sunken in his face now, and his rage seemed gone, lying dormant somewhere deep within him like a pool of blackness lapping at his soul.

There was madness in his eyes—and sadness, too—strangely tempered by an almost gentle smile as he watched the broken little one walk among the sick, then kneel and bend close to them and tell them they were loved. At last, he turned and left the infirmary and mounted the bay war horse that he always rode now, spurring him to a gallop toward the bridge that would take him back to Randall's Bow.

Merrill did not ride The Great Black War Horse on that day. Nor would he ever mount that one again. Nor would any other man. until he chose his rider. And that choice was already made. There was one whom he would fly back home. And in the stables, only Rashan was permitted to come near on his daily rounds.

There was one other in Randall's Bow who would come very near The Great Black War Horse—another one like him whose spirit would not be broken by those who walked another path. These two were truly of one spirit and they would hear each other speak in silence. And they would understand. But the time for that had not yet come.

*   *   *   *

"Joshua! Old Man! I'm back—come and meet Leyla!" Eleanor threaded her way toward them through the tightly packed pallets, followed by a young woman of extraordinary beauty. Joshua rose from the floor and stood beside Old Man, unable to take his eyes off Leyla. They were clearly mother and daughter, yet very different from each other. While Eleanor's beauty was in her strength of character and integrity that was evident in her attitude and the forthright way she carried herself—her's was an inner beauty—her daughter's beauty was of a different kind.

Leyla's hair was black as a moonless night, held away from her high-cheek-boned face by a green ribbon that swept it behind her graceful neck. Her shining hazel-green eyes spoke of a great depth of soul, inviting you to tell her everything about yourself. You are safe, they said. Tell me all your secrets—I will understand. You will find no judgment in what I think or what I say. There is nothing to defend yourself against with me, so you can tell me everything that is in your heart. I have only love for you, Leyla's eyes said. I want to know you as you really are. I will give you comfort, Leyla's eyes said. And I will give you myself, because we are the same. We are one. So let us tell each other the truth about ourselves, so we may come to know each other and ourselves. We will find comfort in our oneness, Leyla's eyes said.

Unlike Eleanor, who was fair of skin with auburn hair held back in a bun, Leyla was darker skinned, with golden honey-tones that gave her mystery and the look of one possessed of ancient wisdom. And yet, as different as the two women were, somehow there was a sameness in their beauty and in the power that came forth from both of them. Peace followed in their path, and arrived with them to the pallet where Joshua knelt.

"Well," Eleanor exclaimed loudly when she reached Old Man. "I expected this place of misery to be empty by the time I returned." She looked down at Joshua. "All the sick brought back to health and stronger than ever is what I expected to find here when I returned. All gone home, and this place as empty as the barn that it should have been in the first place." Her laugh rang throughout the infirmary. "Come. Look at this one, Leyla," she said pointing to Joshua. "This is the one I told you about. He has the gift of healing in him, just as you do. And wait until you hear his voice. It is an instrument of beautiful music. A piper, he is, this little old one. This is Joshua—a piper who will lure you to within hearing of the good things of this life because he knows what those good things are. The things that give us joy. I know you well, do I not old one? Say hello

189

to my daughter now. Her name is Leyla. Say hello to her and let her hear your music for herself."

Joshua felt a sudden emptiness he had never felt before. It was like loneliness, but it was more than that. It covered him so completely that it became his being—who he was at that moment. He looked at the beautiful young woman standing beside Eleanor—she was more beautiful than anyone he had ever seen before. And he knew her. But how could he?

"Hello, Leyla."

Leyla looked down at Joshua and smiled. "How wonderful! How wonderful you are! She knelt beside him and took his hand in hers. "I feel as if we have known each other for many lifetimes," she said and kissed him gently on the cheek.

Joshua touched his cheek where Leyla had kissed him. What had she done? He didn't know how to reply or what to do—or if there was anything he was expected to do or say in reply. He felt the warmth of Leyla's hand on his, and felt again the strange emptiness—the loneliness. He felt as if he had been transported back to another time—a time that was beyond his memory, but one that he wanted to remember. He and Leyla looked at each other in silence, their hands moving ever-so-slightly within each other's grasp.

"And this one calls himself Old Man." Eleanor's voice was a welcome interruption, breaking the spell that both felt and neither understood. "A suitable name, but a curious one. A name that is meant to hide something, if you want my honest opinion." She looked at Old Man, waiting for his reaction.

Old Man smiled but said nothing.

"But no matter," Eleanor continued, when it became obvious that Old Man had no intention of answering her challenge. "We will spend some time together, and you will learn that you have nothing to fear from me. Quite the contrary, as you shall soon see, In time, you will reveal your secrets to us, and gladly, too. I promise you that freedom. Our destinies are connected, and only truth will survive between us." Eleanor looked down at the joined hands of Joshua and Leyla and smiled.

Old Man felt as if a fist of ice had suddenly gripped his heart. It was difficult for him to breathe. Joshua and Leyla seemed to speak to each other in a silent language that he couldn't hear or understand. He felt as if he would faint from the intensity of this unknown thing that was happening here—this mystery that he could see and feel, but couldn't name. He could only stand outside of it and watch, and somehow feel that there was a loss in his life now that hadn't been there before. And there was nothing he could do to reclaim whatever it was that he had lost. If ever he was in need of guidance, that time was now. He listened, and all about him seemed to pass to another time and place. And then he knew it was with Leyla that Joshua had once felt the warmth of the only mother's arms he had ever known. And he had felt her mother-love torn from him as she left him that night upon the forest floor beneath the moon. And Eleanor is the one whose part it was to decide to send her daughter into the forest with Joshua when she had received him into her hands from his mother's womb, though she knew not the true nature of her deed. So bless them both. Each had their part to play.

This one? Leyla was the one? He felt as if this place of sickness and death was taking him to madness, and there was no escape. He looked at Leyla, his heart pounding, as a cloud descended before his eyes and he was back in the forest on that moonlit night of long ago. He saw a young girl gently laying an infant beneath a fallen tree on the forest floor. And as she hurried back down the path towards Randall's Bow, he saw himself step quietly from behind a nearby tree and watch her as she disappeared among the trees beyond the moonlight. And now she had taken Joshua from him in an instant, leaving him desolate and alone.

Suddenly, the sounds of the dying were once more in Old Man's ears and he was thrown out of the void of silence where all is known into the sounds of suffering and death once more. And laughter. Old Man heard laughter. His vision cleared and he saw Joshua and Leyla laughing together. And there beside them lay the boy who had been so near his death, smiling and sighing a sigh that was full of peace. And a little laughter, too.

Chapter 27

A madman stood unnoticed in the shadows of the infirmary, watching—and listening. It was not the first time. And it would not be the last. That little ancient one and his friend who had come into this place unasked had set themselves against a foe the likes of whom they had never known. They would not escape the punishment that would surely come upon them. As for Eleanor and Leyla, well, he would have to think about that.

Merrill looked toward the sound that was obscene in this place of suffering. Laughter? Who dares to laugh in this place where the stink of rotting bodies hangs in the air like a filthy veil before the face of Hell? He stared unblinking through the gray light of the infirmary, his eyes straining toward the source of that unseemly sound. Laughter in this place frightened him. He felt threatened by it—surrounded by danger because of it, as if he was responsible for a sacrilegious act for which he would never be forgiven. He heard the laughter again, and he felt damned by it. Terror crept through his body and he felt weakened by it. He looked around the infirmary, searching for the ones who dared condemn him with their laughter.

No one had seen Merrill enter the infirmary. He came there often in secret, standing unobserved in some darkened corner, watching the fruits of his madness unfold. He wanted to be done with this, and as each new victim of the fever was carried through the doors and passed by him, his hate increased until he thought his heart would burst from the fury of it.

Merrill saw them as they stood together over the pallet of one of the sick. He strained to hear their words of treachery and deceit against him for he had no doubt that was what they were. But the only sounds he heard were the moans of the dying, and then, faintly, the sounds of some kind of strange music. Or was it someone's voice? Was someone mad enough with grief to sing in this place of death? He could not tell.

He wanted to leave this place, but he couldn't tear himself away from the horror spread before him and the knowledge that it was all his own creation. He stayed a while longer in the darkened corner and watched those four who plotted against him. He had no doubt of that. And as he watched, the fire of his hate burned slowly through him, and turned upon itself.

*   *   *   *

Leyla reached up from where she was kneeling and gently touched Old Man's hand. "Hello," she said,. Old Man heard the kindness in her voice and her sweet smile reassured him of her friendship. He smiled in return, but said nothing as she returned her attention to the sleeping boy on the pallet beside her.

"They suffer so," she said. "Children and grown ones alike— it makes no difference. But it is sadder for the children. Their lives haven't really begun, and there is so much joy and happiness that they have yet to experience. Now they are near death and they are in so much pain. It's rare that a child is strong enough to survive."

"What is it like for them?" Old Man asked. "How does it begin?"

"Small, hard lumps—like little stones— all over their body. And there is always severe pain in their joints and muscles. And their stomachs twist and turn because they are so full of bitter juices. Their heads ache so that it seems that only the splitting of their skulls will bring relief, and a thirst that won't be quenched won't let them go." She fell silent then and looked around the infirmary in sadness, anger, and frustration.

Eleanor's voice broke the silence. "Enough of this talk of pain and death. Let's talk instead of life and healing, for that is what we must be about. There's a purpose in all of this, though we don't know what it is. And we have a part to play in it, whatever that may be. So let's get on with it. Not everyone will die. There is hope. There have been times, not many, but there have been times when I have given a mixture of roots and herbs that work for a little while. Especially with the children. Perhaps it's because their bodies are smaller and not as much strength is needed. But the reason, truthfully, is not known to me." She looked down at the still sleeping boy. "Or perhaps it's because their belief is stronger than those who have grown weary with the hard life here, and at a deep level of their being welcome death as a relief from that."

"We will find the answer, will we not?' Eleanor said to Joshua. "We will find the answer in our forest. So let us leave this place and be about our work."

Old Man and Joshua followed Eleanor and Leyla out of the infirmary doors and into the sunlight. They didn't notice the one standing motionless in the shadows, watching them leave.

*   *   *   *

There was a path behind Eleanor's cabin that led to a part of the forest rarely visited by anyone from Randall's Bow anymore. In days gone by, it had been one of the most fertile places for berries of all kinds, but over the years heavy undergrowth had crowded out the berry bushes, forcing the harvesters to find other places for their gathering. Old Man and Joshua followed Leyla down the overgrown path, with Eleanor leading the way.

"Usually, I'm the only one who comes here anymore," Eleanor called over her shoulder. "We're coming to the berry patches where the sweetest and juiciest berries grow but the patches are hard to reach because of the thick undergrowth and other patches have been found—and some even cultivated—in places that are much easier to reach. They are easily found along the riverbank and on the hillsides on the other side of the river, not far from the infirmary. We'll find what we need for the fever untrampled by those who know nothing of the many gifts the forest has for us."

Leyla stared angrily at her mother's back and wished that she would stop her constant talking and just get them to where they were going so they could quickly gather what they had come for and go back to the cabin. She had come this way before, when she was just a young girl. It had not been a journeyshe had made by her own choice—she had been forced to take it by her mother. She had taken the small bundle that Eleanor had handed to her on that night that seemed so long ago yet, sometimes it seemed like only yesterday. She would awaken with a start at night and feel the weight of the tiny bundle in her arms. She had carried the bundle of bloody rags and its contents up this very path and into the night, and had left it in the forest to breathe its last, alone and unloved. He would never know his mother's looks or smell, or hear her voice.

She looked at Joshua, now walking with difficulty in front of her, and tried to forget the thing she knew would always haunt her. It was always with her—always there and waiting to come to her in night dreams or appear to her in full light of day, when it was least expected. She would feel the gentle rise and fall of the tiny bundle as each breath was taken by the infant that lay cradled in her arms. She would see that small and wrinkled face as she lifted a corner of the rags to say a quick prayer and ask forgiveness for the thing that she was about to do.

But now it was not as if it was long ago or yesterday. No. It seemed as if the time was now—this very moment—and her heart ached with the realness of it. It was as if that tiny, innocent face was here before her now, unaware and not to blame for what it was, and now condemned to death, its only crime that it was born. She would leave him to die, knowing he had done nothing to deserve it. The wrong was done by the one who had judged him as not fit to live, and ordered that he be carried into the forest and left to die. And the wrong was done by the one who had left him there. Oh, yes. Perhaps that one was most to blame of all—the one who had done it in the end. Leyla's face was wet with tears. Why had her mother brought them to this place? There were other places in the forest where they had gone to collect herbs and roots for their potions. Why had she brought them here today?

They hurried on, passing berrying places no longer used and overgrown, going deeper and deeper into the forest, until Eleanor abruptly brought them to a stop and looked around her.

"Here," she said. "We will have good luck here."

The afternoon passed quickly as they talked about the roots they were searching for, sharing their experiences with what the forest laid before them now and in times before. Eleanor knew from past experience that in this place they would have good fortune. It vexed her that Leyla would never come with her to this spot. She would have better luck, her daughter would insist, some distance from there in another part of the forest. But every hour was important now, and each one lost would mean another life lost.

Eleanor had decided that morning that Leyla must set her superstitions aside. They would all go to the place that was the most certain to give them what they so desperately needed. This was not the time to let things long gone—things that had been rightly done—be the basis for decisions that would affect the very survival of Randall's Bow. Randall's Bow would survive, and she would not allow Leyla's silly fears to interfere with that.

Eleanor was right. The forest gave them what they needed that day. Herbs from which they could create a solution that would disinfect the pallets and clothing that carried the seeds of the fever, and another one that would be used for bathing the sick, cooling them as it cleansed them of the dried fluids that caked their aching bodies. They found roots that could be gently applied over open sores, and leaves that could be made into healing poultices for the sores after they had been cleansed. They found what they needed to bring the fever down and alleviate the thirst a little—and even a root that Eleanor had thought long lost that would ease the pain of swollen joints and soothe constricting stomachs as they retched their bitter juices from the bodies of the sick. By the end of the afternoon, they had found all they needed to ease the suffering of the sick.

All but one.

"We need the night flower," Eleanor said. "We cannot do without it. We have done well—the forest has blessed us beyond everything we could have hoped for. But without the night flower, we cannot do what must be done. The night flower will expel the fever from our midst forever.

"I've seen it only once," Old Man said., "and it was very far from here—deep in the forest, near the place from which Joshua and I journeyed to Randall's Bow. And when I returned to the place the next day, it was gone, and it never grew there again."

"No, you would not have found it again in that place," Eleanor said. "It blooms only once—and in the night—and then it quickly dies and never grows in that place again. It must be gathered when it's found or it will be lost. Its powers of healing are very strong, and we must have it. These two will return here tonight," she said motioning towards Joshua and Leyla. "The night flower will be here. Or nearby. I'm sure of it. There is something in this place that tells me that. I have found it in other places nearby, and tonight there will be others. These two will search them out and bring them to us."

Eleanor looked at Leyla, and the command was in her eyes. There would be no discussion, no matter how much Leyla objected to what her mother just said. Then she turned and started back down the path toward her cabin.

Leyla followed at a distance behind the others. She knew that on that night so long ago she had no choice about coming to this place. And it would be as It had been on that night long past—she would do as she was told. But this time it was different. This time it was for life that she would be coming here. And she would hold on to that with all her heart. If she did not, then fear would hold her where she stood, to die here as one other surely had done before her. She quickened her step and caught up with the others, following closely behind Joshua until they reached the cabin. She waited until the others had gone inside, then turned and looked at the narrow path that she and Joshua would once again follow into the forest that night. Oh, if only they could search in some other place!

But she knew that they could not.

*   *   *   *

Eleanor and Old Man walked with Leyla and Joshua to the edge of the forest where the path began that would lead them back to the place they were that afternoon. Eleanor was well aware of Leyla's resistance to going back, and she knew the reason why, although they had never discussed it. The unspoken between them had happened long ago, and had it not been God's own mercy that had given her the decision she had made?

Eleanor could never forget that little one she had sent to his final sleep that night. He was always with her throughout the day and as she lay awake at night—even sometimes in her dreams. She had never been able to name the nature of his deficiency and she had not seen another infant like him, though she had delivered many since. That poor little one could not have lived—she had been certain of that as he lay cradled naked and bloody in her arms, fresh from his mother's womb. She knew at once that he was only half complete, not even fully human, somehow—that is the only way she had ever been able to describe him to herself. To her eyes, the infant had been formed in part only, though all its limbs were present. It was an incompleteness from within that she had sensed. Some unseen thing that was not there in that little body. And so she had done what she had done—and it remained unspoken of until this day between herself and Leyla.

"Go now." Eleanor's voice was stern, yet encouraging, "The moon is full and there are no clouds to block its light. You will find the night flower in the place that gave us so many gifts today. I am certain of that. And search carefully. Where one grows, you will find others. We will need them all. This is the only chance we have, so look well." Eleanor looked up at the cloudless sky. "The moon is being kind to us tonight. It will make your task an easy one. Now go. Old Man and I have much to do before you return. The potion must be new and fresh if it is to receive the night flower and reach its full healing power. Go quickly. And when the forest gives you its most precious gift, hurry back and we will do the rest."

Old Man and Eleanor watched until Leyla and Joshua were out of sight, then returned to the cabin to prepare the roots and herbs for the next day. They told each other about themselves as they worked together in the warmth and seclusion of Eleanor's kitchen. There was a distance between them that must be crossed if what they were about to attempt was to succeed.

"They'll find the night flower, I'm sure of it. The night flowers always come to Leyla." Eleanor's voice was soft and reflective as she washed the herbs in fresh cold water from a nearby spring. "The flowers that you see outside that sometimes almost overwhelm us with their beauty and their scent—they are Leyla's. They grow for her without need of tending, it seems, and the weeds stay far away when it is she who sows the seeds. It has been so with her since she was a child—when she first began to help her father, Rashan, and me in our garden. The flowers love her as much as she loves them. Sometimes I wish they loved her less," Eleanor laughed, and then became somber once more. "But tonight that love will serve her well. It will bring peace to us once more. Peace. It seems so long since we have known that here. It seems so very long ago."

Old Man and Eleanor worked in silence then, preparing for the time when Leyla and Joshua brought the night flowers to them.

"There's nothing more for us to do now," Eleanor said when they were finished. "Come. I'll brew some tea and we'll sit by the fire for a while."

After Eleanor had brewed the tea and they were comfortably settled before the fire, she looked at Old Man for a moment and smiled. "I remember you, you know. I remember you when you lived among us. It was many years ago, and when you left, I think none other marked your absence but me."

Old Man sipped his tea, and looked into he fire. For a few moments, he said nothing. It was apparent that the next words were to be his, if any more were to be spoken this night. At last, he returned Eleanor's unflinching gaze. "What do you remember?"

"I remember you as one who prowled about the forest, as I did. As you may recall, it wasn't unusual for me to be summoned to bedsides for births and deaths, and everything in-between. I was drawn naturally to the forest and the healing gifts it offered me. It gave me comfort to see you go about your search there, too—to know that there was another who knew the truths I knew. I had been told that there were those who came to you with their aches and pains too, and that you would always help them in some way, if you could."

Eleanor paused, but still, Old Man said nothing.

"Once I saw you as Randall passed by," Eleanor continued. "It looked to me like you wanted to speak to him and I watched you as your eyes followed him until he was out of sight. I saw admiration on your face, didn't I, Old Man? I'm sure that you were called by another name in those times, but that matters not to me. I never knew it, and this one suits you well. But as I saw you look at Randall—was I right? Was it admiration that I saw? He would have stopped, you know, if you had waved to him that day. And he would have listened to you with great interest and respect, whatever it was you wanted to say. If it was admiration you wished to express, he would have been pleased. If not, he would have listened without judgment and carefully considered your words."

"Yes," said Old Man. "Admiration is as good a word as any, I suppose. But more than that. I saw, as strange as this may seem, my own potential in him if I could find a way to awaken whatever it was that would give me the strength and the courage to live my life as I so longed to live it. Oh, not to do the things that Randall had done—a glance at me confirms that I am not a warrior."

"A warrior of a different sort, Old Man." Eleanor said with a little laugh. "A warrior of the spirit, perhaps?" She smiled at him and gently touched his hand. "Tell me, what would you have said to Randall if he had stopped?"

"I don't know. Randall gave me hope that somehow I, too, would find my purpose in life, as he had. Solitude—perhaps it was really isolation at that point—was calling to me from the forest. I felt that if I didn't go, I would die. I couldn't bear to live here anymore, and the unknown of the forest was more comfort than what I knew was here for me. I was an outcast, a misfit—and I had chosen that—or perhaps I was shaped for it by the nature of my heart. You were drawn to the forest, too. It wasn't entirely of your own choice either, was it?"

"No. You and I didn't choose alone."

"And as you said, no one marked my going except you. I am grateful for that—and I would have my return go unmarked too, if that were possible. But it is not."

"And what of Joshua?" Eleanor asked. "What are the events that have brought your paths together? Was Joshua a misfit too, in some other place? And did he also flee a place that rejected him?"

It had come. The question that Old Man knew would be asked had just been asked, and he did not know how to answer this one who had made the choice that had brought Joshua to him. He would proceed slowly with his answer, and he would listen as he spoke. He need but listen to know the words that were his to speak.

"The forest has been our home for many years," Old Man began. He looked directly at Eleanor as he spoke. Now was not the time to be evasive—he had no wish to be—but he did not know how much of the truth to tell her now. The time would come when she must know everything. Old Man knew that—but that time was not for him to choose.

"We each came to the forest for reasons of our own—driven by choice or circumstance." Old Man watched Eleanor's face, but her expression was only one of curiosity and did not change. "For now, let it be said that neither of us were strangers to Randall's Bow when first we met. I ask for your understanding regarding this, Eleanor. You have much wisdom and the gift of knowing what is in others' hearts. My story—as well as Joshua's—has many facets, and I have no doubt that soon I will gladly reveal them all to you. But, for now, I ask for your patience for just a little while longer. Joshua and I have lived for a long time in the forest, and it gave us peace and joy. And now we are caught up by forces that could destroy us. and none of it is of our making. This kind of thing is new to us, and it sometimes brings terror to our hearts. We are grateful that you are with us now, to be of help in ending this terrible sickness. And we will succeed. But there are some things about which I need to keep my silence for just a little while longer. I will tell you everything—I promise that. And I will answer any questions you ask. But I ask again for your patience."

Eleanor smiled. "Please forgive me. I must admit that I am most curious about you, as we all are, though I am certain that none of the others remember either one of you. Your appearance alone is enough to spark our interest—please forgive me for saying that, but it's the truth—but that is a poor excuse for my prying. Of course I understand your wish to say whatever it is that you have to say in your own time. I know both you and Joshua for the two good men that you are. You are both gifted—that is plain see. And, not to offend you, but there is something in Joshua that contains a power I have never seen before. He has the gift of healing that far surpasses anything I may concoct. He and Leyla will find the night flower. But it is Joshua who has the answers we are seeking, rather than the roots and herbs we have gathered. Or even the night flower. But in that ancient little friend of yours—that is where the power lies. It is Joshua who will bring healing to all of us, whether we have the fever or not."

Chapter 28

The moon was high and full when Leyla and Joshua took the path into the forest toward the place where they had gathered roots and herbs with Eleanor and Old Man that afternoon. Leyla led the way as the moon cast tree shadows around them like protecting sentinels against unknown forces prowling the night. The night birds complained about their intrusion, warning others of the approaching strangers.

This cannot be. This cannot be. Leyla's thoughts raced through her as she relived this same journey that she had made with an infant in her arms those years ago. She had come here that night because this was the place that was the most familiar to her. She had come here with her mother almost every day as a little girl, and played her games among the wild flowers and berries while Eleanor searched for the things she needed for her potions.

Sometimes, when she had tired of playing her games alone, Eleanorwould talk to her about the herbs and roots—how to find them and what they could be used for. But Eleanor would not teach her until she asked, urged on by the healing force within her that yearned to extend itself to those who would be receptive to her powers.

Leyla was not able to name that urging. There were no words to tell her what she was feeling, but Eleanor validated it for her in loving looks as she Instructed her daughter in the mysteries of the forest. And Leyla had heard. She heard the guiding voice that would not be still—the inner voice that had spoken to her forever, waiting for the time when she would be ready to listen. It came to her across the bridge of Eleanor's silent love, and she recognized the voice as her true self, and felt joy because of it.

It was this very path that had led her to the mysteries that had given her a new life. There were no explanations to be found—she knew that—and so she sought none. She had followed the calling of her heart and that was all, and the forest answered with the gifts that she needed to ease the pain of others. And when it was their spirit that was in pain—memories of the past tying the body and the mind in a dreadful knot of darkness—it made no difference. Her guiding voice gave her a word, or sometimes only her presence was enough, and the knot would loosen and ultimately disappear.

This very path had led her to the clearing that held the magic of the forest in its circle, and its silent music had sung to her of the peace and harmony that was all around us if we would only see it. She spent much time in this place, and often Eleanor left her by herself and had sought her mendicants elsewhere, to give her the solitude she needed.

Then there came the night when her journey to this place was not for gifts of healing. No. It had been to take a life that she had come here—there had been no other place she could think of—save the river—and the forest had seemed a kinder place. Though it, too, could offer only death to the little one cradled in her arms. She did have hope—yes, she truly did—that somehow the little one in the bundle she held so close would be spared somehow. That she would be given an answer other than the one that Eleanor had given her.

But no. The only sounds that night had been the soft sigh of the infant's breathing and the pounding of her heart. She had left him beneath the berry bushes and the trunk of a fallen tree at the edge of the very clearing they were going to tonight. She had covered him with branches, hoping to spare him death in the hungry jaws of wolves. A quiet, sleeping death was what she had wished for him, so she had covered him and fled that place, vowing she would never go there again. She had kept that vow until today, when she had no choice but to do as Eleanor wished, just as she had done those many years ago. But she had thought that today would be the end of it—that they would find what they needed and she would never have to go there again.

For a moment, it occurred to her that she could tell Joshua about the thing that had haunted her for all these years—that he would understand why she had done what she had done and he would tell her that she had done no wrong and that she had been forgiven long ago. Joshua would tell her that he forgave her in the infant's stead and in the name of the goodness that was in her heart, and she would have peace at last.

And then they were there, standing in the center of the clearing with the moon's light shining down, the forest's sounds and fragrance curling around them in the cool night air. Leyla glanced quickly in the direction of the bushes at the far end of the clearing, from which protruded the rotted remains of a tree that had been struck by lightning and had long since fallen on the forest floor. Her breath came quickly in small, short gasps. "You must be tired," she said to Joshua, her voice low and barely audible. "Lets sit and rest a moment before we begin to look for the night flower. With luck, our search will be short and we'll be returning to mother's cabin soon. I'd like to sit for a few moments before we begin, if that's alright with you."

"Let's sit over there." The music of Joshua's voice floated through the moonlit clearing like the sound of a little bell in a gentle wind. He pointed in the direction of the fallen tree. She had laid the infant down in that exact spot. It was there that she had hidden him and left him to die. Alone. She followed Joshua to the spot and sat next to him on the soft grass not yet wet from the dew that would gather as the hours passed toward morning.

They sat in silence for a few moments, listening to a nearby owl hoot its greeting—or perhaps it was a warning— to the unaccustomed night visitors. Other night-birds sang to them as flying squirrels swooped above them from tree to tree. Leyla thought she was going to faint. Her heart was pounding in her ears and her mouth was so dry that she could scarcely swallow. "Joshua." Her voice trembled at what she wanted to say. She tried again to speak, but no words would come. It was as if her throat was paralyzed, forbidding her to release the secret that she thought would remain hidden forever.

"Joshua." Leyla tried to speak again, but still the words would not come. She was overwhelmed with shame at what she had done.

Joshua watched Leyla in silence. She held the words within her still, though she longed for their release.

"Are you remembering something that is sad?" Joshua's question, so innocent and so free of judgment, touched her at the very center of her pain.

Joshua watched Leyla in silence once more, then moved close to her and took her hand in his, gently stroking it as he had stroked the hands of the sick in the infirmary that morning, a smile upon his face as if he saw something other than her pain.

And how he saw her filled her with joy—yet, strangely, her sadness remained.

This place," she said, turning to the bushes thick with berries behind them. "I did something terrible—something unforgivable—in this place, and I am afraid it will haunt me until I die. It comes back to me in my dreams and suddenly it is there in my waking hours, too. It shows itself to me without warning, as real as on the night it happened. It is as if no time has passed at all, and yet it happened years ago."

Again, Joshua kept silent. If there was a question to be asked, the question was not his. And so he waited. And said nothing.

The full moon shone down upon them, its soft light covering them like a protective veil as they sat together. "There is something I have not spoken of to anyone, Joshua—not even my mother, though she was part of it. You are my friend—I know the truth of that—you have my trust and I know, too, that if only I could speak of it, your wisdom would help me understand something in that terrible secret that has not come to me and is beyond my own perception. But I cannot speak of it—I cannot, now. The time will come when I will seek your wisdom and your guidance—but now I cannot.

"I feel a love between us, a connection that is very strong," she continued. "I don't know where it comes from, but I felt it from the first time I saw you. It was at Randall's grave, when I only glanced your way. But the feeling was there, even then. And when I saw you from a distance in the infirmary, kneeling beside the suffering child, you had my heart. I felt a healing force coming from you then—the same force I feel within myself. Let that be enough for now. Yes. Let that be enough. We have much to do, and we must do it quickly. The time will come when I will come to you and ask you to listen while I tell you the secret that grieves me so. But let me put aside my selfishness for now, and be about what we came here for. If the night flower isn't here, then we must find another place tomorrow. But time is growing short. And there will be those who will die because we didn't find it tonight."

Leyla reached for the basket on the grass beside her. "Come. Let us look for the night flower. My mother said we would find it here, and if it is here, we will. They come to me. I can hear them calling. Perhaps it's because they know I love them so."

And still, Joshua did not speak. He stood up as Leyla rose, and followed her to the edge of the clearing where a bush holding many blossoms was growing. He felt as if time did not exist, and that this place was not upon this earth. His mind was a void and he remembered nothing of the past. Not even yesterday. It was as if this was the only place that ever was, and that he had ever been—and there had never been Old Man or the cave, or even the guiding voice in his life. Ever at all. There was only now and this place, that was ever in his life, and this one beside him called Leyla, her presence and her voice. They were the only reality that he knew as they looked past the blossomed bush in front of them.

There, shining in the moonlight as with a light that was their own were the most beautiful flowers he had ever see. It was as if a garden had been planted there and hidden out of sight, to be tended and protected for none to see but the ones who had put it there.

"Joshua! Look! The night flower!" Leyla was unable to contain the joy that filled her heart. "We have found the night flower—or the night flower has found us!"

Yes. They had found the night flower. There were dozens of them growing in the little plot of fertile ground hidden behind the blossoming bush.

As they bent to pick the flowers and put them in Leyla's basket, she brushed a piece of rotting wood from the fallen tree that had been there for many years and was nearly entirely in dusty decay save for the part that she had touched. She cried out and stood as if to flee until she saw Joshua looking at her with a beautiful, knowing smile. She began to put the forest's gifts into her basket.

When there were no more night flowers to be picked, they turned toward the path that would take them back to the cabin. Leyla was almost running now, and Joshua could scarcely keep up with her. *If only he wasn't with me,* she thought. *I can't leave this place quickly enough.* At last, she saw the lights from the cabin shining through the trees and then, through the open window, she saw her mother and Old Man preparing to receive the forest's precious gifts.

* * * *

While Leyla and Joshua slept, Old Man and Eleanor ground the petals of the night flower into a fine, white powder, then mixed it with the powder they had prepared earlier in the evening. They put the mixture into a large kettle of water over the fire and left it to boil. As dawn approached, the reddish-brown liquid was poured into small earthen pots that would be taken to the infirmary.

"It has been a long night for both of us, my friend." Eleanor said to Old Man as the last of the pots was filled. "Sleep now. I'll go with Leyla and Joshua to the infirmary and we'll begin. You rest here awhile, and join us when you feel rested."

Old Man began to protest, but Eleanor stopped him. "No. I'm used to strange hours, Old Man. I have a midwife's clock inside me that allows me to remain sleepless for a time, if need be. Not forever," she laughed, "but for long enough. We can do our work without you while you rest. You must sleep now. You must. Go now, and wake Leyla and Joshua for me, and then give yourself the rest you need. Come to the infirmary when it's time for you to come—you'll know when that is. As for Joshua—he will be in our care, so there is no need for you to be concerned. He'll be safe. I'll see that he rests, too, when I sense that he is ready for it."

Old Man began to protest again, but his weariness cut him short. He knew Eleanor was right. He was exhausted. He would rest a while and then go to the infirmary, as she said. Joshua would be safe with her, he was sure of that. He awakened Leyla and Joshua and told them that Eleanor was waiting for them, then he laid down on the bed that Joshua left. Blessed sleep claimed him at once.

* * * *

The sun had just risen over Cold River when Eleanor, Leyla, and Joshua reached the infirmary. As they entered, the stench of sickness and death and the sounds of suffering greeted them stronger than ever. Eleanor stood aside just inside the doors and pulled Leyla close to her. "Let him

207

decide," she whispered. "Let him go to those he chooses. We'll follow and do what he tells us to do."

Leyla nodded her agreement, but said nothing. She knew what Eleanor was saying. She knew that what they had gathered and prepared was the least of it. The potion was but a symbol—necessary, but still just a symbol—of what was to take place here. Yes, the salvation of Randall's Bow was here. Now, and in this place. But it was not a mixture from the forest and water from the spring that would save them. It would be done through that little old one and the mystery of the power he possessed. There was a lightness in her heart now that had been absent for many years. She knew the time would come when she would confess her secret to Joshua, and he would understand. And in his understanding would come her own healing because, somehow, through that old one named Joshua she would be forgiven.

"Joshua." Joshua turned at the sound of Eleanor's voice and looked at the small clay pot she held out to him. He took the pot in silence, then turned away and began to make his way slowly through the filthy pallets.

Eleanor handed one of the baskets with more of the little pots to Leyla. "Follow closely behind him, but give him the potion only when he asks for one. If he doesn't ask for one, don't offer it. Is that what you would have us do, Joshua?"

"Yes," Joshua said, his back still to them. Leyla followed him to a corner of the infirmary that was farthest from them, where he knelt beside a man of middle age. They continued in this way throughout the day, with Old Man joining them in mid-morning. Joshua moved from pallet to pallet, taking them through the infirmary without any apparent pattern or purpose to his selections. He knelt next to each person beside whom he stopped, bent close to them and looked into their eyes for a brief moment. Then he would whisper words that only the two of them could hear. Sometimes he would ask for the potion, and, at other times, he would not. Some of the sick he attended to heard him and responded to him, their expression of suffering turning to one of peace and contentment when they heard his words and felt his touch.

Others seemed unaware of his presence and remained in a fitful sleep without any change at all. There were times when Joshua stopped beside a pallet and looked at the one lying on it for a moment, then pass on without kneeling to talk to them, or even smile. It was as if he had experienced something that he wanted to quickly leave behind, and his walk would quicken until he found someone beside whom he chose to kneel and talk to for a while.

The sun was at its highest when Old Man finally spoke. "Are you tired, Joshua? Would you like to rest for a little while?"

"Yes," Joshua said. "And I'm hungry too, Old Man." He smiled at Eleanor as she held out one of the baskets she had filled with food. "And this basket holds the potion for that," she laughed. "We can all use some of this, I'm sure.

Lets sit by the river while we eat. The day is one of beauty and it will wash away some of the sadness of this place that has attached at least a little of itself to us." They followed Eleanor to a spot near the gentle flow of the river, under a tree that blossomed and gave them shade, then sat upon the soft grass to eat what Eleanor had prepared.

"So! Are we saved?" Their quiet respite was interrupted by Shannon's loud voice as he called to them from the opposite bank of the river. His flowing blue tunic billowed behind him as he waved and crossed the bridge to their side, following behind a wagon bringing yet another load of the sick to the infirmary.

"Are we saved?" he said again, a look of disgust on his face as he looked back at the wagon. "Have you brought the magic from the forest that will save us?" He walked over to where they were sitting and took one of the baskets.

"Here. Let me help. Ones such as you," he said to Old Man and Joshua, "should have servants to carry these baskets for you. I assume this is the magic elixir. Your years have earned you relief from heavy work, and I see no servants about, so I shall do their work."

Eleanor took the basket from Shannon. "Thank you for your kindness, my friend," she said, smiling. "but you would be depriving me of my function if I allowed you to carry out your most generous offer. I am the basket carrier here, as is Leyla. We have had the morning to practice that most difficult duty, and it would be shameful now for us not to take advantage of what we have learned." Eleanor and Shannon kept their smiles, but couldn't conceal their coldness. Shannon let go of the basket and Eleanor put it on the grass, well within her reach.

"I've arranged a feast for us," Shannon said, addressing them all, his laughter forced and without merriment. "Just for us. Let's have supper at my cabin tonight and we'll talk about what we will do next. I must be kept informed of everything." His voice lowered, and he sat on the grass next to Eleanor. "Have you seen Merrill today?" he asked.

"No. I spent the night at my cabin, and haven't been to the manor yet today. We came directly here. I haven't seen him at the infirmary. Why do you ask?"

Shannon looked across the river in the direction of Randall's Bow. "I went to the manor early this morning and he wasn't there. Rashan told me that Merrill had asked him to saddle his mount before the sun was up. He told Rashan that he would ride about the countryside today to let the workers in the fields see him and know that he was one of them, just as Randall had done. Rashan said Merrill told him that soon this place would feel his hand upon it—that today he will mourn his father's death for the last time. Tomorrow will be the beginning of more than just another day."

Shannon looked around him as if someone might be listening—someone he didn't want to hear what he was saying. "Come tonight. I have a stew cooking over my fire at this very moment in anticipation of your visit. I've told Rashan that you will be absent from Merrill's table tonight, if Merrill should ask where you are. I hope you don't think me presumptuous, but if I know more about your intentions, it will help you, as I can assure Merrill that you wish him only good. It will make it easier for us all."

"I'm sure you know by now," he said to Old Man and Joshua, "that if it is not made easier for Merrill, he will make things difficult for us beyond anything we can imagine."

Eleanor knew they had no choice. Shannon was not their ally, despite anything he might tell them to the contrary. It was clear to her that he had cast his lot with Merrill, and that didn't surprise her. She also knew he had decided to play both sides for a while, to see what it would gain him. They did not need him for an enemy—he could be dangerous and even cruel. She had seen the capacity for destruction and deceit in him before, but Randall had been there to hold him in check. To underestimate Shannon and the lengths he would go to in order to protect his own interests would be a grave mistake. They would go to his cabin tonight. Perhaps they would learn something that would help them in their work. Time was growing shorter by the hour, and the risk was worth it.

Eleanor had decided to play both sides, too— she had no choice, really. Merrill was Randall's son and she had been the only mother he had ever known. Yes, she feared his madness, but she loved him as if he was her son. They had a closeness they both treasured and there was Jude, too. He was a loving child and she couldn't separate herself from him now. Jude dearly missed Randall—she knew the truth of that— and in recent days she had not been with him to help him through his sadness. And Merrill couldn't help him now. There was an answer and she would find it—perhaps tonight at Shannon's.

"Thank you, Shannon." Eleanor spoke gently, and the others looked at her in surprise. "We will be happy to join you. We must work together or we won't survive. When Randall's Bow has found its peace again, as indeed it will, we will look back on these days as if a bad dream had possessed us for a while. And it will leave us, too, never to return again."

Shannon made no effort to conceal his relief at Eleanor's acceptance of his invitation. "Eleanor, I've watched you long enough to know that the magic you work with your potions is a gift that is given to only a few— certainly not to me. You have done much good here, and I cannot say the same for myself."

"You were Randall's friend, Shannon," Eleanor said. "You gave him much. He trusted you and you were worthy of that trust. You found solutions to things that needed to be set right when Randall couldn't find the answers. You have your own gifts, as do we all, and we must take great care that our use of them is not misplaced."

"Yes. I know that what you say is true." Shannon was moved by what Eleanor had said, but, at the same time, he hadn't missed her warning.. His voice softened. "But I must go now—I have much to do before I see you all tonight.. Come as the sun is setting."

They watched Shannon cross the bridge, standing aside to make way for yet another wagon carrying more of the sick to the infirmary. As he walked along the riverbank on the opposite side, he waved and then disappeared down the path that led to Randall's Bow.

"I've offended him." Eleanor said as she watched Shannon go. "He isn't all that he appears to be when you first make his acquaintance. You should know this about him—he has an appetite for power and he doesn't wear its mantle well. Indeed, there are few who do. And jealousy easily overtakes him. He will question you closely about what has happened between us, and you may be certain that your answers will quickly reach Merrill. So beware. Know that what you reveal to Shannon you reveal to Merrill, too. Be honest and forthright with him about what we have done here in the infirmary today, and about our time in the forest yesterday. But say nothing about yourselves that you haven't said already. If you have told him all, then so be it. If you haven't, then be cautious.

Our concern now is for the welfare of the sick. Nothing more, and certainly nothing less. We must be as free of conflict among ourselves as possible. Our focus must be on what we do here, not on avoiding the raging of a madman or the jealous plotting of one who is concerned with nothing but his own safety and gain. We shall leave the struggle for power to Merrill and Shannon and whoever else may wish to involve themselves in what always is a losing battle in the end. A peaceful evening is before us, if that is what we decide we want. Now come. Let's be about our business here. It's not that far off before the sun begins to set. Let's change our methods now, shall we, Joshua? We will distribute the potion with you, and we will see if our hands and hearts can do what you have done,. Tomorrow and the next day will tell us if we have been of any use here, or if we have done nothing more than fill empty wishes with empty hopes."

Joshua looked at them all and smiled, then turned and walked toward the infirmary. He left them at the doors with the baskets of potion and didn't seek them out until he heard Eleanor calling to him that they were finished for the day. He arose from beside a woman sleeping peacefully and he and Leyla slowly made their way toward her and Old Man.

The rays of the setting sun lay upon the waters of Cold River, turning them red as blood as they met outside the infirmary. The day had been long and hard for all of them. It seemed that the line of wagons bearing the sick was never-ending. The floor of the infirmary had become so crowded that there were no longer enough pallets for everyone who needed one. Some were just laid in the dirt. The ones who were lucky enough to have a member of their family with them at least had a makeshift pillow of straw, the only bit of comfort that was left. More men were sent for to walk about the infirmary to find the ones who had already breathed their last. It was the only way pallets, as filthy as they were, could be made available for those who still had a little life left in them.

The sky above the pits was black with smoke as the day ended, and the grotesque parade of wagons filled with the dead from the infirmary became as endless as the one that rumbled across the bridge from Randall's Bow.

"Come," Eleanor said when Leyla and Joshua had joined her and Old Man. "Let's rest for a few moments before we go to Shannon's. The day has been long and we've worked hard—and there is something that I must say to you. It has been on my mind, and I feel that I must tell you now."

Eleanor led the way to the place by the river where they had sat earlier in the day. "I want to tell you something about Merrill that may surprise you," she said when they were all comfortably sitting on the grass. "In many ways, he is a good man. You should know that I love him as I would love him if he were my own son. Yes—there is goodness in Merrill. He could not be otherwise, having come from a father such as Randall." Eleanor looked across the river where she could see the straight path at the edge of the forest and there, through the opening at the far end, she could see the village green where Randall lay buried.

"Merrill has done things that have brought much sorrow to the people here. Many say he is evil—that an evil force possesses him that is not of this world. They say it will destroy him and, as it does, it will destroy all of us, too. The people here have superstitions about such things, and who is to judge them wrong? What has happened since Randall's death has given us little hope that he will lead us in the way his father did—but there is not a man alive who could do that. The essence of Merrill is good—I have no doubt about that. We have spent much time with him and he has revealed himself to us as he has to no others," she said, looking at Leyla. Then, to Old Man and Joshua, "And there is Jude, too—you have seen him only once, at Randall's grave. Merrill has no wife—Jude was born out of wedlock. His mother's family left him on the doorstep of the manor and then left Randall's Bow in shame. They haven't been heard from since. There is beauty in the way those two love each other."

Old Man's voice, a whisper, broke the silence. "But his mind is full of storms. And Shannon fears him. Merrill is sick with grief, and he is fearful, too. And his cruelty is obvious in the bloody mount he rode to his father's grave. What you say surprises me."

"Merrill understands." It was Joshua who had spoken, and they looked at him in surprise, not knowing what he meant. Old Man shook his head as if to silence him—a look that did not pass without Eleanor's notice.

"Let him speak, Old Man," Eleanor said. "Why do you think you can silence him? Are you the elder? Is that it? Or perhaps you two are of the same blood and you are the older brother who thinks he still holds the power over the younger. Is it that?" she laughed. "Come now. Let us speak freely with each other. You see a mother and her daughter here—we are your friends, not your adversaries. We are equals here, free to say what is in our hearts. Deceit between us will only interfere with what we are trying to do. I am sure you know that."

Old Man nodded to Joshua, then waited to hear what he would say. Eleanor was right. They must be free to say whatever was in their hearts now. He knew that. But this was a place of superstition and fear, and they must use caution— even with Eleanor and Leyla—about how much they revealed about themselves. At least, for now.

"I knew that Merrill would understand," Joshua said again, "and so I wasn't afraid when I spoke to him at Shannon's—when I told him that the forest held the answer. And when I spoke to him, we looked at each other—it was an intended thing for both of us, and from our eyes, we spoke beyond the words. The true talking between us was in our eyes because it came from our hearts. What I said to him and what he answered in that way, I don't know how to explain it—I don't have the words. But what we spoke was truth. I know what Eleanor says about him is true. Merrill is fearful now and he is sad—that's the reason for his madness. Randall is gone and Merrill is left alone except for his son. Except for Jude. And Merrill is afraid and so he sees us all as his enemy. But in his heart, goodness lives. And there will be a way for him to let it out."

"For one whose experience with others was confined briefly to two people, and then me, until a few short days ago, you seem quite sure of what you say." Old Man's words escaped him before he realized what he had said.

Joshua looked at Old Man as if he was observing a stranger about whom he knew nothing, and would wait for a while before coming to any conclusions. And as Joshua looked at him, he knew a question would be asked that he must answer now—whatever the consequences.

Eleanor's question came as no surprise. She missed nothing, so there was no reason for him to hope she would not ask the question he did not want to hear. He had thought the revelation would come from Joshua. It had not. It had come from his own lips and now he must tell them the truth, whatever it might bring. There was no longer a choice.

"What is that you said? Two others?" Eleanor waited for Old Man's answer.. Still, Old Man did not speak.

"My friends, whatever is going on here must end." Eleanor would not be satisfied until she had a truthful answer, and Old Man was well aware of that. "There are things you have not told us—things you are concealing from us, and you have your reasons, I'm sure. But hear me now. If we are to continue together, you must tell me everything. I feel the weight of lies here—or truth not spoken—it's all the same. I feel it coming from you, Old Man. You are living in your past, whatever that may be. You reek of fear, and I must know why. We must clear the air of this, or we must separate from each other now. There is much to do, and we need your help We need your wisdom. The decision is yours."

Eleanor turned her attention to Leyla. "I feel that the miracle will come through these two, if a miracle is to come to us at all. But they must be freed by the truth first. There is no other way."

Old Man kept his eyes fixed on the grass at his feet as Eleanor spoke. He heard her words and he wondered what had happened to him. What had become of that part of him that he had found in the forest. His true self. He had thought he couldn't live without it, once he had felt its power and the peace it had brought to him. And yes, the joy. The joy of life and of knowing himself, who he really was, at last.

He looked at Joshua and his heart filled with sadness. This little one is my teacher now, he thought. And what would he have me do? If he knew the truth I have to tell—some of which even he does not know—what would he have me do, this teacher of mine?

Joshua looked back in silence at Old Man. Old Man did not find the answer in his teacher's eyes.

They listened as Old Man told his story. When he had finished—when there was nothing more to tell—they sat in stunned silence for a while, looking at the gently flowing waters of Cold River that had brought Old Man and Joshua once more to Randall's Bow.

Eleanor looked at Leyla and Joshua at last, and they turned to meet her tear-filled eyes with their own as they looked upon each other in a way that they could never have imagined before this moment. Leyla reached out and took Joshua's hand in hers.

The depth of Eleanor's sadness seemed to have added years to her face. "Yes. We have met before, haven't we?" she said. "And that night when first we met—for a moment I saw you as a child, Joshua, for that is what you were and what you are. My dear one. You are the child—my dear one, Joshua, it was I who took you from your mother and judged you not fit to live. I was the one who wrapped you in filthy rags and laid you in Leyla's arms and commanded her to do what I had decided must be done. For whose sake? Certainly not for yours. I ask forgiveness for what I did. From you, Joshua. And from you, Old Man. And you, my dear Leyla, can you ever forgive me? And can I ever forgive myself? I don't know. And even as I ask for your forgiveness, I know that somehow I should be asking for something else, but I don't know what it is. What I did is far beyond forgiveness' reach, and I don't know what it is that I really seek from you. You owe me nothing but contempt. Or worse, if you were capable of it. And I know you are not, for you are goodness. All of you. Goodness, and nothing else.

"And you, my dear one," Eleanor said to Leyla. "I know how you have suffered all these years for the thing I had you do. Now you are redeemed. This life of beauty that sits before you now, this little Joshua— this beautiful Joshua— has redeemed you."

Leyla was unable to take her eyes off Joshua as disbelief and joy filled her heart to overflowing.

"And you, Old Man," Eleanor continued. "You must love this dear little one with all your heart to have left your peaceful forest to come here with him and confront the things from which you fled to save your own life—to come back here and be with ones like us. You came at the worst of times to be swept up in our madness once again. It is far worse now than when you left it."

Eleanor looked at Joshua again. A loving look. A pleading look, too. You are but a child," she said, smiling. "You have the same years as Jude, Merrill's son. Joshua, there is something that I must say to you. It was into my hands that you were born, and I saw that you weren't like the other newborns that had come into my hands. I couldn't name the difference, but it was there, and so I made the decision that I made. No one else helped me with that. It was by my judgment, and mine alone, that you were carried into the forest and left there to die alone. It was I who wrapped you in rags and gave you to Leyla and told her to take you into the forest and leave you there. It was there that you were meant to die, according to my will. That was my intention. I told your mother that you were born dead and, shortly after, she left this world. Your father had died shortly before, claimed by the waters of Cold River after a storm. Leyla did what I told her to do. She had no choice. And the two of us have not talked of that night until now. But the memory of it has haunted us without ceasing all there years. And now here you are.

"Joshua, Dear Joshua. There is one thing more," Eleanor continued. "In the place where you were left to die—in the very place where Old Man found you—it was in that very place that you and Leyla found the garden of night flowers."

They waited for Joshua to speak. Until now, he had sat and listened quietly to Eleanor—it seemed at times without really hearing what she was telling him. There was no expression on his face to reveal what he was feeling. And no words.

There was only joy in Leyla's heart now. She leaned over and kissed her mother on the cheek, than she kissed Old Man. "Thank you," she said to him. Then she turned to Joshua. She put her face close to his, as he did with the sick in the infirmary, took both of his hands in hers and softly kissed him on the cheek. Still, Joshua said nothing,

At last, the music of Joshua's voice broke the silence. "We have a special thing to do here, you and I," he said to Leyla. "And it would not be so if all that has gone before this time had not happened." He looked at Eleanor and smiled. "That is what makes it so. That is why we are who we are now, and why we are together here. It is a thing of great beauty that we will do together. We are a part of the healing miracle—for ourselves and for everyone in Randall's Bow. Everyone. We will see our miracle happen because of who we are—because of who you are, Eleanor, and you, Old Man. And Leyla, it is for us now to finish the work through which the miracle will come. Yes. Our miracle has begun." Joshua stood up and looked toward the infirmary. "Old Man, I am very tired," he said. "I need to rest before I begin again."

"There is no need for you to go with us to Shannon's," Eleanor said to Joshua. "I will deal with him. Go to my cabin and rest. It has been a long day for all of us and we will stay at Shannon's for only a little while."

They walked together across the bridge and down the path that took them to the village green. Eleanor, Leyla, and Old Man watched Joshua as he turned from them and went in the direction of Eleanor's cabin, then they continued on to Shannon's.

They knew Shannon would not be pleased that Joshua was not with them.

*   *   *   *

Night was falling as Joshua painfully made his way back to Eleanor's cabin. A pounding, unceasing ache filled his head and he could no longer ignore its presence. It was difficult to keep his attention on his purpose here because of what he had learned about Old Man and himself. He knew it was all for good, but for now, he was full of conflicting emotions. It gave him joy to know that Eleanor and Leyla had been in his life since the very beginning. He had felt a special bond with Leyla since the first time he had seen her—and how could he have not? It was her arms he had felt around him on that long ago night that was beyond his conscious memory. And as she had laid him on the forest floor to die, it had been with tenderness and love. He had felt that love, and he had carried it with him ever since that moment. And Eleanor. Yes, to know her now was a thing of joy too. She had been the one who had taken him from his mother, but he knew her as a wise and loving woman. She had done what she thought was best for his mother and for him, even though she was not without fear. And it was because of what she had done that he had spent his life with Old Man in their beloved forest.

But it was so much for him to think about. To feel and absorb. His head hurt so much from the force of it all. And his body, too. The pains in his body were getting worse, and he didn't want to tell anyone about it. He wanted to spend his days among the sick now—he knew that was what he was here to do. But there was so much pain in his body now, and there was pain in his heart too, from the confusion of all the things he had learned today.

He struggled to stay on the path in the growing darkness, walking slowly and with great effort. The soft bed at Eleanor's cabin would feel good to him, and he would take some of the powder he had brought with him from the cave. It always helped his pain go away. He was glad to be alone for a little while. He wanted to lie down in darkness, in the quiet of the empty cabin, and listen to the silence that would come to him. Perhaps the silence would take him from the loneliness that he felt so deeply now that he wished he would pass from this place in sleep and never see another morning's sunrise. But he had work to do here, and he must not think such things.

He reached the place where the path forked, the left fork leading to Eleanor's cabin and the right fork leading to the manor. He stopped and looked toward the manor for a moment. He could see its iron gates only a short distance from where he stood. The pain in his joints was growing more intense now, and it would take all of his strength to reach Eleanor's cabin, which was farther away than the manor.

Past the manor gates, through the courtyard and in the stables all was quiet except the sounds of contentment as the horses nuzzled through the grain and hay Rashan had put into their stalls. And in one stall at the far end of the stables, The Great Black War Horse paused in his feeding. He raised his head and looked toward the manor gates, his ears brought forward to listen to the silence that spoke to him in quietness and strength, and he sent that strength out through the gates to one he knew who was not far off. The Great Black War Horse whinnied softly into the night and sent his welcome across the courtyard and through the gates, where it was received by the heart to which it was sent.

Joshua turned from the path that would take him to Eleanor's cabin and slowly limped toward the manor gates. He wept from the agony of his swollen joints and aching head, the pain shooting through him like bolts of lightning. He entered the dark courtyard and slowly made his way toward the stables, where he would soon be safe with his spirit brother.

And The Great Black War Horse waited in the silence of his stall for the little one—the innocent of innocents—to come to him.

Chapter 29

"I will deal with Shannon alone." Eleanor's voice shot through the darkening light, bringing Old Man and Leyla to an abrupt stop. She turned and faced them, then looked toward the lights of Shannon's cabin. "Yes," she said again. "I will deal with Shannon alone."

"Mother. What do you mean?" Leyla stepped toward Eleanor to stop her from knocking on the cabin door.

Eleanor ignored Leyla and looked at Old Man. "Shannon knows, doesn't he? He knows that Joshua is a child." It wasn't a question. It was a statement of fact and she knew it.

"Yes. Shannon knows."

Eleanor said nothing, waiting for Old Man to tell her more.

"I didn't intend to deceive you," Old Man said to her. "It was after Randall's funeral—after the night that Merrill came here uninvited—that it was revealed to him. By me, directly, perhaps. Or in the manner I treated Joshua, taking care of him as if he was a child. I trusted him. He was the only friend we had here, or so I thought. He said that our secret was safe with him—that he would tell no one. Please forgive me, Eleanor. I had no other choice at the time, or so it seemed."

"That explains it, " Eleanor said. "I sensed terror in Shannon when we spoke last. He feels like he is caught between two forces now, with no way to escape because he has kept his secret from Merrill for too long. Something is happening in the infirmary now. I feel it, though we won't see the results for a few more days. But it is there. We've won. I have no doubt of that. And it is through Joshua that the healing powers come. Tomorrow, with Leyla by his side—and the love that is between them now—that love is even stronger because of what we've learned today. He is very strong, and will become even stronger. Soon, all will be well again and we will be safe. But when the healing becomes evident, Merrill will see it. The people will know that he was wrong, and he will choose Joshua as the mark for his revenge. He has done so already. I'm sure of that.

"Joshua will be the one to pay the price that Merrill will demand, whatever that may be. And when the people learn that Joshua is a child, they will react from superstition and fear of anyone or anything that is different from them. We won't be able to protect him. Shannon will insure his own safety by revealing Joshua's secret to Merrill, for that is the only currency he has. He has nothing else with which to buy his safety. And so I must be alone with Shannon tonight. I decided that on our way here. I will try to dissuade him from using what he knows. I have no control over what he will end up doing, but I know he fears me almost as much as he fears Merrill, and he knows that if Merrill has to choose between the two of us, he will side with me. Go back to my cabin now. I'm going to do this alone. It's the only way."

Eleanor turned and walked the several remaining steps toward Shannon's cabin without waiting for them to answer. Old Man and Leyla watched her go until she reached the door then turned and walked back the way they had come. Neither one spoke until they passed the village green, where they stopped and looked toward the mound of dirt that marked Randall's still-fresh grave.

"It seems so long ago that he was with us," Leyla said in a trembling voice. She took Old Man's hand and held it tightly as they walked together through the darkness to Eleanor's cabin.

* * * *

The Great Black War Horse raised his head and whinnied softly to the small, thin shadow that limped slowly toward him through the darkness of the stables. He sensed the little one coming closer and closer to him now—the one for whom he had waited. The one he knew would come. And he knew his little spirit brother was in great pain.

There was no blood on the horse's flanks and withers now. Rashan had cared for him well when Merrill left the stables after the grim parade to Randall's grave, and then the return here at full gallop, whip and spurs lashing at his torn and bloody hide. Rashan had bathed his entire body with warm water, then spread a healing balm over the wounds. The pain was gone now, and there would be only the slightest evidence of what had happened that bloody night when Merrill had spewed his rage upon him.

Joshua limped toward The Great Black War Horse's whinny and stood at last before the open stall. He heard the sound of the other horses as they shifted in their stalls, an occasional hoof knocking against wood as they changed positions or swished their tails at the few annoying insects that buzzed about them. Slowly, the form of The Great Black War Horse came into sight, looming before him as his eyes became more and more accustomed to the darkness. He had been drawn to this place, as he knew he would be, by a power not his own. There had been no choice in his coming here, no more than there had been a choice about whom he would kneel beside or pass by that day in the infirmary. There was only the knowing that guided his actions now, and he followed it with clarity and without doubt or hesitation. There was only the doing of now—without choice or resistance—and that was all.

The Great Black War Horse whinnied softly again, and Joshua came closer to the sound. There was gentleness in it and a welcome, and suddenly he felt the wet-warm softness of a muzzle against his cheek. Joshua looked up at the horse's eyes as they looked knowingly down upon him, and he felt peace and strength of spirit, and a kinship that bespoke of a oneness that covered them. He was safe here. There was much pain, but The Great Black War Horse knew *wh*at it was to suffer pain and yet to have done no wrong.

The Great Black War Horse moved forward in his stall. He was untethered, and at first it seemed to Joshua that the horse was moving out of his stall toward him. He pressed his withers against the side of the stall then wheeled to leave the greater part of the stall open. He stood aside and looked at Joshua, bending his powerful neck and again softly brushed his muzzle against his cheek. Joshua moved slowly past The Great Black War Horse and went into the far corner of the stall, where he fell upon the soft straw, weeping softly. His joints felt as if they were on fire. His head and his heart pounded, and he was frightened and confused.

The Great Black War Horse positioned his massive body lengthwise across the front of his stall and stood like a mighty sentinel carved from black marble, his head held high, ears forward, eyes upon the darkness ahead. He stood so quietly that it seemed as if he had even ceased to breathe. Soon, Joshua's pain would go away and he would return to Eleanor's cabin and sleep. But for now—for just a little while—he would lie here on the sweet-smelling straw beneath the unmoving form of The Great Black War Horse and feel the comfort of his presence.

Chapter 30

"You play games with me, Eleanor!" Shannon's voice rang through the cabin. Sweat poured down his flushed face in little rivulets, turning the collar of his tunic a wet dark blue. "You play games with me!" he shouted again., rising from the table and knocking his chair backwards to the floor. "I am not an enemy you want to have! You know that well—and now I wonder whose side you're on!"

"What do you mean, whose side? Merrill's? Yours? But that remains to be seen, doesn't it?" Eleanor spoke quietly, though her heart was pounding with fear. Yes, what Shannon said was accurate. He was, indeed, not an enemy to have. And yes, she knew it well. She had seen the extremes of deceit and treachery he had gone to in the past to avenge himself against those whose wrongs he had felt, whether those wrongs were real or imagined. It made no difference, because the results were the same. None had survived Shannon's wrath unscathed when he had determined to take revenge. Everyone he had pursued left Randall's Bow to settle elsewhere rather than face the constant misfortune that befell them as long as they stayed.

Eleanor was not so naïve as to believe she would survive Shannon's fury should he decide that she must leave Randall's Bow. But she had gone too far to retreat now. She had to learn what he was planning. Shannon knew that Joshua was a child and he would use it for his own purposes when the time came.

"And whose side are you on, Shannon?" Eleanor said quietly, concealing her fear. "Mine? Would you tell me that you are on my side, if indeed there are sides to take in this tragedy that could kill us all? You have known the truth about Joshua and you let me believe otherwise. Why? Whose side are you on? It seems to me that the question is more mine to ask than yours."

Shannon stopped pacing about the room and stood facing her. "So," he said. "You know." He had calmed himself somewhat and Eleanor thought she heard relief in his voice. Even a little sadness. "It's just as well. Yes. I'm glad you know." He smiled then looked at the floor like a child who had been caught in a lie, and was attempting to use his charm to get out of it. "When and how did you find out?"

"By the river today. We were sitting by the river resting from the morning—Leyla, Old Man, Joshua, and I." She stopped speaking and said nothing more. She would not be specific about how she came to know that Joshua was a child—nor could she be. She didn't even know, herself. It was almost as if she had told herself the things that had been revealed to her today. And yet, Leyla had been told too. And Old Man and Joshua knew that they hadn't been the ones who had spoken the words she had heard so clearly.

"I didn't think the truth was mine to reveal, Eleanor. And what we know frightens me. What does it mean? Who is this child who looks so old?

Where did he come from? Our ways are built on superstition and ritual. We don't easily accept things that aren't familiar or can't be explained in ways we can understand. You are well aware of that, I know. And because we are the ones who have welcomed him here—no others have, and certainly not Merrill—you and I would be in danger of sharing any consequences that would befall the child if he is perceived as something evil who has come to do harm to Randall's Bow. Maybe even the cause of the fever itself. Joshua arrived here on the day after Randall died. Perhaps that wasn't a coincidence." Shannon became silent then and waited for Eleanor's response.

But Eleanor said nothing. She would not be a part of whatever Shannon was planning—and she knew he had a plan—a plan that would concern only himself and his own safety. She would not play his game. So she held her silence, looking at him without expression.

"Joshua's life would be in danger if the people knew the truth of who he is," Shannon said, almost pleading with Eleanor to agree with him. "They would demand his life, believing that in some way there would be an exchange—his life for the fever leaving Randall's Bow. That's how they think. And Merrill would see it as a convenient way to rid himself of the one who had proven him wrong. If indeed Joshua's presence at the infirmary is having any real affect on the fever. Do you know what is happening there?"

"No. We'll know in a day or two, when the fever has had time to break—if that's what it's going to do in the ones who have been given my potion."

"Potion? Surely you don't think that any change will be because of a mixture of leaves and berries, or whatever it is you've concocted? Or that the people will see it that way. They'll see it as being caused by the new ones here—Old Man and Joshua—not to anything that you've done, Eleanor. You must know that."

"Joshua," Eleanor said. "It is he alone who is treating the sick, with Leyla standing by with the potion if he asks for it. Which isn't often."

"But how can that be? Can't you see where that puts him? It gives him the power to directly oppose Merrill if he succeeds. How can you allow such a thing to happen? If Merrill sees Joshua as his enemy, then he see you an I as his enemies too. We are the ones who befriended him, and we will pay the price along with Joshua. Can't you see that? There is no way out if the sick are cured. Merrill will strike. And if it is discovered that Joshua is a child, the people will demand a cleansing of this place, and that will mean his life. There will be no escape from that—and we are connected to him in the minds of everyone. You must take him out of the infirmary. You must keep him away, and I will force Old Man and Joshus out of here. They will be no longer welcome here. And you must do the same. There is no other way. Let them go back where they came from."

"They came from Randall's Bow. This isn't the first time Joshua and I have met," Eleanor said calmly. Her voice was almost without feeling, and the power of her words struck Shannon hard, as she intended. She had made her decision and, for her, there would be no going back. Shannon would be alone in his schemes—she would not cast her lot with him.

"What do you mean?"

"Nor Leyla and Joshua. They, too, have met before this time."

"What are you saying, Eleanor? What do you mean?"

"Joshua was born in Randall's Bow. I mid-wived his birth. I told Leyla to take him into the forest and leave him to die, because I sensed something about him that was incomplete somehow—something I hadn't seen before, and it frightened me,"

She was telling Shannon more than she had intended, and she knew it wasn't wise, but she couldn't stop once the words started to come out. What she had held inside for so long needed purging, and she could not stop herself.

"I told the mother, a barmaid at the tavern, that her baby was stillborn. She never knew the truth, and died shortly afterward. I was frightened. And I well know that what you say about the people of Randall's Bow is the truth. I felt the fear they would feel if they knew that this little one who looks so old is only a child. I know because I felt it and I tried to kill him as you have said the people here would do. There is no difference. Yes, Shannon, I know you speak the truth, because, as you can see, I have been a part of that truth. But I will not be a part of what you plan. I cannot. I will fight you. I will fight you, and Merrill will stand by me. I will see to that. Oh, I know you will try to win him to your side, but so will I. It will be of great interest to see where his allegiance falls, will it not? But of course, we know that it lies with none other but himself. Whichever one of us he chooses, if he chooses at all, will tell us nothing, because he will be using us as we will be using him. Isn't that true?"

"You are a good woman, Eleanor," Shannon said. "What you did then didn't come from evil intentions, for I know there are none. And now we have this most remarkable child in our midst. Yes, I will admit that. Joshua is truly remarkable. But to think a misshapen child will deliver us from the monster that is killing us is insane. And to believe that if he works the miracle that you hope for, and then is discovered for who he really is—to believe that he will survive is insane. It is impossible. Can't you see that?"

"You and Merrill are very much alike," Eleanor said. She knew she was in control now, and Shannon knew it, too. "Did you know that? Merrill wants a throne, of sorts. And you, Shannon, you want the power behind the throne. To whisper secrets in Merrill's ear. And he will believe you and do as you advise because you two are so much alike. You will be whispering his own thoughts to him. If things go wrong, he will have you to blame. You will be Merrill's scapegoat, for that is the price you must be willing to pay. You will dance with one another, never sure where the music is coming from, and each of you will be serving his own ends while pretending to care about this place Randall loved so much. There will be no trust between you, and you both will fall, but not until the others have been hurt and have paid a heavy price they had no say in. You both can be a part of the destruction of Randall's Bow. I will say no more tonight, Shannon. We will talk more about this at another time, if you wish. I pray that we will, for we must. Despite what I have said, nothing is final, and there is some truth in what you have said. But now it's late, and I'm going home. I'm tired. And there is much to do tomorrow. Come to the infirmary or not—as you wish."

Eleanor rose from her chair and abruptly left, leaving Shannon standing in the doorway, watching her disappear down the path toward home. "In truth, I do not wish to do battle with you. Eleanor. No. I truly do not," he said softly to himself as he watched her go. "I would not be certain of victory, any more than if the battle was with Merrill himself."

Shannon turned and went back inside, closing the door on the world. At least for a little while.

* * * *

The touch of a wet muzzle upon his cheek awakened Joshua from his sleep. The pain was gone from his joints now, and the vicious pounding in his head had ceased. He looked up into the face of The Great Black War Horse hovering just above him, and smiled.

"I must go now," he whispered. "I must go to my bed at Eleanor's now. I have much to do when morning comes." He rose slowly to his feet and took a step. There was still a little pain, but he could bear it now.

The Great Black War Horse stood aside as Joshua hobbled from the stall and out the stable doors into the night. He turned back in the direction of a soft whinny that reached out to him through the darkness. "I'll come back," he whispered. "I promise." He crossed the courtyard, keeping in the shadows near the wall, and went out the gates of the manor, turning down the path that would take him to Eleanor's.

Joshua approached the cabin quietly, opened the door without a sound, then crept silently into his bed. The only sound was the steady breathing of

Old Man, who was fast asleep. When Old Man had returned to the cabin with Leyla earlier that evening, he had assumed that Joshua was asleep beneath the pile of blankets on his bed. He hadn't lit a candle, so as not to awaken him and had gone to his own bed unconcerned, certain that Joshua was with him, safe and sound.

Joshua hadn't noticed Eleanor following quietly behind him up the path to the cabin, then standing in the shadows as she watched him enter the cabin and close the door behind him.

*   *   *   *

The next several days in the infirmary were days of revelation and hope. And sadness, too. The fever had begun to break in those beside whom Joshua had knelt. The others—those whom he passed by—began to die.

"Joshua, why do you pass some of them by? There are some you barely look at, yet there are others with whom you spend a long time, even while others nearby are suffering." Leyla and Joshua were sitting by the river, resting from the morning, when she asked the question that had weighed so heavily on her heart since their first day in the infirmary. It seemed to her that Joshua didn't care about some of the sick, and at times he even seemed to purposely avoid some parts of the infirmary. She felt anger when she knew he was doing that and would go herself to those he wouldn't kneel beside. But her presence did no good. They needed Joshua by their side, holding their hand and whispering to them, and she intended to do whatever she could to persuade him to give even just a little attenti9on to everyone.

"Why, Joshua?" she asked again, unable to hide her anger. "Doesn't everyone deserve to get well?"

"Some have already embraced death in their hearts."

"What do you mean? I don't understand what you are saying."

"They don't want me to stop and be with them. They have embraced death."

"But I see them, Joshua. I see them." Frightened and confused, Leyla was weeping now. "Look at them. Their eyes speak of the fear that they have been judged by you, and you have condemned them to a fate they

229

can't escape. And so they give up. They give up because you have passed them by. And then they die. I've watched the ones you ignore and they die. They all die."

"Yes, they die. And I can't save them. There is nothing I can do. I know the ones you mean, Leyla—do you think I don't see them? Do you think that I choose the ones who are to die? Is that how you've come to know me in the time we've spent together here?"

"I don't know what I think, Joshua, but I do know what I see."

"No. No you don't, Leyla. You don't know what you see."

"Then tell me. Tell me."

"There is something in those I pass by that speaks to me of the death they have already embraced. Even welcomed. In their hearts, they have chosen death and it has nothing to do with the sickness in their bodies. If I knelt beside them, they wouldn't welcome my presence. If I gave them words of comfort, they wouldn't be comforted. And if I held the potion to their lips, they wouldn't drink. And if they did, their stomachs would reject it, and they would throw it up. Their lives have become such that they don't want to live anymore, and it has nothing to do with the fever. They would take from me, Leyla. They would take everything I have to give them and replace it with their own poison if I let them. But I will not. I cannot. There is no other choice for me. I will not embrace their death, and they cannot embrace my life. Remember on the river bank, when we learned the truth about ourselves—that I wasn't a stranger to Randall's Bow and we weren't strangers to each other?

"Do you remember how we learned that? How we heard a voice inside us speak the truth to us and we knew it was the truth even though we didn't know where it came from and we couldn't see it? That perhaps we only felt it and didn't really hear it at all? But we felt the trust in our hearts and we knew that we had heard a truth that would change our lives forever and we trusted that. Without question. That's how I choose in the infirmary, Leyla. I listen to that same spiritvoice that we heard on the river bank. It's the same voice that told Old Man and me that we would return to Randall's Bow. We listened and we followed, just as I am doing here. And the voice tells me, 'Pass that one by,' or 'Stop here, and only speak,' or 'Kneel, and speak the words I give you, then lift the potion to that one's lips.' So to some, I give the potion, and to others, I don't. To some, I speak the words that are given to me, and to others, I say nothing at all."

"I don't decide these things, Leyla. I don't choose. I only listen and do what there is for me to do." Joshua's entire body was trembling now. There was so much sadness in his heart that he thought he could no longer bear it. He was talking about himself, too—he knew that—and he couldn't express it because of the almost unbearable sadness that he felt. How could it be? How could it be that he could give to others what he couldn't give to himself? He could give himself no words of comfort to ease the heart-pain that he felt almost all the time now. There was no potion that could give him relief—there was no wonderful gift from the forest that would suddenly appear and take away his pain.

"Forgive me, Joshua," she said. "Please forgive me for the way I judged you." They stood together beside the river, looking at the water as it flowed past them. "Very soon, Joshua, Cold River will no longer carry the ashes of our dead," said Leyla. "And it will be because of you and the work you're doing here. But what about you? There are things you haven't told me, aren't there? I can see you're in a lot of pain. What about you, Joshua? What will become of you when your work here is done?"

Joshua looked upriver for a moment in the direction of the place where he and Old Man and Goat had been so happy together, and he knew he would never see that place again. It was gone from his life forever. He turned and looked in the direction of the open doors of the infirmary, where he saw Old Man and Eleanor waiting for them. Without answering her, Joshua hobbled toward them, with Leyla following slowly behind, frustration and sadness on her face.

As Leyla looked at the fragile form of the little one walking ahead gf her, she fought back the terror that seemed to have hands that gripped her throat. She loved him so much. She heard a horse's whinny carried to them on the wind from the direction of the manor. When Joshua stopped to listen, she thought she heard him answer the whinny with a cry of pain, but he started walking toward the infirmary again before she could catch up to him and ask if he was alright. She had imagined it, she knew, but it had seemed so real.

* * * *

231

It continued in the same way for the next several days. They would arrive at the infirmary soon after the sun had risen over Cold River. Eleanor, Leyla, and Old Man would carry the baskets of potion, even though they knew now that it wasn't really needed anymore. Nor was their presence. Old Man and Eleanor would return to her cabin at mid-morning because it was clear that Joshua wanted only Leyla beside him as he walked among the sick, although he never said so in words.

Joshua tired easily and often during the day, and he would turn to Leyla during these times to see her smile as she came up to him and gently touched his cheek. When his pain became too great, he would silently leave the infirmary and sit by the river for a while with her beside him. He never spoke of his pain, but she could see it in his eyes and in the way he walked, each step sometimes so painful that he couldn't walk alone. Leyla would put her arm around him then, and they would walk slowly to the riverbank to rest in the shade.

Often now, Joshua said nothing to the ones he chose to spend a little time with. He simply held their hand and leaned close to them so they could see his smiling face, for when he was close to one of the sick, he felt no pain. He felt only peace. Only joy. And joy and peace were the gifts he gave.

As the days passed, the faces of those on pallets began to change, and even here and there a pallet lay empty. No longer was the sky thick with black smoke over the pits, although some still died and were burned. People were coming from the village more often now to help a loved one rather than bid them a tearful farewell. And the dead were fewer—no more than two or three a day.

Then there came the day when the pit-fires at the edge of Cold River were fed not even once. Wagons still brought the newly stricken over the bridge, but the numbers became fewer and fewer until at last no wagons came across the bridge, for there had not been even one in Randall's Bow who had been claimed by the fever the night before. And soon after that, there were no dead to be taken to the pits and burned.

Joshua was often spoken of now around the home-fires in the cabins of Randall's Bow. Who is that old one, they asked each other? Who is that

232

ancient one, so small in stature, who is delivering us from an evil so great that we had thought we would all be carried in its jaws from this earth—our lives and homes and families destroyed forever, with not even a marked grave to tell others who might pass through that we had ever existed?

Who is this one called Joshua, they asked, who heals with words and smiles and gentle touches—who looks as if he has walked through time from the land of the ancients to be with us in our misery and lead us back to the abundance we knew in earlier days in this place upon the river?

He was sent to us by Randall, someone said. Was it not just a day or two after Randall died that this ancient one appeared as if from nowhere? And the other one, the one who calls himself Old Man—perhaps it is his role to carry the spirit within his body that protects Joshua from harm and sickness while he is here with us.

And his voice, they said. Surely his is not the voice of one whose origins are of our time and place. His is the voice of times when men first came upon this earth—their voices were still pure because they had not learned to speak words that are not the truth. Joshua's voice holds the music of purity in it, they said—the purity of first man, from times when sadness was yet unknown. Oh, the joy in Joshua's voice—his voice sings with it, and the fever flees before its purity.

The only people who came to the infirmary now came to bring their loved ones home or to stand and watch Joshua perform his healing miracles. Or so they called them

The wagons were gone, and as the filthy pallets began to disappear the people stopped coming to the infirmary. Peace was returning to Randall's Bow, and upon the frail shoulders of Joshua—without his knowing—was cast the heavy mantle of savior.

Without his knowing, too, he was given the task of conforming to the people's wishes in all his ways—to be as they wanted him to be—rather than who he really was. And the people of Randall's Bow required him to know their wishes in his heart, without those wishes having to be spoken.

Above all else, he must not be different from them—except as a perfect likeness of themselves as they aspired to be. He must be like them—and even more. He must be perfect. To be any less than that—to be different from them in a way other than the perfection they desired for themselves—would be to mock them in their wisdom of appointing him to his lofty position among them.

And they would not tolerate mockery, any more than difference—for in that, Joshua would condemn them to their truth.

Chapter 31

Merrill stood in front of the stall of The Great Black War Horse and wondered why he had come there. He hadn't entered the stables since he returned the horse to his stall, his blood mixed with the white foam of exhaustion, after Randall's body had been given to the earth. Since that day, he had instructed Rashan to ready the buckskin stallion and bring it into the courtyard each morning at sunrise, to be tethered to one of the posts near the water trough at the far end of the stables.

It was never to be the bay war horse that he would ride, Merrill told Rashan, for he had been Randall's favorite mount after the black stallion. Nor would it ever be necessary for Merrill to enter the stables. The memories of Randall that were awakened by the bay and the stables, even when he chanced to look inside through the open doors, brought pain to his soul followed by a blackness of need that overwhelmed him and sent him to his bed to suffer in a sleep that tortured him with grotesque dreams.

And now he stood before The Great Black War Horse and didn't know how or why he had gotten there.

He had spent the afternoon unobserved in the infirmary, watching Joshua and Leyla as they walked among the sick. He had been told by some of the councilmen that something extraordinary was happening there that he should know about. The number of those who were recovering from the fever was increasing with each passing day, and soon the infirmary would no longer be necessary. There were murmurings in the village, Merrill was told, that perhaps the cruel measures he had ordered had not been necessary after all. There wasn't a family in Randall's Bow that hadn't been touched by sorrow because of the course Merrill had chosen. If they had followed Joshua from the beginning, some were saying, many who

235

had died would have survived—or at least they would have a grave upon which to lay their flowers.

Some were saying, Merrill was told, that the two old ones from the forest had showed them another way. More than that, perhaps Merrill wasn't fit to take Randall's place. Perhaps a council should be appointed by the people to direct the affairs of Randall's Bow. Randall had power because the people had given it to him, some said, and if they chose not to give that power to Merrill, that was their right.

Merrill had kept watch in the infirmary for several days, hidden against the wall in a darkened corner. There was no question that the fever was being defeated. As he watched, he saw that after the first day Joshua rarely gave the potion to anyone. He would merely stop and talk to some while he passed by others, seemingly not even noticing them. Sometimes Joshua touched the ones beside whom he knelt, sometimes he would lean close and whisper to them. And sometimes he did neither, only kneeling close to them and staying with them for a little while. But Joshua almost never gave them the potion after the first day—even to the ones who had just arrived.

Merrill noticed, too, that Old Man and Eleanor were rarely present after the first few days, and that Leyla followed after Joshua with the basket of potion, but usually did nothing more than stand by and watch.

He saw for himself that fewer and fewer were being brought to the infirmary each day, and that not as many were dying—until there came the day when there were no more dead upon the infirmary floor. And soon thereafter, no more wagons came across the river.

Finally, Merrill saw that there were no more fires in the pits. They were no longer needed.—the fever had been defeated and it was because of that strange little old man who had boldly told him to his face that he wasn't afraid of him. Yes, the fever had been defeated. And so, too, had Merrill, and he knew it. What little power he still had left was only because he was Randall's son, and he knew that soon that would be weak currency indeed.

And now Merrill stood before The Great Black War Horse, and he couldn't remember how he had gotten there. The only thing he remembered was that only a short time before, he had stood in the darkened corner of the infirmary, searching his mind for a way to take his vengeance on that old, misshapen one who was destroying his world.

Merrill looked at The Great Black War Horse and felt the bile rise into his throat. He had not broken this one—he knew that. And he knew that he would never sit astride the horse again. He could try, if he was fool enough for that, but one of them would die before the bit was put between the stallion's teeth. Merrill knew that The Great Black War Horse had won as surely as if he had crushed his body beneath his hooves.

The stallion stood unmoving and looked at Merrill. Merrill's gorge rose higher in his throat until he thought that he would choke from it. That taste had come to him before—today, when he watched Joshua walk among the sick, and had seen them look at him and smile their grateful welcome.

The Great Black War Horse looked down at Merrill from a lofty height that was born as much from spirit as from his huge, magnificently muscled body. Merrill looked up at him and knew that he had lost much more than just a noble mount. Yes, he had had lost much more than the satisfaction of his vanity—but he couldn't name it. Only the all-consuming emptiness that he felt—the emptiness that he could never fill— seemed to matter any more. It would bring him to his death if he didn't find a way to fill it. He thought of Joshua, and he knew the answer somehow lay with him.

Merrill walked from the darkness of the stable into the sunlight of the courtyard, and saw Shannon standing on the manor steps, waiting for him. Shannon came quickly toward him, almost at a run, and met him in the middle of the courtyard.

"Merrill! There is something you must know!" he gasped. "We have him, Merrill! We have him! Once again, it will be as it should be. As it is meant to be. Randall's son will direct the fortunes of this place that bears his father's name, and no one will question that!"

"What are you talking about, Shannon?"

"It's about Joshua. He's not what he appears to be. Come. Let's go inside and I'll tell you something that is most extraordinary—something that is most extraordinary, Indeed!"

*   *   *   *

Joshua was awakened by the sound of his own cry as pain cut through him like a dagger in the center of his chest. For a moment, he couldn't breathe and the darkness whirled around him, bringing nausea to his stomach. He tried to call out to Old Man, who was asleep on the other side of the room, but no sound would come. His head pounded and his arms and legs jerked in spasms as the pain ripped through his body. He felt crushed by its fury and cried out again. Still, Old Man didn't awaken. Then, as suddenly as it had come, the pain disappeared. He breathed deeply and felt a numbness in his arms, but that was all. His body was soaked with sweat as he lay under the blanket, growing cold from the wetness.

As his strength slowly returned, he knew that he must go now to The Great Black War Horse. He would be safe there from what it was he feared but couldn't name. The stallion's strength would nourish him and give him strength in turn, and he would go again to the infirmary with the morning sun.

It would be the last time he would go there. Only a few remained now, and they would be taken home by their families, where they would become strong and well again. The fever had left their bodies and no one would be brought across the river anymore. The infirmary would be taken down soon, and the pits fired for the last time to burn its timbers, its ashes thrown into Cold River to follow those who had died within its confines. His inner voice had told him so.

But now, he must go to The Great Black War Horse.

Joshua crept quietly from his bed and left the cabin, painfully hobbling down the path toward the manor. He went through the iron gates and entered the courtyard, keeping in the darkness along its edges as he made his way toward the stables. He heard a whinny in the darkness to guide him to his place of peace and rest. When he reached the stall, The Great Black War Horse moved aside. Joshua crept into the farthest corner and laid down on the fresh straw Rashan had spread there only a few hours before. He could breathe easier now, and he sensed the large head of The Great black War Horse just above him as he came near his face and gently brushed him with his wet muzzle, whinnying softly in thedarkness to reassure him.

The Great Black War Horse moved to the front of the stall then and stood across it, a massive wall of strength and power protecting the little one—the innocent of innocents—who had sought sanctuary with his spirit brother.

*   *   *   *

In the manor, Merrill laid upon the bed in which his father had died. And if one was asked to choose who felt the greater pain—the one named Merrill who laid upon his father's death bed, or the one named Joshua who curled himself into a corner of the stall of The Great Black War Horse—if one could know the truth, there was no difference in their pain. One does not suffer more than the other. One's pain is of the body—a body that is a prisoner within the process that nature has foretold for it. It has nearly run its course now, and will soon release the spirit that it carries as it fulfills its purpose upon this earth. The other's pain is of the spirit, a spirit that is prisoner of a mind that twists and turns and will not let the spirit be. Twisted body or twisted mind—who is to say which bears the greater pain?

There is no Great Black War Horse to stand guard for Merrill and keep him safe as he lays upon his father's death bed and suffers in his madness and his grief. No. Merrill lies alone in darkness and listens to the beating of his heart, the heart of a deeply wounded child, even now, and he searches his tortured mind for the ones who have left him all alone.

He had a mother once, or so he was told. She was gone within hours after his birth and Randall took her place, or tried to, for just a little while. Then he was alone again, until Jude came into his life and somehow this son of his, beautiful in body, mind, and spirit, brought Merrill and Randall together once again.

Oh, father. Why did you go away again? Why did you surrender to death and let it take you from me, as it took the mother that I never knew? I miss you so. You thought you could defeat the fever as you had every adversary you had ever faced. But neither sword, nor shield, nor battle ax could save you in that last battle, and you were felled like so many lesser men before you. You believed you were invincible and you were not, and now you are gone. Oh, father. I suffer so in your absence.

I sought to pillage and burn the enemy that took your life. I sought to take revenge upon the bodies that housed your enemy, to separate them from the others, and then to burn them and let the river take whatever was left to wherever it would take them. Far away from this place that bears your name. I would carry your banner, father. Yes—I would take your banner and hold it high, flying in the wind that brings the memory of you to me. And the people here would say "Look there—there rides Merrill—and surely he is the son of Randall." And when the time came for me to join you in that other place where you have gone to be with your Judith once again—and my Judith, too, my mother who never knew me—it would be Jude's place to carry on.

Oh, father. I feel life slipping from me. I am lost. I don't know what to do. I cannot bear it, father. If the choice was given me to take from this place where you once lay, your wisdom or your death, I would choose death and be with you now, wherever you have gone.

Who is this strange one named Joshua, who has taken this place from me and has turned the people's love for you into hate for me? Shannon told me that he is just a child—that his years and Jude's are the same. How can that be? He looks like one with many years, and he does not have a child's fear of those who are his elders. Yet Shannon swears it is the truth—and that Eleanor will stand beside him in this.

What will I do, father? Is Joshua the fever's force made into a form that resembles ours? Is that the reason it fled from him, though there was nothing toprotect him from it? What should I do with Joshua? Should I take him and hold him up alone for all to see, as the aberration that he is, and then give him to the fire and let the wind take his ashes from this place forever? Oh, help me, father. Come to me and tell me what to do.

And then he slept. And dreamed. In the dream he heard The Great Black War Horse whinny as he kicked against his stall. He saw the stallion move aside, and then he saw Joshua slowly uncurl in the far corner of the stall and finally stand. And then he saw a shadow leave the stall and hobble toward the stable doors, left open to the moonlight.

Merrill awakened then, soaked with sweat. Coldness embraced him in the night as he looked out the window at the full moon hanging high above the courtyard. When he heard The Great Black War Horse whinny and kick against his stall, he hurried to the window and saw Joshua come through the stable doors and into the moon light, slowly making his way toward the manor gates. And as he watched, he knew what he would do.

Whether the whispers that he heard that night were sent to him by Randall—or by a madness that had doomed him lost to all that was right and good and kind—he didn't care. He took his sword into his trembling hands, and ran his fingers along the cool sharpness of its blade.

He would be waiting at the manor gates when Joshua reached them.

PART THREE

Chapter 32

"Old Man! Come quickly!" Eleanor woke Old Man from a deep sleep. He could hear the urgency in her voice—something was very wrong. He looked across the room at the pile of blankets on the other bed to see if she had awakened Joshua, too. There was no movement—he must still be sleeping. Yet, it seemed strange. Eleanor's cry had been loud and sharp, something they were unaccustomed to from her, and Joshua hadn't been sleeping well because of his pain.

Joshua had tried to conceal his pain from Old Man, but he couldn't hide the tears that came unannounced throughout the day. He would suddenly stop and stand still until the pain subsided enough to allow him to move on. Old Man said nothing to him, waiting for him to talk about it when he was ready. That was Joshua's way and Old Man had promised that he would respect his wish to talk about the pain only when he brought it up himself.

Old Man walked over to Joshua's bed and slowly pulled the blankets back. Joshua wasn't there. He hurried down the stairs calling Joshua's name as he went. "Joshua! Joshua!"

"He's not here," said Eleanor. Her face was white and drawn and her voice trembled as she spoke. "Come. Come with me. Something terrible has happened. Merrill has taken his revenge, and we must hurry." Eleanor quickly left the cabin and ran down the path toward the village green, with Old Man following behind her. He walked as quickly as he could to keep up with her. The world was a blur in front of him.

When they reached the end of the path and stepped onto the village green, they were met with chaos and confusion. They pushed their way through the crowded ring of people who had gathered there, moving slowly closer to the object of their attention. When they finally reached the inner circle of people, what thy saw wasn't possible. It was beyond belief—but its horrible reality could not be denied.

Many years before, Randall had constructed heavy wooden stocks in the center of the village green as a warning to the people. He told them if any man or woman was found guilty of actions that endangered the welfare of the people of Randall's Bow, they would be putinto the stocks and kept there to bear their pain and humiliation. They would be released only when Randall himself deemed that they had paid their debt to his satisfaction. But no one had ever been locked within its jaws, to feel the pain and ridicule of all who passed by.

Until now.

There before them, locked within the heavy, rough-wooded stocks, was Joshua. His head protruded from a hole near the top, with his arms and legs sticking out through holes lower down, at angles that were unnatural and grotesque. He appeared to be asleep or oblivious to the activity and noise around him. Leyla was kneeling at the further end of the stocks, talking softly to him and wiping tears from his face. When they reached her side and knelt beside her, they said nothing, so great and incomprehensible was the horror of what they saw.

Joshua opened his eyes and saw them kneeling next to him. "Old Man, what's happening to me? What have I done? I don't know what I've done. Old Man. Help me. Please help me. It hurts so much. Old Man. Please."

Old Man began to speak, but Leyla put her hand on his shoulder. "Wait," she said. "Look there. Merrill. He's coming. Let's listen to what he says."

Merrill walked toward the stocks, paused at Randall's grave for a brief moment, then continued toward them. He seemed to be talking to himself.

"He's mad." Eleanor's whisper cut through the now silent green. No one moved or said a word. Every eye was on Merrill now, waiting to hear what he would say.

Merrill stopped in front of the stocks and looked down at Joshua. He seemed unaware that anyone else was there. He placed one hand on the stocks, just above Joshua's head, and smiled. Then he turned and faced the people, who had circled closely around him.

There was one among those in the circle whom Merrill would have had by his side to observe the consequences of what he had done. He would have liked to have known that the informer was close by, waiting with the others to hear what he would say. But Shannon kept hidden on the outer edge of the circle where Merrill couldn't see him. Merrill would have had Shannon next to him as his comrade, standing there for all to see. It would have given him pleasure for Shannon to see up close the consequences of what he had done, because he knew Shannon could never have imagined that this would be the result of his revelation the night before. But it wasn't necessary. He didn't need anyone standing with him to support him in this action. It was enough that he stand alone for all to see him now in what was surely his finest hour.

And what, after all, had Shannon expected? An outburst of rage, perhaps, and certainly the banishment of Joshua and Old Man from Randall's Bow forever. That, surely—but that and no more. It would be over then, and the people would soon forget what really happened. Life in Randall's Bow would return to the way it had been before the fever, and memories would grow dim from full bellies and peaceful evenings around the hearth.

As for those who would not or could not forget, they would hold their silence, lest they bring disaster on their neighbors, for Merrill's wrath did not discriminate. All would feel his fury, even if it was just a few who voiced their discontent. And so they would remain silent and take their cowardice to their graves.

But this? No. Never this. Shannon was horrified by what he saw. What good could ever come from putting this misshapen child into the stocks? Why punishment so cruel for one like this? Joshua had, in truth, done only good here. Shannon knew that. He didn't reveal to Merrill that Joshua was a child because of some evil thing that he had done—something that he should be punished for. No. It was only for his own good—his own position with Merrill—to stand beside him as a trusted confidant because he had done what he had done. Shannon waited for Merrill to speak, and in that moment he would have taken the place of the little one crushed beneath the weight of the rough-hewn stocks. Yes. He would have taken the punishment as his own.

There was one other there who had kept himself well-hidden at the circle's edge. Had Merrill seen him, he would have sent him home. He hadn't intended for Jude to witness this event. It had nothing to do with him, and he didn't want it to intrude on his son's life in any way. This was not a pleasant thing to see.

But Jude didn't keep hidden for long. He pushed through the circle to stand full-center at the front as Merrill turned and faced the people of Randall's Bow. Merrill didn't see his son as he began to speak.

"You have been deceived!" Merrill's voice rang across the village green. One hand held his unsheathed sword while the other rested upon the stocks just above Joshua's head, still gently cradled in Leyla's arms

"He is a child! Joshua is a child!"

Merrill looked around him to see the people's reaction to what he had said. They turned to each other in confusion, whispering among themselves. This made no sense to them at all. Who was a child? Who was Merrill talking about? Surely not that ancient one held prisoner now. The one who had chased the fever from their midst. The one who was now imprisoned in the stocks. What did Merrill mean—that Joshua is a child? Is he mad?

Merrill waited for the whispers to die down before continuing. When all was silent, he slowly, almost reluctantly, removed his hand from the stocks, as if not to disturb the one locked within its grasp. He moved closer to the people at the edge of the circle. Shannon stepped back even farther out of sight, while Jude moved a step closer to his father. Merrill saw neither one of them, so intent was he upon the secret that he was about to reveal to the unsuspecting crowd—the secret that would return to him the mantle that was rightfully his, bequeathed to him by his father's death.

"You have seen Joshua as he moved among our sick," he said, his voice soft and cold now. It was necessary to focus intently on his words to hear him, he spoke so softly. As one, the people moved even closer to him. And in that moment, unknown to them, they joined with him in purpose and were allied with the son of Randall once again.

"You have seen the way he moves, with halting steps as if he carries the weight of many years upon his back. But Joshua is a child. He is not aged, as he would have you believe. His years are the same as Jude's."

The people gasped as one at what Merrill was claiming, moving even closer now. His voice swept through them, moving over them like the wind.

"Yes. He is but a child." He raised his voice, sensing he had the people with him now. "But what kind of child is he? Can one such as he wish us any good? Has he put a curse, disguised as healing, upon us? Why should I not take action to protect us from him?" Merrill lowered his voice even more. "What place of darkness has this devil-child come from? Yes. Devil-child! And if you doubt my word, then ask the mother of the one who cradles his head now in her arms. Ask Eleanor, for it was into her hands that he was born. Yes. Eleanor received Joshua from his mother's womb. Yes. Yes. It's true! It is the truth I'm telling you now!"

The people knew that what Merrill said was true. The truth was written on Eleanor's face for all to see. No words from her, affirmation or denial, were needed.

"Eleanor was the midwife for Joshua's birth. Look at her now and listen to her silence, for it is in her silence that you will hear her say yes, what I say is true.

This one has not saved you," he shouted, pointing to Joshua. "He has laid his curse upon you, for what else can come from a creature such as this? No one is dying now, that's true. The fever is gone, and the infirmary has been torn down and burned. The pits that held the fires are cold. But would you believe that this one showed you another way—without quarantine or fire—to defeat the fever, and so bring healing to Randall's Bow? Is it your belief that Joshua has saved you and that I, Randall's son, would lead you down the path of pain and destruction until all were dead and burned and carried away by the river's waters, and Randall's Bow would be no more? How could that be so? As this one's power gripped the fever, so, too, has it taken you and made you his prisoner."

There was only silence in response to Merrill's questions. They waited for him to tell them more. Coming even closer to him now, they moved as one.

"This little one named Joshua has power—that's true. Where does his power come from?" Merrill looked at the faces of the people gathered around him, one-by-one, and waited for an answer. But no one spoke. His eyes lingered on Shannon, who had forgotten to hide himself now, so drawn was he to the horror of the moment. He looked at the ground, unable to look Merrill in the eye. Merrill smiled at his victory, then turned and stepped close to the stocks behind him.

Suddenly a stone flew through the air. It hit the stocks near Joshua's head and fell at Merrill's feet. And then another. And then another.

Merrill stepped in front of Joshua and raised his hands. "No!" he shouted. "Now is not the time for that. We must let him ponder what he has done here. He will remain here day and night, with only water to sustain him, until I declare that he be released to whatever fate I decide."

Merrill reached down and pulled Leyla to her feet. "Go," he said to her and Eleanor, pushing Old Man after them. "Come back with water when the sun is at its highest, and then again before night falls. Then again, in the morning. I don't want you here at any other time. Now go."

As Merrlll turned to leave, the people quickly parted to make a path for him and he saw Jude standing next to Randall's grave. He stopped and stood as if frozen to the spot as his son looked at him and then ran in the direction of the manor. Merrill ran to his mount, looking neither right nor left, and rode after Jude, his whip beating hard upon the horse's flanks, spurs digging deep into his hide.

*   *   *   *

And what of Joshua?

When Merrill put him in the stocks and tightened the heavy locks around his neck, wrists, and ankles, it was as if he was in a dream. He felt no pain at all. There was only darkness in his mind, without memory or fear of what was happening to him.

But it was different when others discovered him as the sun rose over Cold River and the people of Randall's Bow began their day. One-by-one, they gathered. And as the rays of the early morning sun reached the village green, the pain returned to Joshua's limbs and joints stronger than ever. Then, at last, a numbness began to seep through his body, giving him a strange kind of relief in another kind of pain, until he fell into a shallow sleep. He was barely conscious of anything around him except the rough wood of the stocks pressing down on his frail and trembling body.

Merrill's words had no meaning for Joshua as he spoke to the people of Randall's Bow. He felt the warmth of Leyla's hands as she held him and he took comfort from her voice as she whispered softly to him. Everything will be alright, she told him, and Merrill would let him go soon, and he would be in his warm bed at Eleanor's. He would be safe there. She would see to that. Old Man and he would return to the forest soon, she told him, and all that had happened here would seem like a bad dream, soon to be forgotten. She would come to visit them, Leyla whispered to him, and he could show her the cave that he and Old Man loved so much, and she would taste the sweetness of the vegetables from their wonderful garden and drink Goat's rich milk. And Joshua believed her, because she would never speak words that weren't the truth.

Then Leyla's warmth was suddenly gone, and Joshua was left alone. He slowly turned his head and saw those who had remained to mock and ridicule him, and he couldn't understand the meaning of what they were saying, nor why they said such things to him.

A child, he heard them say. He is but a child—as if to be a child was a bad thing, a thing to be reviled and driven away. What was his crime? What had he done? Was being a child the thing he had done that was so wrong that he should be imprisoned here and tortured in front of everyone, so they could bear witness to the justice being done and contribute painful reproaches of their own?

Joshua lowered his head again and rested his neck and chin on the stocks. The rough wood rubbed against him, making raw sores on his neck, wrists, and ankles. Darkness came upon him then. He felt his thirst for just a moment and then was lifted out of his pain and into the sweet relief of unconsciousness.

Throughout the day, some looked at Joshua in scorn, others in confusion. Some laughed at him while others wept. Still others sighed and looked away and said that it had nothing to do with them and was of no concern. None of those who came to look realized that they looked upon a child who was like themselves, and he was innocent.

Joshua was awakened when Old Man, Eleanor, and Leyla brought water to him. He took what they offered, then slipped back again into a dreamless sleep. They gave him words of comfort, but his ears were closed to them. He stayed within the dreamless sleep, without pain or feeling of any kind.

Just before darkness fell, a boy walked to the edge of the village green and hesitated there for a moment—then began to slowly approach the stocks. He stopped after taking several steps, turned and ran back down the path that led to his father's manor.

And in his stall, The Great Black War Horse waited. He stood without moving, looking out the stable doors in the direction of the village green. His ears were pointed forward as he snorted the hot breath of battle and pawed the ground. Then he whinnied softly, knowing that the one to whom he spoke had heard.

*　*　*　*

"You have been to the village green!" Merrill was waiting on the manor steps as Jude came through the gates and across the courtyard.

"Joshua has done nothing wrong, father." Jude walked past Merrill and into the manor without stopping. His eyes were red and swollen. What frightened him most was his own powerlessness. There was nothing he could do to help Joshua or his father or anyone. And most of all, there was nothing he could do to help himself.

Old Man had come to the manor earlier in the day, and Jude had hidden in a corner of the Great Hall and listened while he pleaded with Merrill to let Joshua go. He promised that they would return to their home in the forest ay once.

"Joshua has done only good here," Old Man told Merrill. "Somehow, he has brought healing to this place. No one is dying now and the fever has gone. What does it matter where the healing came from? There is no harm done here—only good. The true nature of Joshua is unknown to me. Why his body is like one who has many years, and yet is only a child, is a mystery to me. I have raised him as my own. He is a son to me, as Jude is a son to you. You found Jude abandoned on your doorstep, just as I found Joshua abandoned in the forest, not even an hour after he was born. Merrill, I beg of you—look upon the little one who is imprisoned in the stocks and know that there is only goodness in his heart. There is power within him, yes—I don't know what it is. Sometimes it frightens me, as

I believe it frightens you. But its fruits are only a gentle good. There are many here who have been spared death because of it. I ask you for your mercy in something that none of us can understand. Release Joshua from the stocks and let us go back to our home in the forest. We will never return. Please, Merrill—release him. Let us go home."

When Old Man had finished, Merrill, who sat and listened without expression to everything he said, rose from his chair and left the Great Hall without saying a word.

Old Man looked up at the portrait of Randall and Judith above the fireplace. "Would that you were here, Randall," he said, "so that your wisdom could deliver us from the madness of your son." Then he turned and left the Great Hall, He had done all he could do. For now.

And in a far corner of the Great Hall, Jude crawled from behind the large chest where he had hidden and watched Old Man as he walked across the courtyard and through the manor gates. When Old Man was out of sight, Jude ran to Merrill's private quarters. He would speak to his father about Joshua, and Merrill would listen to him and know that he was right, and he would let Joshua go. Jude knew he would—and then everything would be alright again is Randall's Bow. There could be no doubt about that, because his father was a good man.

His father was Randall's son.

*   *   *   *

Jude opened the door that led to the part of the manor that Merrill had claimed as his own private quarters. Entrance was granted only with Merrill's permission. Jude was the only exception. He was allowed to come and go as he pleased. Even Randall had been required to knock and wait before being granted entrance, and it was a rule he never violated.

Jude walked down the long, narrow hallway that opened into a large room with windows along one wall that looked out over the courtyard and the stable. Merrill sat in front of the fireplace, looking into the flames. He held a tankard of ale in one hand and a wooden carving of a young boy in the other. Randall had given the carving to him on his twelfth birthday, along with a horse that was full-grown and had yet to be broken. Merrill was to break the horse himself, Randall had told him, for he was a man now and he must mold his mount to suit his own desires. The carving had come from the wood of the first tree Randall had felled along the river when he first came upon the place that would soon bear his name. It was a likeness of Merrill, his father told him, so that he might look at it in times to come and remember the day he had become a man.

Merrill looked at the likeness of his own young face that Randall had carved and was startled at how much it resembled Jude. He had never noticed how alike he and his son looked. Jude was the same age now that he had been when Randall carved his likeness into the wood, and if he had been told that the figure was of Jude, he would have believed it.

"Father." Merrill looked up in surprise as Jude walked into the room. He was not pleased to see his son at that moment. He wanted this thing with Joshua to be done with, and he wanted him and Old Man gone from Randall's Bow. By exile or by death, it made no difference to him.

He looked again at the carving. How was it possible? Jude and Joshua are the same age, really—his son and that strange one who has come out of the forest and has changed his life and the lives of all who live here. I will have him gone. He will be rid of him. He will find a way and it will be soon. Merrill looked up at Jude, who was standing silently in front of him. "What do you want?" Merrill asked. He made no effort to conceal his annoyance at Jude's intrusion.

"Joshua, father. He's done nothing wrong. What's wrong with being a child? He's a child—like me."

Merrill was in no mood to discuss the matter. "Jude, you cannot understand. Leave me now." Shannon had come to the manor earlier in the day, and Merrill had refused to see him. Shannon wanted absolution from all responsibility in this matter, and he would not get it. He wouldn't give Shannon the chance to deny his part in what had happened and he wouldn't give Jude the chance to accuse him of something that had elements in it a boy couldn't understand.

"But father...." Jude's voice was trembling now. His father must listen to him. He must.

"No. Leave me now. Your presence here displeases me." The coldness in Merrill's voice cut through Jude and pierced his heart with its cruelty. His father had never talked to him like that before.

"I'll go, father," Jude said, holding Merrill's eyes with a look direct and unflinching. "But I will do something. I will—and Grandfather would have done something, too. I know he would have."

Merrill watched Jude turn his back on him and leave the room. He stood and walked to the windows that looked out over the courtyard. The stable doors were open and he could see Rashan working just inside. "What would you have done, father, if this burden was yours to bear?" he asked out loud, looking at the storm clouds gathering above him like an omen of things to come. "What would you tell me if you could give me your counsel now—and if I could hear you?"

Merrill listened, but the only sound he heard was the echoing of the hooves of The Great Black War Horse pounding against his stall. He shivered with a sudden chill, then returned to his chair before the fire to warm the cold that chilled him to his bones.

*　*　*　*

Thunder pounded against the midnight sky as Jude awoke with screaming in his ears. Was it his own? Or was it Joshua he heard? He didn't know because his dream had been about both of them. He looked out the window as lightening forked down near the manor and sent a tree crashing through the gates and into the courtyard, its wounded trunk charred and smoking on the cobblestones. Rain came down in torrents through the blackness of the night.

"Joshua!" Jude's scream was drowned out by another crash of thunder as lightening made the courtyard light as day. He got out of bed and went to the window. The courtyard was like a river as water rushed across the cobblestones, creating small rapids of whitewater as it hit fallen trees and branches.

Jude dressed quickly and took the blanket from his bed, rolling it as tightly as he could. He held the blanket against his chest, left his room and went quietly down the stairs to the main floor of the manor. He stopped next to the heavy doors of the Great Hall and looked at the suit of armor standing like a gleaming metal sentry. A blood-red plume was on the helmet, anda long white scarf was tied to the lance that stood by the armor's side. This was the armor worn by Randall when he rode into battle for the last time. He had placed it there for all who came into the Great Hall to see, that they would be reminded he was once a man of war. He wanted them to remember he was a warrior to be reckoned with, he said, so they wouldn't be deceived by his peaceful ways and mistake them for weakness.

The scarf was Judith's. Randall had tied it there himself, so all might know he was now a man of peace in his heart, not merely in word or action—for a woman such as Judith wouldn't be with him if that wasn't his truth. When he was on his deathbed, Randall had asked that the armor and the lance remain there so that he and Judith wouldn't be forgotten. He wanted everyone to remember the two who gave so much to this place upon Cold River.

Randall would not have permitted what was happening now to happen. Jude was sure of that. Joshua would be safe now if Randall was alive. Jude would go to Joshua now. Old Man, Eleanor, and Leyla were prisoners somewhere in the manor, confined by Merrill for the night, so they could do nothing. But he could. He would go to the village green and be with Joshua and he would stay with him until the morning so Joshua wouldn't be alone on this terrible night.

Jude slipped quietly out of the manor and ran across the flooded courtyard, water splashing almost to his knees, then out the manor gates and down the path that would take him to Joshua. He crossed the dirt road that circled the green, now turned into a small river of mud. He looked through the unrelenting sheets of rain that pounded against his face, trying to locate the stocks but saw only a watery blur. Then his feet broke free of the mud and touched grass. He ran toward the place where he thought the stocks would be. Jude's feet went out from under him on the slippery, water-soaked grass and he fell to the ground, sliding on the grass that was completely covered with water. It was as if the village green had become the bottom of a small lake in the center of Randall's Bow. Jude got to his feet, still holding the rolled-up blanket tightly against his chest, and for a moment, disoriented by the fall, he didn't know which way to go. He tried to locate the stocks, but he had no idea where the center of the village green was.

"Joshua! Joshua!" Jude's voice was thrown back at him by the wind and rain as thunder rolled across the sky. Lightning forked down in front of him, lighting up the village green as if it was the middle of a sunny day. There in front of him, only a short distance away, were the stocks, holding Joshua's limp body. He ran to the stocks and lifted Joshua's head in his hands so he could see his face. "Joshua! Joshua! It's Jude! I've come to be with you. Look! I've brought a blanket. It will cover us against the rain!"

Joshua slowly opened his eyes and looked at Jude through the water pouring down his face. Was this real, or was he in a dream? Was all of this just a horrible dream, like the one he and Old Man had walked in when they learned they would go to Randall's Bow? It was as if his senses had been taken from him and he couldn't focus on anything that was happening around him. He didn't even feel the coldness of the rain anymore. His body was numb as the rain beat down upon him, and he had fallen into a blackness without dreams. He looked at Jude as he unrolled the blanket, then smiled as he put the blanket over the stocks and crept under it with him.

"The blanket is wet, Joshua. I'm sorry," Jude said. "But I'll stay here with you and protect you. And you will protect me, too. We are children. You and I are children."

Lightning forked down again. Jude and Joshua looked into each other's eyes and sew each other's pain. And something else. Yes. They could not name it, but they knew that they were the same, somehow. They were one—and there was no threat nor danger that could harm them now. They knew that they were safe here together on the village green, as the rain pounded down and lightning flashed around them. They were safe, and there was no need to worry now.

Jude rested his head next to Joshua's and gently held his hand in his. The two children fell into a sleep of innocence there together, as the storm raged around them.

And in his stall, The Great Black War Horse snorted into the wet air and tossed his noble head in a challenge toward the manor. But the one he meant the challenge for did not come forth to meet him. The stallion was not destined to taste the combat he longed for until another time. A time that was soon to come.

*   *   *   *

Merrill slumped in a drunken sleep in his quarters before a fire long grown cold, an empty tankard on the floor beside him, where it had fallen from his hand.

"Merrill! Merrill!"

Merrill awoke to the sound of someone pounding on his door. His head ached and he felt a pain behind his eyes as he looked at the early morning grayness and the rain hitting the windows like thrown pebbles. Was it Shannon's voice he heard? He had nothing to say to Shannon and he wasn't disposed to welcome him here at the manor under any circumstances. Shannon's intentions would surely be self-serving and he didn't have the patience to hear whatever it was he had to say. He stumbled over the empty tankard as he struggled out of his chair and headed for the door. His body was stiff and sore, and he felt the lingering unpleasantness of disturbing dreams that he could remember only vaguely.

"Merrill! Wake up! Come quickly!"

"Hold your noise, Shannon! Hold your noise! I'm coming!" The anger in Merrill's voice brought silence, and the pounding abruptly stopped. Merrill opened the door and found Shannon holding Jude in his arms. His son looked as if he was dead, and both he and Shannon were soaked through to the skin.

Merrill was unable to comprehend what he saw. He was paralyzed with fear, and nausea clawed at his stomach. What was left of last night's ale rose in his throat. "What happened? What are you doing with my son?" He stepped toward Shannon and took Jude in his arms. Jude's head hung limply, his rain-soaked body cold and unfeeling. "What happened to my son?" Merrill's voice rang through the manor. He carried Jude into his quarters and put him on a small couch near the fireplace. "Tell me what happened while I build a build a fire," he said to Shannon, who had followed after him in silence.

Shannon covered Jude with a blanket that lay nearby as he watched Merrill build a fire with trembling hands. "Jude was with Joshua," he said. "I found him at the stocks, beneath a blanket he had covered the two of them with to protect them against the storm. He must have gone there sometime during the night to try and help Joshua. There was a terrible storm last night—the river overflowed its banks in some places and turned the village green into a small lake. Didn't you hear it?"

"Go on," Merrill said, without answering Shannon's question. Flames began to build beneath the kindling in the fireplace, sending a little heat into the cold room.

"Early this morning, a little before dawn, I went to the village green. The rains were very heavy, heavier than I had ever seen them, and there was lightning. Trees were falling everywhere and I was afraid for Joshua, that he couldn't survive such a storm. Merrill, I fear your wrath, but Joshua doesn't deserve what you're doing to him. He's so frail—he'll die from the wet and cold out there. I couldn't stay away. I couldn't leave him alone there any longer. I don't know what it was that I thought I could do, but I had to go to him so he wouldn't be alone. I knew that you had confined the others and they couldn't go to him. How they must have suffered with that. And so I went."

Is he listening to me, Shannon wondered as he watched Merrill poke at the burning logs with the point of his sword? He seemed completely unaware of the urgency of what Shannon was telling him—that Joshua's life was at stake. He would die if he wasn't released from the stocks at once.

"I took a lantern, but when I got there I couldn't see anything," Shannon continued. "The wind was very strong and the lantern couldn't stand against it and went out. I stood at the edge of the village green but couldn't see the stocks, and Joshua didn't answer my call. After a while, I couldn't even tell where I was and so I waited for the light. As dawn approached I saw a form appear where I thought the stocks should be, but the shape was different. As I got closer, I saw they had been covered with a blanket, and when I removed it, I found Jude there with Joshua. I thought they were asleep, but when I tried to awaken them, I couldn't. I brought Jude here, and I beg you to release Joshua. Let me bring him here, Merrill, so he can be cared for. Please, Merrill. Release the child. He can do no harm and he is near death. I have no doubt of that."

* * * *

Merrill stood at the edge of the village green and looked at the stocks. He could barely see Joshua, his unmoving form slumped over the rain=soaked wood. His eyes went to Randall's grave and he moved slowly toward it as if it was a living thing that would harm him if given the chance. When he reached the grave, he fell to his knees and clawed at the dirt, now an oozing mound of mud.

"My son is yours now!" he shouted. "You've taken him from me. It's you he loves, not me! I will honor his wish and bring you back from the dead!"

Lightning hit the ground nearby, its shock waves throwing Merrill off balance, He fell into the mud as thunder rolled across the sky in deafening intervals, jolting Joshua awake. Joshua looked at Merrill through bleary, half-closed eyes, unable to comprehend what was happening. Lightning struck again, revealing a large wolf trotting toward them from the edge of the forest and coming to a stop next to Joshua. He looked at Merrill, snarled through bared teeth, his ears laid back and half-crouched as if ready to strike.

"Father!" Merrill screamed, clawing frantically at the mud. "Help me, father! Help me save my son!" Eleanor, Old Man, and Leyla, released by Merrill before he left the manor, ran to his side. "Your answer isn't there, Merrill," Leyla told him, kneeling at his side. She pointed to Joshua. "Your answer is there!"

Merrill lifted his head and looked where Leyla was pointing.

"No!"

"Joshua is our only hope, Merrill. There's nothing left. There's nothing any of us can do. Without Joshua's help, Jude will die."

Merrill crawled through the mud toward the stocks. The wolf crouched lower, his eyes a blazing yellow now, his growl low and menacing. He began to advance toward Merrill.

Merrill struggled to his feet, but instead of going closer to the stocks, he ran across the village green to a church that was boarded up when the people lost all hope that the fever would be defeated. He threw himself against the locked doors, then slumped to the ground.

"Take me, if you must take someone, but please, please spare my son," he whispered against the wet wood. Merrill looked at the sky. "Please," he moaned. "Please." Then all was silent. He looked across the village green at Joshua. Leyla was kneeling beside him, cradling his head in her arms. He began to crawl towards Joshua. "Please. My son is dying. Can you save him?"

The wolf moved around the stocks and faced Merrill, blocking his way to the stocks. He was ready to strike if Merrill came any closer.

Seemingly from out of nowhere, Old Man stepped between Merrill and the wolf. He turned to the wolf and patted him gently on the head, then knelt and lookd into the wolf's eyes. "You've done well, old friend," he whispered. "It's over now. Joshua is going home. You've traveled far and must be tired. Rest awhile by the river, then return to your home near our cave. Your work here is done."

The wolf trotted to the stocks, looked at Joshua for a moment, uttered a gentle growl-whine in greeting, then trotted to the edge of the village green. He turned and gave a last, lingering look at Joshua, then disappeared down the path toward the river.

Chapter 33

Merrill stood by Jude's bedside with Joshua in his arms. "Jude. Jude. Joshua is here. I've brought Joshua to be with you. It's alright now, Jude. Joshua is here with you." Jude lay beneath the blanket as still as if death had already claimed him. For a moment, it seemed as if he had stopped breathing. He suddenly gasped, opened his eyes and looked at Merrill and Joshua, then sank into a deep sleep once more.

"Jude...Jude." Merrill tried to reawaken him, but Jude didn't respond.

Leyla put her hand on Jude's forehead. "He's burning up with fever," she said. She took a cloth and wet it with water from a kettle nearby that Eleanor had brought from the kitchen and pressed it to Jude's parched lips. "Jude," she whispered. "You are such perfect children, you and Joshua. You are both so beautiful." But Jude didn't hear her.

Eleanor knelt beside her, holding a cup of hot broth. Leyla lifted Jude's head while Eleanor held the cup to his lips, but the broth couldn't tempt him to consciousness. His body shook with chills as he fought for every breath.

"What is it, Eleanor? What's wrong with him"?" But Merrill knew what Eleanor's answer would be before she spoke.

"It's the fever, Merrill." Eleanor's voice could barely be heard—her answer was barely a whisper. "It's the fever," she said again through her tears. "Jude.

Jude," she pleaded, holding the cup of broth to his lips. "Drink, now. Just a little bit. Just one little sip. And look, Jude. Joshua is here with you."

But Jude did not answer.

*   *   *   *

"In there. I'll stay with Jude. Leyla will go with you.." Eleanor pointed to a half-opened door as Merrill left Jude's room with Joshua in his arms. He put Joshua on the bed, his thin chest barely moving through his rain-soaked clothes. Short, gasping breaths and an occasional rasping cough were his only signs of life. "Treat him as if he is my son," Merrill said softly to Leyla, then returned to Jude, kneeling by his side and taking his hand in his.

"Go to Joshua now," he said to Eleanor. "I told Leyla to treat him as if he is my son and I say the same to you."

Eleanor hurried into the room where Joshua lay and looked down at his still form. "Quickly—remove his clothes," she said. There was something different here—something she was unfamiliar with—and it frightened her. "And then we shall see." She put her hand on Joshua's forehead. "Yes. Then we shall see."

Leyla began to remove Joshua's wet clothing. His frail body quivered at the first touch, and then became still once more.

Eleanor touched Joshua's forehead again. "This is not the fever," she said. She looked at Old Man, who had been standing in the corner, strangely quiet and keeping his distance as the two women administered to Joshua. "Yes." she said to him, a touch of anger in her voice. "This is something different." She returned her attention to Leyla. "Quickly now— we must make him warm. Put him under the blankets. I'll warm some stones for him and Jude, and then we'll see." She bent close to Joshua and felt his forehead again. There was no fever. She shook her head, puzzled by what she saw—or didn't see—then hurried to the kitchen to heat stones to keep the beds warm beneath the blankets.

When she returned, Merrill was at Joshua's bedside, looking down at him. "Will the fever take him, too?" he asked. "Or does he have enough strength to fight it?"

Eleanor put a warm stone under the blanket near Joshua's feet. "I have done the same for Jude," she said. "It wall help him awaken.. But Joshua— it's not the fever." She looked at Old Man again, who hadn't moved from the corner of the room. "I haven't seen anything like this before. Is this the first time he's been like this?"

"Not in this way," Old Man's answer came in a voice that trembled with the anticipation of tragic news. This was new to him, and he was very much afraid, expecting the worst. "There have been times when he has seemed more frail than others, but he would stay awake and we would talk and then, at night, he would fall into a peaceful sleep. But this is different—this is not what I have seen before. Sometimes in the forest a sickness would suddenly come upon him. It wasn't the fever, although sometimes he would be burning up with fever. But it was different that the fever that was here. It seemed to be a part of him, and when it left we knew that it would return again. It was different than what we see here. The stocks, the storm, the unjust punishment...."

Merrill knelt close to Joshua. "What can we do?" he asked. "Will Eleanor's medicine help? Will it help him as it did the others?" After a long pause, he whispered. "I would give my own life if I could undo what I have done."

Eleanor touched Merrill gently on his cheek, as if he was a hurt child once more. "It wasn't my medicine. It was Joshua who somehow helped them heal themselves. There's nothing we can do but keep him warm and wait and see what tomorrow brings."

The night was long as they watched Jude suffer through it. His fever rose then suddenly fell, and toward morning he began to convulse. He opened his eyes for a moment during the night and looked at his father. "It hurts so much," he said, then fell into a fitful sleep once more.

Eleanor forced a little of the potion between Jude's lips, hoping that it would ease his pain. If only for a little while, but she knew that it was no use. They were as helpless now as when the fever had taken Randall: And they were helpless with Joshua, too. There was no way to tell the nature of his sickness and he couldn't awaken to tell them.

Another day passed and Jude's breathing became more and more labored. He was awake for short periods of time now, but there was no hope in that. His joints were swollen and he suffered without relief. They knew that if things continued in this way, Jude would soon be in the final stages of the fever. He would last for another day—possibly two. One of the times when he was awake, he asked for Joshua. Merrill assured him that Joshua was safe and that he had been freed from the stocks.

"I want to see him, father."

"Joshua will come to you soon," Merrill answered, avoiding Jude's eyes. "He is resting now, but he will come to you soon. And now you must rest, too, so that when he's here you will be strong enough to talk to him for a little while."

"Will you punish him again?'

"No, Jude. No. I won't punish anyone ever again. I promise you. Now rest. Joshua will come to you soon, but you must rest now."

Merrill stood up and looked at Leyla. "Stay with him." he said and left the room. He entered Joshua's room, where Old Man, Eleanor, and Shannon were gathered at his bedside with smiles of surprises on their faces. Joshua's eyes were open. "Hello," he said, looking at Merrill and smiling.

Without answering, Merrill looked at the others. "Leave us," he said quietly. He sat down in a chair beside Joshua as they closed the door behind them.

*   *   *   *

Merrill returned Joshua's smile, but it was not a happy smile. It was a smile of sadness and contrition. And hopelessness. Hopelessness because he knew now that what he had done to this little one was unspeakable. And yet he knew that forgiveness shone through in Joshua's smile of greeting. And he knew that he must speak to this little one whom he had punished so cruelly. And so unjustly. This little one who was innocent of any wrong. But what was he to say? What words were there that could say what was really in his heart and would undo what he had done? Joshua had done only good here—he knew that now. What was he to say? That he had acted as best he could? That was not the truth. Rage and grief had possessed him—somewhere he had crossed over into madness and he was unable to return. Or could he have? He didn't want to, truth be told.

"Hello." Merrill was taken from his thoughts when Joshua spoke to him again. The way Joshua looked at him touched him deeply and brought him back to the time he had watched Jude tell Randall that he had decided to be like him—a man of greatness. He would be like his grandfather because that is what he decided. There was sadness in Merrill's heart too as he recalled that day when he and Eleanor watched from a window in the manor. And now he realized that he, too, could have made that same choice. But he had not. And perhaps he could not make it even now.

"Hello, Joshua."

They looked at each other in silence for a moment, and then Joshua tried to sit up a little in the huge bed, but couldn't. Merrill put his arm around Joshua and helped him into a sitting position, propped another feather pillow behind him then sat down again in the chair beside the bed.

"Jude," Joshua whispered. His voice very weak. There was none of his music in it now. "Jude came to me in the storm. I saw him, but I couldn't talk and then I fell asleep. Where is he?"

"Jude asks about you, too, Joshua. I told him that he will see you soon, and so he will."

Merrill fell silent then, and looked toward the closed door. He wished that Leyla was there to help him with what to say next. "There were some you passed by," he said at last.

"Yes."

"Why?" Why some and not others?"

"Some had embraced their deaths already. It was death they welcomed. They would not have welcomed me."

"And you saw this? You knew this?"

"Yes."

"How could you know?"

"I did what I was told to do. From deep inside me. Sometimes I feel very sad about that, but I know there was no other choice."

"Who told you, Joshua"

"A voice that I hear inside of me. In my heart. Inside of me."

"And this voice you hear, Joshua, what does it tell you of me and the thing I have done to you, and the pain I have caused the people here? Would you pass me by, too, Joshua, if you saw me lying on a pallet on the infirmary floor? Would that voice say pass this one by, for he has already embraced his death and he will not welcome you?"

"You have not embraced your death, Merrill. Not yet."

Joshua's words washed over Merrill like clean water from a forest spring, and he smiled through his tears. What power did this strange little one possess? He felt as if a crushing weight had been lifted from him, and for the first time in a long time he felt hope. Hope for what? He didn't know, but it wasn't for anything upon this earth, except for something that might dwell so deeply in his heart that he had never been aware of it. He felt a warmth fill his chest and he reached for Joshua's hand as if he was the child and Joshua was the man who would lead him safely from the darkness.

"And what of my son, Joshua? What of Jude? Would he be one of those you would be told to pass by?" Merrill could hardly breathe now, as he waited for Joshua's answer.

Joshua did not answer Merrill at once, as the whinny of The Great Black War Horse echoed across the courtyard and washed over him with its coolness as a gentle breeze came in through the open window. Joshua and Merrill turned their heads in the direction of the stables and listened together as the stallion's hooves thundered against his stall. He whinnied once again, then all was silent.

After a moment, Joshua turned his attention once more to Merrill. "No, I would not pass Jude by," he said, his voice barely above a whisper.

"Jude has the fever, Joshua. He is very sick. We fear that he will die."

"He will not die, Merrill."

"Can you help him as you did the others? I have done much to harm you Joshua, and you have a sickness, too, though Eleanor says it isn't the fever."

"No, Merrill. It's not the fever. How can I ask you to take what strength you have and use it for my son's good rather than your own after what I've done? But I do, Joshua—I do. I'm asking you to save Jude's life."

"I have never saved a life," Joshua said, smiling. "Those who haven't embraced their death have embraced life, and so they save themselves. I only see them as they really are, and tell them so. That's all I do."

"Will you go to him? Will you let me take you to him so he can see you? That's all I ask. And when you are well, you and Old Man will see your cave in the forest once again. I promise you. Will you let me take you to Jude?"

"Yes."

"He's sleeping now. Sleep is the only relief he gets from his pain. When he awakens, I'll come for you. Now rest, Joshua. I'll leave you now".

Merrill rose from his chair and crossed the room. When he reached the door, he turned back towards Joshua. "You have my father's heart," he said. "I would have had that good fortune to be mine, but there was nothing I could do to will it—I didn't know how." He turned then, and left the room.

Across the courtyard, carried on the wind, came the sound of The Great Black War Horse. It sounded like a child's cry

* * * *

Eleanor stood at the window and looked across the courtyard at the new day's sun coming up over Cold River. The brightness of the morning gave her new hope somehow, and she breathed a long and weary sigh. Would it ever end? There had been too much death, and it was time for it to stop. She prayed that the dying would be finished before the child who lay behind her in the fever's sleep was taken from them. And Joshua—what could be done for him? His sickness was so strange. It was a mystery to her.

"Eleanor...." Jude's voice came faintly and she walked quickly to his bedside. "Yes, Jude," she said, bending close to him, hoping that somehow her strength would become his strength, too.

"Joshua...."

"It will be a little while yet before Joshua can come to you. But he will. I promise. You did well, Jude. You did well when you went to him. It's because you were so brave the he's still alive. You saved Joshua's life, Jude, but he's sick from the rain and can't leave his bed yet. But he'll come to you soon. Soon, Jude. Soon." But, even as she spoke, Jude slipped back into the grips of the sleep that brought him ever closer to his death.

And across the courtyard, The Great Black War Horse stood quietly in his stall, feeding his spirit with memories of Randall, the only one he has ever carried on his mighty back—and of Joshua, whom he would carry from the battle that no one upon this earth can turn away from. It must be fought by all who come here—the final battle of their lives where we surrender all we know and go to meet the Mystery.

* * * *

Merrill sat before the fire in the Great Hall and looked up at the image of his father. As the firelight shimmered across the portrait, it seemed to bring changing, lifelike expressions to the face imprisoned upon the canvas. Randall's hair seemed to move as if caressed by a gentle breeze, while Judith's white silk scarf floated like a dove upon his sword, offering peace to all he looked upon.

In an hour it would be dawn and, as he looked up at his father, Merrill wondered whether his son would see this day through until the sun would set—or if this day would be Jude's last. Sadness gripped his heart and would not let it go. He grieved for both Jude and Joshua, two innocent children who did not deserve the fate that threatened to claim their lives. He grieved for Randall—for the father he had never been and for the father he had finally become. The paradox blanketed his heart with confusion.

But the one for whom he grieved the most—and it seemed so strange to him—was himself, and he couldn't find the reason why. He felt so lost and all alone, and now he knew he had felt this way for all his life. Rage and rebellion had been his escape until his own son came into his life. He gave to Jude, and in this giving, he was giving to himself. He knew that now, as he sat beneath the portrait of Randall that seemed to look down upon him with eyes that still held the light of life. He didn't remember that first year Randall had spent with him, as Judith had made him promise. Eleanor told him about it, but, strangely, he couldn't remember the things she said he and Randall had done together. Rather, his memories began on that day when Randall didn't come to him as he always had—the day that marked the beginning of another year. His world changed on that day. His heart had pounded from the terror of it. And that terror still haunted him in his dreams. Even now, his heart pounded in that way, and it was all for himself.

It seemed that Joshua held the key to all that was precious to him now.. Eleanor said it wasn't the fever that had brought that little one down. No, she said, it was something else—something strange to her that she had never seen before. Joshua had no fear of the fever, nor of those whom it had claimed. Because of that, it would not survive within his body. As fragile as he looked, Eleanor said, Joshua possessed a greater strength than she had seen in any man. And that included Randall. Eleanor had looked directly into Merrill's eyes when she told him that, and he knew her words were the truth.

But Joshua would die from whatever it was that warred within him. Eleanor had no doubt of that. That was the only thing she was certain of—that he would die. That he was dying now. He might not even last as long as Jude.

Merrill had looked in on Joshua before he had come to the Great Hall. He had walked quietly to the bed and looked down at him, hardly visible beneath the blankets. If someone had entered the room and hadn't known that Joshua was there, they would have thought the bed empty. He looked closely at Joshua and, for an instant; it looked as if he wasn't breathing. Panic gripped him as he thought Jude's last hope for life had gone, swiftly and without a sound, as if it had flown out the open window like an imprisoned bird suddenly freed to find another home where it would be more welcome. When he leaned closer, he felt Joshua's hot breath on his cheek. He was alive.

Merrill left the room quickly then, for the memories of the nights he had spent with Randall before he died were too painful for him to bear, and it frightened him because he couldn't remember everything that had happened there. He remembered standing next to Randal's body holding his sword in his trembling hands, but he couldn't remember how blood came to be smeared upon its blade. And he remembered the morning only slightly, when he had entered the stables as if in a trance. He had seen the marks of whip and sword upon the hide of The Great Black War Horse as blood dripped upon the straw and he knew he had put them there. But he didn't know why, nor did he remember doing it.

And now he sat alone and watched the sun rise outside the windows of the Great Hall. He would go to Jude now and sit by him until he awakened—and he would bring Joshua to him. He would wait no longer. There was nothing else he could do. There was no power in him that could undo what he had done.

Then Merrill wept, alone with his sadness and his grief, beneath the impassive eyes of Randall and Judith hanging high above him.

* * * *

Merrill sat in the straight-backed wooden chair next to Jude's bed, while Leyla slept nearby in a large, cushioned chair next to the window, her long black hair shining in the early morning light. He looked at Jude's face, flushed with fever, and put his hand on his forehead. Jude stirred and made a little crying sound when he felt his father's touch. There had been no change from the night before. Eleanor had told him that the fever must break during the night or sometime today before the sun sets, or all hope that Jude would survive must be abandoned. His body couldn't endure much more of the fever's onslaught before it began to collapse.

Merrill looked again at Leyla and was stricken by her beauty. He remembered how she looked as he had watched from a darkened corner of the infirmary when she and Joshua walked among the sick. Sometimes she had knelt next to one of those whom Joshua passed by and had raised a cup of cool water to their cracked lips. She would hold their hand for a moment and give them a word of comfort before continuing on behind Joshua. It seemed that she was a mother to them all then—to the sick and to those who were there to do whatever they could to ease the pain of the dying.

Leyla stirred in her sleep, then opened her eyes and looked at Jude. She closed her eyes again for a moment, holding her breath and listening. Something was different in the room. Something was there that had not been there before.

"Oh!" she said with a start, opening her eyes again and looking at Merrill. "I was so tired—how long have you been here?" She rose quickly from the chair and sat on the bed next to Jude. "Is he alright?" she asked. "Has anything happened?" Merrill's presence in the room without her knowing when he arrived frightened her.

"No. Nothing has changed." Merrill spoke softly and Leyla looked at him, confused at his demeanor. It was as if his concern was for her at this moment, and not for Jude. "I'm going to see how Joshua is feeling," she said, walking to the door. "If Jude wakes up, come and tell me at once."

"Leyla." Merrill's voice brought her to a stop. She turned and faced him, holding her hands together in front of her to keep them from shaking. Her face was white and drawn.

"What?'

"You are very tired. Thank you for what you are doing for Jude. And for Joshua. I want you to know that I deeply regret, more than I could ever say, what I have done. I…."He began to say more, but no words would come.

"I know, Merrill. And yes, I am very tired. We all are. But now we must do all we can for these two precious children who are so near death.

That's the only thing that must concern us now until whatever is going to happen, happens." With those words, so final and so true, she hurried out the door.

After a few moments, Leyla came back into Jude's room. "He's asleep. He looks so peaceful. Perhaps we still have time."

*   *   *   *

Joshua lay under the blanket without pain now. The sun's first rays coming in the window across the room reminded him of the times in the forest when he walked from the cave to see the sun's first light bathe the clearing in its warmth.

Although there is no pain now, Joshua's heart is gripped with fear. A new lesson is coming to him soon and the unknown of that lesson has made his anxiety so great that he feels as if he cannot bear it any longer. Old Man can't help him because he, too, is afraid, and it seems as if Old Man knows something about what the lesson will be. But he won't talk about it. And Eleanor and Leyla, too. They seem to know something that he doesn't, and their secret makes him sad and afraid. If only he could see Jude. If only he could talk to him. Perhaps the answer is there. Joshua closed his eyes and felt the sun's warm rays come through the window to cross his bed.

Suddenly, Joshua's fear was lifted—gone as if it had never existed as the warmth spread throughout his body. His mind was clear and his body felt as if it was floating above the bed. It was as if he had no weight and was made of the air itself. And then he knew. It would be like this when The Great Black War Horse carried him home. And there would be light and he would know all there was to know, for he would be all there was for him to be.

He would sleep now. He would awaken when it was time.

And in the stables across the courtyard, The Great Black War Horse stood unmoving in his stall. There is no snort or whinny now, no flash of hoof or toss of head—for only silence has words for what is soon to pass.

*   *   *   *

No words would pass between these two, for perfection needs no words. It need only be, and that is all. These two—the one named Joshua, the other, Jude—are the children of the world, perfect in their beauty and in their brokenness.

Old Man stood in a corner near the door watching the two children and felt the peacefulness of the forest fill his heart once more. Oh, he had missed it so! It was gone forever—he had been certain of that in recent days. He had talked to Goat about the joy they had felt in their forest home as she had given him her sweet milk each day as the morning sun warmed them both. And then again as evening came, and the sun disappeared over the trees, announcing the end of another day. He would tell Goat of his sadness and confusion because the little one he loved so much was disappearing from this place too, like the setting sun—in silence, sinking slowly from the earth. Oh, Joshua. My little Joshua, he sighed as he gently pulled upon Goat's full udder and watched her sweetness fill the wooden bucket between his knees. There was no more that he could say or do but that. And now he stood and watched as Joshua and Jude sat together in the light that surrounded them.

Jude sat propped up on his bed by feather pillows. Merrill had carried Joshua to the large, soft chair Leyla had slept in the night before. He had put Joshua down like a gentle, loving mother, his movements were so filled with tenderness and care. Both of the children were covered with fresh, warm blankets and a fire burned brightly in the fireplace nearby. The sweet smell of soft pine filled the room and there were little popping sounds as the flames licked at the sap running freely from the burning logs.

Leyla and Eleanor stood next to Old Man and watched Merrill as he knelt for a moment between Joshua and Jude, holding a hand of each in his. He looked from one to the other, then stood and left the room in silence. The others followed after him as if he had commanded them to do so. No words had been spoken since Merrill had carried Joshua into the room. Leyla was the last to leave, closing the door softly behind her. Their leaving was not noticed by either of the children.

*   *   *   *

The children are alone now. The fire enfolds them with a gentle light that protects them from the world. The aroma of burning pine is like a sacred incense before the altar of their perfection. The only sound that can be heard is the whinny of The Great Black War Horse as it crosses the courtyard on a warm and gentle wind.

Chapter 34

The moon is high and full as Joshua looks out the window from beneath his blankets. He's back in his own bed where Merrill carried him from Jude's room just as the sun was setting.

He had fallen asleep for a while and then had eaten a little of the supper Leyla brought to him. She sat at the foot of the bed while he ate, assuring him that he and Jude would be well soon and that the three of them would have a picnic on the river to celebrate. Joshua had little appetite because the pain had returned after he left Jude. He was glad when Leyla finally left so he didn't have to hide how he really felt.

Old Man came into the room a little while later and they talked of their time in the forest together—the peace and happiness they had known there not so very long ago and would know soon again.

After Old Man left, Leyla returned. "Sleep now," she said. "You must be strong when Jude and I come to visit you in the forest so you can show us the beauty of your home there." She kissed him on the cheek, pulled the blankets snugly around him and left.

Old Man sat quietly for a while, waiting for Joshua to fall asleep. Joshua closed his eyes at last and his breathing, though very weak and shallow now, came at regular intervals. He felt the coolness of Joshua's forehead and was satisfied that he would be safe during the night. He would come back at morning's first light and resume his vigil. Joshua would be well—he was certain of that—and when he was strong enough, they would return to the forest where they belonged. They would be rid of this place forever.

Old Man left the room, quietly closing the door behind him. He would rest a while and try to sleep. They would be home soon, and his heart was warm with knowing that.

* * * *

And now Joshua watches the midnight moon rise high above the courtyard outside his window. There is a fullness in his chest and he feels as if he will burst from the joy of it. Jude will be well and strong again—their inner voices told them so. When they sat together that afternoon, they had embraced the life that was in their hearts and, through the strength of both of them, that life embraced itself. The sickness that held Jude prisoner fell away. Both of them felt it—they had known the instant the fever left Jude's body and they smiled at each other in silent joy.

Jude looked at Joshua then, and his eyes said "Now we will do the same for you." He held his breath and looked into Joshua's eyes and waited for their hearts to join as one. Together, they would defeat the enemy that lived within the broken body of his friend—they would chase it away forever, just as they had done with him. They would play together soon on the village green where they had come together to do battle against a force that was too strong for one of them alone, but would crumble before their oneness.

As Jude focused his newfound strength upon him and waited for their joining, Joshua saw Jude's eyes fill with tears as he received the silent message that came to him. No. It cannot be for me as it is for you, Jude. It cannot be and, in truth, I do not want it so, for there is a voice that calls me home, and I must go. But I will be with you, Jude, and I will talk to you and you will hear. You will hear me and you will do great work upon this earth, for that is why you have come. That is your purpose, for you will become as great a man as Randall was, as is your wish. And more, Jude, more. You will be an even greater man than Randall in years to come, and we will talk together, you and I, as you ride to your greatness upon the back of The Great Black War Horse and his son, who is yet to come. But it cannot be as you wish it now. It cannot be.

Jude's eyes closed then, and he fell into a deep and healing sleep.

Merrill came into the room and looked down upon his son, at peace for the first time in what seemed to him a lifetime. He took Joshua in his arms and held him close as he returned him to his bed. He laid Joshua down, covered him with warm blankets and kissed him on his forehead. "As is Jude, Joshua, so are you my son," Merrill said. "And you will be my son from this day forward. This I swear to you. On my father's honor and upon Jude's life, I swear to you that I will keep you safe from harm forever."

And now the midnight moon is high above the stables as Joshua rises slowly from his bed and wraps a blanket around him against the coolness of the night. The joy that fills his heart is greater than any he has ever felt—greater even than the joy he felt with Old Man when they worked in their garden in the forest, the morning sun warming their backs. Quietly, he moves past Jude's room, then down the stairs until he comes to the heavy doors of the manor. He pushes against them with all his remaining strength and then stands quietly, listening to see if the groaning of the hinges has awakened those who sleep above him. Only silence comes from the floor above. He walks through the open doors and down the steps of the manor to the courtyard, Then in the direction of the stables, the moon guiding his way.

He enters the stables and stands just inside the doors, looking into the darkness. A soft whinny comes from the far end of the stables, and Joshua follows it to the stall of The Great Black War Horse. He is going home at last.

*   *   *   *

The Great Black War Horse steps aside when the innocent of innocents enters his stall. He stands unmoving as Joshua creeps beneath his belly into the farthest corner and lays down in the darkness on the fresh straw Rashan had spread there before he left the stable to watch the sun set over the river.

Joshua wraps his blanket tightly around him and breathes a breath that surprises him with its depth. His breath had come in little shallow gasps when he left Jude's room only a few hours before, and his ribs had pained him as they strained to help him pull the air he needed into his lungs. When he crossed the courtyard only moments before, he had felt faint from the effort and feared that he would collapse upon the cobblestones before he reached the one who called to him from his stall.

Joshua breathes in the sweetness of the straw and pulls the blanket tighter around him. Though the night is warm, he feels so very cold. He can see the golden fullness of the moon beyond the open stable doors, its light casting in silhouette the form of The Great Black War Horse standing above him. The stallion whinnies softly and turns facing the night so that his great body blocks the front of the open stall. He tosses his head and snorts at the moon, then turns and gently brushes Joshua's cheek with his wet muzzle. He turns and faces the moon once more, and stands unmoving in the night.

The Great Black War Horse is ready now to do what he was born to do. He will carry this little one—this innocent of innocents—beyond the stars to safety and to peace. And he will bring him back again when it is time for that. But now, they will fly together above this earthly battlefield to the end of time.

And so The Great Black War Horse stands with spirit wings extended, and feels the weightless presence of innocence upon his mighty back. This is the rider he was born to bear. And the battle they will win this night will be bloodless, without sword, or lance, or battle ax.

They look back only once, these spirit two, and softly breathe farewell to the frail and earthly form still curled there beneath them in the straw. It was on a night like this that he had been placed upon the forest floor beneath the moon and his journey here had begun, to grace this place upon the river with innocence for just a little while.

And then they fly as one to the place where only truth abides, and all else is forgotten as if it never was.

*   *   *   *

The Great Black War Horse was restless in his stall when Rashan walked through the stable doors only seconds behind the light of the day's first rays of the sun coming up over Cold River. He had heard the stallion kicking against his stall when he entered the courtyard. He became aware of the sounds at once, as it was the horse's habit to rest in the early morning, laying on the straw until Rashan turned him out into the rolling meadow reserved for him in back of the stables. He would graze there in contentment, galloping to the river at the far edge of the meadow to quench his thirst.

"What is it?" Rashan asked softly as he approached the stall. "What is it that disturbs you at this early hour?" The stallion stopped his restless movement when he heard the familiar voice that he had learned to trust. This one, he knew, did not mean him harm. This was not the one who, with whip and sword, had scarred his midnight hide for as long as he would live.

The body of The Great Black War Horse blocked the front of his stall as Rashan reached out to touch him gently on his neck before coming closer. The stallion pulled back and wheeled so that he and the stable master faced each other. Rashan let the horse position himself in the center of the stall, still facing him, then stepped forward again. The horse reared up and whinnied loudly—Rashan would have thought it was a human scream had he not known the source. He stepped back. This was not the animal he knew. Something was wrong. The stallion stood in the center of his stall, pawing the ground. He whinnied and snorted again—then looked at Rashan and moved slowly to one side, head up, ears forward.

Rashan knew that The Great Black War Horse wanted something from him—there was something he was commanding him to do. He looked into the stallion's eyes, keeping his focus there without moving. And then, without knowing why—it was something that he suddenly felt compelled to do—he took his eyes from the stallion and looked into the corner at the far end of the stall. There was a formless something there.

He took a step into the stall, then was frozen to the spot. Merrill, he thought. Merrill. What has he done to this noble animal that he hasn't already done? He looked at the stallion's withers and flanks for signs of blood—the hide was clean and shining in the sunlight that now filled the stables, flecks of dust dancing in its golden rays. He looked at the stallion again, then walked slowly into the stall toward whatever it was that lay in the straw. His shoulder brushed against the horse and he felt the animal's heat cover him with a reassuring warmth. Somehow, he knew that he was safe. Whatever it was that awaited him in that darkened corner, it was something he was supposed to find. He felt the stallion's eyes follow him as he approached the crumpled pile.

Rashan thought it was only a blanket that somehow had been dropped near the stall and had become entangled around one of the horse's legs before falling where it now lay. Then, as he examined it more closely, it looked as if there was something wrapped in it. He could see it only dimly, but he was certain now there was something in or under the blanket. He bent and touched it, then quickly drew his hand back and watched the blanket for a sign of movement. When there was none, he took a corner between his fingers and slowly pulled it back. He heard movement behind him and looked over his shoulder. The stallion had turned around and was looking at the blanket over Rashan's shoulder. He nudged Rashan's back with his muzzle, as if to urge him on in the thing that he was about to do.

Slowly, reluctantly, Rashan pulled the corner of the blanket back until he saw the face of Joshua within its folds. His eyes were closed as if he was sleeping. He had a smile on his face as if a dream had brought him back to the peace and joy of his beloved forest once more.

"What are you doing here?" Rashan whispered, gently touching Joshua on the shoulder. "Come. I'll take you to the manor. This is no place for someone who needs protection against the early morning chill."

There was still no movement, and Rashan touched Joshua's shoulder again, this time shaking it gently.. "Joshua, come. I'll take you to the manor." He touched Joshua's cheek, then quickly withdrew his hand from the unexpected coldness of his skin. "Joshua!" he said again, this time louder, as he pulled the blanket back all the way and put both hands upon the still form's cold and lifeless cheeks.

The Great Black War Horse snorted and pawed the ground as Rashan gathered the small bundle in his arms and stood, then stood aside and let him pass.

Rashan didn't know what had happened here last night, but he knew that it was far beyond his understanding—as was the peace he now felt, and the joy within his heart. He paused and looked into the eyes of The Great Black War Horse, then walked slowly through the stable doors toward the steps of the manor with the lifeless body of the innocent of innocents cradled lovingly to his breast.

Chapter 35

Eleanor awakened slowly, and looked at the gray, pre-dawn light outside her window. She lay quietly for a few moments, taking comfort in the warmth of the blankets that covered her. As she enjoyed the early morning quiet, she felt protected somehow from the days that had piled one upon the other without relief from the presence of death that had hung over Randall's Bow for so long. Harvest time was close upon them, and everyone's strength would be needed to bring the crops in from the fields and to make Randall's Bow safe for everyone for the winter.

The days were growing shorter now, and the sun was going down over Panther Mountain, far in the distance, earlier and earlier. It was time for Merrill to step forward and lead the people in the harvest that would take them through the winter and into the new-birth time of spring and ease their memories of the things that had happened here. There was not a person in Randall's Bow whose heart was without scars left in one way or another by the fever and the swath of death it had left behind.

The rooster's crow brought Eleanor from her thoughts, and she looked out the window again to see the day's first rays of the morning's sun. Suddenly, she remembered Jude. She had awakened in the night and gone into his room to put her hand on his forehead to feel the hotness there, and then to put a cool, wet cloth upon him to ease him in his sleep. But instead of fever, she felt a coolness in his skin. She had held the candle close to his face and had cried out when she saw that the flush of fever was no longer there. She felt Jude's forehead again and then saw Merrill sleeping in a chair nearby. There had been healing here, and the father had joined his son in the circle that Joshua had drawn around him—large enough for all who were willing to enter without fear, or guile, or evil in their heart. She had returned to her bed and slept soundly for the first time in many months.

She rose quickly and returned to Jude's room. Had she been dreaming? Or was the memory that was with her now from something real? When she entered the room, Merrill was standing next to Jude, looking down at him and smiling. "It's gone" he said. "The fever is gone. My son isn't going to die." Then he knelt next to Jude, put his head in his hands and wept tears of joy that replaced the despair that had kept him bound as its prisoner since Randall's death.

Awakened by the noise, Leyla hurried into the room, followed by Old Man. "Where is Joshua?" she asked, looking around the room as if she expected to find him there. Her face was drawn and white with fear. "Joshua isn't in his bed. Where is he?"

"Leyla? What's wrong? Has something happened to Joshua?" Jude had awakened and he pushed against Merrill's arms as he struggled to get out of bed.

"No, Jude. Stay in bed. Stay where you are. We'll find him. He can't have gone far." Merrill stood and looked at Old Man. "Come with me," he said and left the room with Old Man following behind him. When they reached the bottom of the stairs, Merrill turned to Old man. "Do you know where he could have gone?" he asked.

Old Man could barely speak—his mind was frozen in confusion. He didn't know what was happening here. Why would Joshua leave the manor? Why would he leave without telling anyone? "Perhaps the forest," he said, but in his heart he knew that Joshua had not gone there without him.

Merrill walked to the manor doors and pushed them open. He started down the steps with Old Man by his side then stopped. They stood on the manor steps together and watched Rashan walking slowly toward them. They did not need to ask the nature of the small bundle that he held gently in his arms. They knew their search for Joshua had ended before it had begun.

When Rashan reached the bottom of the steps, he stopped. He held Joshua's body tighter, as if he did not want to release him to another's care. He began to speak, but no words came. He could only stand and shake his head in disbelief and sadness.

Merrill and Old Man hadn't moved. They looked at Rashan, and only at him. After a few moments, when they had the strength to bear the finality of it, they looked upon the gray and lifeless face of little Joshua, a peaceful smile upon his lips, as if he had been found sleeping in the sun upon the soft, green grass of the river bank and had been carried safely home.

*   *   *   *

There are no stocks on the village green now. Those whose lives have been given back to them by the little one who had been imprisoned there have torn them down, and in their place have dug his grave amidst their sorrow—and shame. The people of Randall's Bow who ring the village green now remember that day not so long ago when they had gathered there and uttered not one word in defense of the innocent of innocents who had been locked within the grinding jaws of the stocks.

They are silent here today too, but now, instead of the voice of madness proclaiming the reason for their presence, they hear the distant beat of a single drum as Joshua's journey from the manor to the village green begins. The flower-lined grave stares unblinking at them in its emptiness—as empty as their hearts feel now. The drum they hear is the drum that had beat cadence as Randall was carried here on his last journey upon this earth, too. And the one who is carried here this day will be laid to rest beside that other one of greatness who had put his name and mark on this place on the banks of Cold River.

As the drummer comes into sight, there is something else that brings them back to the day when Randall had been returned to dust. Behind the drummer, prancing on the dirt as if he danced on air is The Great Black War Horse. And on his back a rider sits, as still as if the stallion and the boy upon his back are one.

This is not to be the way it was before. No. This time there is no blood upon the stallion's gleaming, midnight hide. This time it is by his own desire and design that he carries a rider upon his mighty back. It is the will of The Great Black War Horse that he sent upon the wind to the only one now left upon this earth who will ever sit astride his back again.

Yes. It is Jude who sits astride The Great Black War Horse as if the stallion is his throne and he is king of all that meets his eye—and far beyond. He keeps the reins held firmly to hold the stallion at a pace that meets the cadence of the drum. Jude looks ahead and sees the people circled around the village green, and he remembers the last time he came here and huddled beneath the storm-soaked blanket with Joshua while thunder rolled over them and lightning struck the earth around them. He looks up at the bright blue cloudless sky and feels the sun upon his back, and he gives thanks for The Great Black War Horse prancing beneath him now, bringing him back to the place where sadness would crush him if he had to come here alone. He feels the stallion's strength course through him as the heat from his hide seeps into his body like lifeblood, filling him with more strength than is his own. And as The Great Black War Horse prances toward the village green, Jude feels his own body become one with the horse, and he knows that this mighty one who was bred for war needs him upon his back as much as Jude needs this one beneath him. Together, they will fulfill their purpose upon this earth, as they are doing now.

It had been Merrill's intention to lead The Great Black War Horse behind the open carriage upon which rested the small wooden coffin, but the stallion would not be held back. He had broken free from Rashan as he was led from the stables and he had sought out Jude. When Jude was in his sight, he walked up to him and stood in the courtyard in front of him, pawing at the cobblestones and gently nuzzling Jude's chest. He whinnied softly, nuzzled Jude again then wheeled and trotted back into the stables. When Merrill and Rashan reached him, he was standing by the saddle that had been Randall's.

The Great Black War Horse then trotted from the stables back into the courtyard and stood at Jude's side. He returned to the stables and stood by Randall's saddle once more. Jude followed him into the stables and walked up beside him to take the bitless bridle in his hands and lead him to his place behind the carriage in the courtyard, but the horse sidestepped away, then approached him again. He pushed his muzzle gently against Jude's chest and returned to Randall's saddle, where he stood unmoving. It seemed as he was scarcely breathing, he stood so still. Then Jude's words confirmed what they knew. The Great Black War Horse told them too, as surely as if he had the power of human speech. "He wants me to ride him. father. He wants me to ride upon his back. With Grandfather's saddle, too!"

Merrill started to walk in the stallion's direction, but the horse whinnied sharply as if in warning, snorted, and stood waiting next to Randall's saddle. Rashan put a saddle blanket, followed by the saddle, on his back, tightened the cinch, then lifted Jude into the seat and handed him the reins. He adjusted the stirrups to the length that would give Jude a firm seat and then stepped back and stood next to Merrill. The two of them watched in silence, knowing they had no choice. The Great Black War Horse would lead them to the place where Joshua's body would be laid to rest. And more. In The Great Black War Horse and Jude, somehow the one whose lifeless body lay within the small coffin still lived and would be among them as the mighty stallion and the young boy went before them, each at ease with the saddle that had carried Randall first, to war, and finally, in peace. It was beyond their understanding—but they knew it to be the truth.

*   *   *   *

The Great Black War Horse leads the cortege onto the village green now, no longer prancing but slowly walking toward the open grave, high-stepping as he goes. The carriage bearing Joshua's is drawn by eight white horses, their harness black and shining, with Rashan riding a black mare at the front and side, to guide them. Merrill follows next and walks alone, followed by Eleanor, Leyla, and Old Man walking side-by-side. Shannon follows last, after the servants, his head bowed, his blue tunic replaced by one of mourning black.

The people part and make a path as the cortege continues toward the grave, then they join together again as the coffin is gently lifted from the carriage and placed on the ropes that will lower it into the ground.

Merrill walks to the side of The Great Black War Horse and holds his hand up to Jude to help him down. Jude's voice is strong and clear. "I will remain mounted, father," he says firmly and Merrill hears the joy in his son's voice as he holds his father's eyes with his and pats the powerful arched neck of The Great Black War Horse.

Merrill walks now to the head of the grave and stands there in silence, head bowed and hands clasped before him. The people wait for him to speak, but what words does he have to give them? He has given them only pain—what words are there to ease the memory of what he has done to them? And what of this innocent child that lays lifeless before them now because of what he has done? Merrill's mind is dark, as if all memory has fled from him. When he opens his mouth to speak, no words come. He looks around at the people who have circled around the grave, every eye upon him. Anger and accusation are on their faces, but it is not all for him. It's for themselves, too, for they share the responsibility for what has happened here, the thing that has brought them to this place for this purpose. They kept their silence when they could have protested, but they did not.

And they know that, but for the innocent and persecuted child who now lay in his coffin, there would have been two innocent children buried here today.

Merrill looks up at Jude astride The Great Black War Horse. Jude looks back, waiting for his father to speak. Merrill glances at the nearby grave of his own father a few short paces away and he is swallowed by an emptiness that paralyzes his throat. He cannot speak, even if he had the words.

Then a sound—and only one—escapes him, and that sound will haunt the dreams of all who hears it—but none will ever speak of it again. It is as if an animal is about to breathe its last, and all the agony of its species, from the first instant of its existence upon this earth until this day, has gathered in this tortured one before them. The cry that issues forth from Merrill is supernatural in its intensity, as if he is not a man at all, but a beast from out the sky and can speak but only once—and only in a howl of pain that stops the hearts of all who stand here with him.

They know that Merrill is howling for them all, and that the grief he hurls against the sky is as deep as ever life itself can be. There is not one among them who does not bear the weight of what has happened here in this place upon Cold River. There is not one among them whose voice of grief is not contained in Merrill's dreadful howl of deep and everlasting pain.

Old Man, standing across the grave from Merrill, tries to speak, but hears only a growl upon the wind. Did it come from him? How could he not know? He tries to scream, but yet another growl echoes in his ears. He has no tears to shed, for they had come upon him in a sudden rush when Rashan carried Joshua's lifeless body to the steps of the manor the day before, continuing through the day and into the night until he could weep no more. His pain is even worse now, striking him even deeper, because it is final. Joshua is not here.

Then through the agony that engulfs him, Old Man hears a far-off howl, as if in answer to his own, It comes faintly on the wind from that place among the treetops where the river widens and then curves in the shape of a warrior's bow. It comes from the wolf, who loved the innocent of innocent as much or even more than any human could.

Suddenly, silence wraps itself around the village green of Randall's Bow. And who is this we see? The body of Joshua, innocent of innocents, will be laid to rest today, but it is his body that we see, is it not? Surely, it is he who died that night, alone within the comforting darkness of the stall of The Great Black War Horse as the mighty stallion stood like a silent sentry above him.

And the voice that whispers to us now is his voice—there is no mistaking that. It is the voice of Joshua we hear. How can that be? And yet—it is.

*   *   *   *

All on the village green seem to float above the forest, yet they feel the ground beneath them as they look upon the empty grave that awaits the innocent child who died because of what they have done.

Joshua seems to be everywhere—around and within them. How can this be? The piping voice they hear—yes, it is his.

Look about you now—all of you—as you go into a dream. It is a dream of forgiveness from which you will awaken and not remember, except in little parts as you walk along your paths, brothers and sisters on the same journey, for you all are one. Look about you now as you love each other and give forgiveness to all you see. And so too, you will forgive yourselves.

The dream will be but for an instant, though it will seem a lifetime, and then I will awaken you.

The people look about them, gathered in one place now, and see all with their senses, as they had seen before. And something else—for now there is an inner vision too, a seeing with the heart, not just the eyes—and the world as they have known it is now changed. The old world is not removed, but that world does not matter anymore, for there is a truth beyond it that they see. It is a truth they have longed for—it is the source of the peace of mind they seek. There is no judgment here. No condemnation of any kind. Forgiveness is entire—for themselves and for all others—not attained by merit or force of will, but received as gifts along the different paths that take them on the journey that is the same for all. They were always one, but had to reach this place to know it.

Awaken now, all of you, from this forgiving dream where you have felt the weight of condemnation and of guilt lifted from you for just a little while. And know that this gift is yours. It will embrace your hearts more and more as you walk your paths upon this earth, until it is no longer just a dream but is your life and the lives of all you meet upon your journey home.

It is time now to give this frail and broken body that lies before you to the earth.

*   *   *   *

It's as if a cloud has lifted from around those who stand upon the village green. Each one feels a new peace, but cannot tell the reason why. They look upon the grave that is now no longer empty, and can't remember lowering Joshua's body to its final resting place, nor placing flowers upon the blanket of earth that is freshly piled there.

Each one turns in silence and walks from the village green. What happened here is but a pleasant memory, almost forgotten, as soon it will be. Each one knows this, and each one knows that their life has been changed forever. They know, too, that they are on a journey that will bring them the remembrance of what they learned this day.

Old Man knows he has said goodbye forever to his forest home. He and Goat will make a new home in Randall's Bow. They will make a life here and see what it will bring. It is a wonder to him, how it has come to this. Yet, there is a memory, ever so faint, that stirs and then lays quiet, leaving only the knowledge that it is time to forsake forever his beloved forest and be here in this place upon Cold River that is Randall's Bow.

Chapter 36

It's mid-day now in Randall's Bow, and the townsfolk are busy with the thoughts and things that take them through the day into the evening, and then to sleep and dreams that come to them from a time not long ago that changed their lives forever. The midnight hide of The Great Black War Horse shines like water in the moonlight as Rashan brushes him down before he is turned out to pasture for the day. Jude rides the stallion every morning now—Randall's saddle beneath him as they prance and gallop through the meadows and along the river bank until they are far down river from Randall's Bow at the place where the river forks and continues on its way to places they have never been.

The horse responds to the gentle pressure of Jude's spurless boot and firm yet gentle touch of rein upon his neck and turns back towards Randall's Bow. He prances through the town and past the village green, everyone pausing in whatever they are doing to look in wonder at The Great Black War Horse with a boy upon his mighty back. They feel a stirring in their hearts of something they have forgotten but will remember as the days and years pass. They are certain of that, somehow.

The people look then toward the village green where Joshua is buried, and they remember him and smile. They wonder why they miss that little one so much. That little one they hardly knew. Then they turn once again to the tasks they had been attending to but had left forgotten for just a moment, though it seems like days have passed. The task seems unimportant now. Some would hold themselves to the work before them, while others walk to the village green to tend the flowers there upon the graves of two unlike any others they have ever known.

Randall's grave is marked by a warrior, sword raised above his head, astride a rearing war horse carved from stone as black as night. The massive stallion paws the air, proclaiming victory over all who are foolish enough to challenge them. Judith rests nearby, the eyes of Randall covering her.

A small white wooden cross in a bed of brightly colored flowers marks the grave of Joshua. Some kneel and part the flowers to reveal a flat white stone of the finest alabaster. And upon its surface they read these words:

> *Here rests the child Joshua*
> *Whose innocence of heart and soul*
> *At first we could not see*
> *But when at last we could*
> *We changed for good*
> *And here he rests with us*
> *And lives with us*
> *As we remember more and more*
> *The forgiving dream we dreamed with him*

Back at the manor, when Eleanor and Leyla hear the hooves of The Great Black War Horse clatter upon the cobblestones of the courtyard, they walk to the window and look at those two who have just arrived with so much announcement. They smile at each other and take an apple and some freshly baked sweet cakes to the stables, to be with Jude and The Great Black War Horse for a little while. When the apple and sweet cakes have been eaten, they go about their day again, tending to the manor and all that needs doing there—and some that do not—to fill the emptiness they often feel yet can't explain.

Then suddenly—for just an instant—they remember something. Was it long ago? They do not know for certain, and they smile and feel a surge of hope and they know there is a purpose to their lives, though they don't know what it is. There is no need to know, a voice within them whispers, for each day will tell them more.

Old Man has lost all track of time. He spends his days with Goat, tending Eleanor's garden in front of her cabin, which is now his home. Her garden is the same, somehow, as his beloved forest garden, and he loves it dearly. People come by to visit him, for none was closer to Joshua than he, and sometimes they need to be with him for just a little while. The richness of his life surrounds the sadness that he feels because Joshua is no longer with him, and he is grateful for their company.

And yet, sometimes, in the early morning sun as he takes Goat's sweet milk into the little wooden bucket held firmly between his knees, or when the sun is setting over Panther Mountain and he walks toward the manor in pleasant anticipation of the supper Eleanor has prepared for him there, the trees whisper in a way that bring the music of Joshua's voice to his ears. He pauses then, and looks into the branches and all around him, as if that little one he loves so much—yes, even now and even more than when he was here—would walk out of the forest and call to him, and tell him he is safe, and he is at peace and without pain, where he has gone.

A memory stirs in Old Man then, and he tries to remember something that he knows but has forgotten. He cannot remember what it is, although it seems so near. Then he smiles and shakes his head and continues toward the manor and the ones who are waiting for him there.

Shannon's days are long and lonely now, and his nights hold terrors that he has never known before. Strange voices echo in his mind, and when he goes into the village, the others make way for him and look away when he passes by. The betrayer feels betrayed. He is without a friend—except for one.

Sometimes on an afternoon, he walks the path that takes him to Eleanor's cabin, though she rarely comes there anymore. Old Man is working in the garden near the edge of the forest, or is tending the flowers that Leyla has planted along the path that leads up to the door. And when Old Man sees him coming, he rises from his work. He smiles at Shannon, calls him friend and asks him to sit and spend some time and talk a while. Shannon calls Old Man friend in return. He experiences his only pleasant time in the slowly passing days with this old one who has cause to hate him most of all, but thinks of him as his friend instead. And Shannon sometimes weeps at the wonder of it.

They speak of little things—the garden and the flowers, the warmth of the sun, the river's flow after a heavy rain. The meaning of their words lies underneath somewhere, in something that they both remember only dimly. They cannot keep their silence and so they speak of unimportant things common to the day and look into each other's eyes and see the memory of something far away yet very real and close to them.

In the quiet of their softly spoken words, Shannon's pain leaves him for a little while, and he breathes the faintest breath of hope that each day will bring him closer to the unknown thing that he has always longed for. He lives with that. He lives with the mystery of not knowing, until he knows, if that time will ever come. He has no power over that—the time, or place, or even what it is— and he does not want that power anymore.

There is a time each day in Randall's Bow—a little space of time when the sun has done its setting, yet evening hasn't yet begun—when Merrill goes to the village green. Sometimes he's alone, and sometimes Jude is by his side. He stands between the graves of Joshua and Randall and, if he is alone, speaks their names, whispering softly in the fading light as if calling them from the earth, invisible and in secret there, to tell him what he longs to know again—what was revealed to him in the forgiving dream. But there is only silence. And, after a moment, he cannot remember what he has asked. And then he turns to Judith's grave and whispers, "Mother."

Sometimes Merrill stands with Jude and watches him put his hand on Randall's boot on the statue. They look at each other and Merrill sees the greatness in Jude's eyes, not manifested yet, but he knows that day will come as sure as day follows night. And as they stand there, they remember the morning not so very long ago when Jude looked up at Randall mounted on The Great Black War Horse, put his hand upon Randall's stirruped boot and announced, "I've decided to be like you, Grandfather." The battles Merrill and Jude will fight in days to come will be mighty ones. The war between good and evil will once again be waged in Merrill's mind—and the victor will claim his heart and soul. Jude will lead the way in Randall's Bow, and in the struggle for power between the father and the son, there is one who will return to earth, born anew. No longer frail and looking like one born long ago among the ancients, Joshua will stand tall and strong in body and in spirit and will grace Jude's journey with his wisdom and his innocence.

Merrill and Jude turn and walk the few steps it takes to reach the bed of flowers and the small, white wooden cross. They stand there a while in silence and they think of Joshua and what his presence in their lives has meant to them.

Old Man looks up from his work of caring for Joshua's flowers, as he calls them, and watches Leyla as she steps onto the village green and approaches Merrill and Jude.

"There's Leyla!" Jude's voice echoes across the village green as he runs to greet her. They hug and Leyla kisses him lightly on the cheek. Their laughter brings smiles to Old Man and Merrill as Leyla and Jude approach them.

"Well. What brings you here, Leyla?" Merrill asks, laughing with them now. "Were you lonesome for your young friend…or possibly even me? Or have you come to assist Old Man with his gardening?"

"Both, Merrill. But most of all to tell you mother has freshly baked sweet cakes and her special blend of afternoon tea waiting for you when you return to the manor."

"Well, my friend," Merrill says to Old Man, "shall we go and see what Leyla is talking about? You know you are welcome. We treasure your company."

Old Man looks at the words carved upon the alabaster covering Joshua's grave. "You all go and enjoy what Eleanor has prepared," he says softly. "I think I'll stay here a while longer and tend the flowers. Perhaps share some thoughts with Joshua, too. I know he hears me, although I must appear to be a babbling old man to those who hear my voice yet see no one in my company." He looks at Jude. "You know what I mean, don't you? You talk to him, too. Joshua tells me so."

Jude steps close to Old Man and touches him affectionately on the shoulder. "Yes," Jude says, and says no more for no more needs to be said. He takes Leyla's hand and they start off toward the manor.

Merrill follows behind them, then moves to Leyla's side. "You're Jude's mother now, you know."

Leyla smiles. "Yes, I know," she says.

Merrill takes her hand and gives it a gentle squeeze. Leyla looks up at Merrill, smiles at him…and squeezes back.

Old Man watches them cross the village green hand-in-hand and start down the path to Randall's Manor. Their obvious love for each other fills his heart with joy. "Yes," he says softly, standing and looking at the small, white wooden cross. "And to tell the truth, Joshua," he says with a little laugh, "I have a grumbling stomach that tells me I'm hungry. I think I'll join them, after all. But I'll be back tomorrow. I promise." A gentle breeze caresses Old Man as he speaks and he looks at the sky streaked with reds, blues, and grays as if put there by a master painter's brush as the sun sets over Cold River. "Oh, Joshua," he whispers, "Will we ever meet again?" And yet, somehow, he knows they will, in another place or even another time, perhaps. Yes, they will meet again.

And as Old Man starts down the path to Randall's Manor, the gentle breeze answers, "Yes."

Author's Note

Some years ago, I saw a thirteen-year-old boy with the disease of progeria being interviewed on television. I had never seen anyone so in the moment and so full of joy. His voice had a musical, piping, flute-like sound, and he deeply touched my heart. He looked like a little old man despite his tender years, yet his being transcended his affliction. It was miraculous. I was to later learn, from seeing other children with progeria interviewed, that what emanated from that boy is typical of progeric children.

Progeria is a genetic condition that produces rapid aging in children and is extremely rare. An afflicted child has a shrunken, wrinkled face, baldness, no eyebrows or eyelashes, short stature, a head that is large in proportion to a small face, a small jaw, dry, scaly skin, teeth that are crowded together and rapidly decaying, and a body with a limited range of motion. The average lifespan is thirteen years, with the cause of death related to the heart or to a stroke.

I wondered what it must have been like in ancient times for a child with progeria. Were they feared? Revered? Abandoned? Put to death as evil—a devil-child?

In an instant, the concept of a trilogy that takes place in ancient times was given to me by, I believe, the Divine. My inner voice told me the stories would be given to me as I wrote.

And so it was—and will be. There is more to tell. Much, much more.

Printed in the United States
By Bookmasters